International Human Resource Development

A leadership perspective

Elaine S. Potoker

 Routledge
Taylor & Francis Group

LONDON AND NEW YORK

First published in 2005
by South-Western, part of the Thomson Corporation, as
Managing Diverse Working Styles.

Second edition published 2011
by Routledge
2 Park Square, Milton Park, Abingdon, Oxon, OX14 4RN

Simultaneously published in the USA and Canada
by Routledge
270 Madison Avenue, New York, NY 10016

*Routledge is an imprint of the Taylor & Francis Group, an informa
business*

© 2011 Elaine S. Potoker

The right of Elaine S. Potoker to be identified as author of this work
has been asserted by her in accordance with sections 77 and 78 of the
Copyright, Designs and Patents Act 1988.

Typeset in Times by
RefineCatch Limited, Bungay, Suffolk
Printed and bound in Great Britain by TJ International Ltd, Padstow,
Cornwall

British Library Cataloguing in Publication Data
A catalog record for this book is available
from the British Library

Library of Congress Cataloging-in-Publication Data
Potoker, Elaine S.
International human resource development: a leadership perspective /
Elaine S. Potoker. – 2nd ed.
p. cm.
Includes bibliographical references and index.
Previously published under title: Managing diverse working styles.
1. Diversity in the workplace–Management. 2. Intercultural
communication. 3. Organizational learning. 4. Organizational
effectiveness. 5. Multiculturalism. I. Title.
HF5549.5.M5P68 2010
658.3008–dc22

2010010145

ISBN 13: 978–0–415–45901–3 (hbk)
ISBN 13: 978–0–415–45902–0 (pbk)

To the "turtle's work," and the joy that creative management and transspection bring to make life "good."

International Human Resource Development

Workforce mobility and cultural diversity within contemporary international organizations pose unique challenges for managers and HR professionals. Overcoming the challenges of developing and training such a workforce requires the ability to bridge diverse working, learning, and communication styles.

In contrast with conventional organizational approaches to international HRD, *International Human Resource Development: A Leadership Perspective* explores workforce development from a personal perspective, challenging practitioners to develop their own leadership, learning, and communication skills. As a point of departure, the book uses a demographic analysis of the workforces of a number of key countries in order to examine cultural implications for training and development, and for best practice.

Drawing on a unique anthropological perspective and complete with case studies, exercises, and an extensive glossary this text will prove an important resource for students of human resource development, human resource management, and international business.

Elaine S. Potoker is a Professor in the Loeb-Sullivan School of International Business and Logistics at Maine Maritime Academy, USA. She has extensive experience as a practitioner in international business and cross-cultural management and training. Her research focuses on management across cultures, workforce development, international management, and marketing.

Table of contents

About the author

ELAINE S. POTOKER BA, SUNY, Potsdam, N.Y.; MAT, the University of Chicago; Ph.D. The Ohio State University is a Fulbright Award recipient (2007), Lecturer/Researcher, Costa Rica, Senior Specialist Fulbright designate in Business Administration (2010–2015), and Professor in the Loeb-Sullivan School of International Business and Logistics at Maine Maritime Academy, Castine, Maine, where she teaches in both the undergraduate program and the Dept. of Graduate Studies and Research. Additionally, she is owner of Interloqui®, an organization that provides domestic and international trade service assistance (e.g., business planning, assessment, executive education workshops). Dr. Potoker has traveled in a management, sales and marketing capacity for over 30 years, and has extensive experience as a practitioner in international business and cross-cultural management and training. She is formerly Coordinator of Central American Sales for Reed Mfg. Co., Erie, Pennsylvania. Her recent presentations, practitioner and academic interests focus on management across cultures, workforce development, anthropology as applied to business assessment and strategic planning, and international management and marketing (Focus: Latin America). Her professional affiliations include: Rotary International (former Board member), Board Member, Fulbright Association (Maine Chapter), and Judge for the Niagara Moot Court Competition. She is recognized in *Who's Who in International Business, Who's Who, Women in Education,* and *Women in Business.*

Illustrations

Figures

Tables

Maps

Introduction

It is with a great deal of satisfaction that I write this Introduction to *International Human Resource Development: A Leadership Perspective*, a new and revised edition of its forerunner of 2005, in association with a new publisher, Routledge. Ironically, while the face and mobility of the workforce continues to change and evolve due to regional trade agreements, cross-border trade and investment, and integration of physical and virtual worlds and advanced technologies, the core need for this book continues to be the same. In other words, as much as business environments may have changed, certain others remain constant, and hence the importance of this book.

Why this book? An overview

Integration of technologies, industries, nations, cultures,[1] relationships, and interests continue to characterize the twenty-first century workplace. Leadership in this dynamic environment depends upon the ability to bridge diverse working and communication styles that may be different from one's own. How to do it, and, what influences these styles? These remain important considerations addressed in this book, and important to those entrusted with international human resource development.

Feedback from readers of the first edition strongly supported the usefulness of the book as an eclectic toolbox for those dedicated to development of diverse and mobile workforces. Therefore, the new edition continues to navigate individuals through a self-discovery process of personal working and communication preferences to enable the trainer to develop. Along the way, the book provides historical background and theory to enhance understanding and case study for application of broadened communication skills in both physically and virtually interconnected organizational environments. The book and the journey aim to:

a   Broaden communication skills for integrative roles and dynamic, changing, and diverse cultural environments.
b   Illustrate that personal working styles and design preferences may not be the most informed or effective in integrated physical and virtual,

computer-based, interactive worlds. Leading change begins at home with self-assessment. By popular request, this book continues to guide the readers to perform that self-assessment and flush out personal biases.

c   Illustrate that personal working style and design preferences are culturally constructed; they are *learned*. Working styles, which refer to preferred ways of accomplishing work, learning, and communicating, for many reasons are not universally shared. These styles and learning preferences are explored in this book.[2] Each new setting requires individuals and groups to "break the code"—that is to assess what may be similar and/or different, however subtle these constructs might be—and decide what their implications are for workforce development.

d   Provide further insight into best practices in the field of human resource development and the *intensely* creative design process it can and often does entail. Conceptualization and communication of complex individual, group and/or organizational agendas are challenged, indeed, in multicultural/national environments. In this regard, *International Human Resource Development* points to the limitations of language in human interactions, and illustrates how and why breakdowns in communication can occur when people of difference meet. It is argued that dynamic and diverse collaborative forums require individuals to be armed with communication skills that go beyond spoken and written communication. Strategies are presented that aim to bridge working styles by optimizing the communication process. These include, but are not limited to, the use of visual cues and relational diagramming, and the creation of "learning landscapes"—a proprietary term that is discussed and illustrated throughout the book.

e   To show that the environment of the contemporary workplace requires multiple disciplinary lenses to deconstruct—audit, analyze and chart—developmental paths for organizational development, growth and change. In this regard, the book's rationale continues to be grounded in literatures that frequently go unnoticed by one another—e.g., the literature of training and development, anthropology, linguistics, sociology, management, adult learning theory, art education, global education, and intercultural communication. This multiple disciplinary lens was regarded as unique in the earlier edition, and important to the sequel.

"*Why,*" new readers may ask, "*are these literatures important? Isn't the business of business enough?*" Isn't it enough to know accounting, finance, how to manage, how to organize, and so on? Or, alternatively stated, what insight do they provide?

For starters, writers from each of these disciplines have grappled with, agonized over, and researched issues that address potential roadblocks and provide insight into gateways to communication—defined herein as the exchange of thoughts and ideas through *shared* symbols. The field of adult learning theory, as one example, considers the role of cognition, or how individuals perceive and mentally process information. If cognitive processes are not generally shared among adults, then it is important to know where similarities and differences can be bridged since these influence patterns of learning and productivity. The literature of intercultural communication helps here. Intercultural communication is grounded in theory derived from empirical study of verbal and nonverbal exchanges between individuals and groups of individuals. Bridging border zones between peoples of different cultures involves conscious choices of *which symbols to choose?* If we know, *or can learn about that*, then we are further informed by the research and practice of training and development (T&D). T&D professionals can plan and implement learning experiences, approaches, and/or design procedures that help the organization, groups and individuals to achieve a common, or *shared* purpose.

As cognitive processing is largely determined by the way individuals perceive and respond to the world around them through culture and experience, the literature of anthropology, sociology, art education, and adult learning theory enrich insight into how and why adults learn they way they do. Together they provide guidance when attempting to discover one's *own* (perhaps) unconsciously preferred working and communication modes. They also provide insight into how one might go about learning and employing other (perhaps unfamiliar) modes. Research in these fields also has much to offer to designers of computer-based technologies in the global Information Age.

Anthropologists and sociologists have also studied how people understand the meaning of work. Flex-time, travel, and virtual communication blur lines between home space and workspaces. These scenarios raise many questions about the relationship between organizational design, to include virtual designs, and group and individual performance.

As workforce(s) continue to transcend national boundaries, the field of global education provides additional insight into workforce development as it focuses on the interrelationships between peoples of the world. Research from this discipline has still not generally been applied to business; functional areas generally tend to ignore the communications tasks and knowledge of culture that may be necessary to achieve organization, group, and personal goals.

In short, the information provided herein is applicable to a wide variety of settings. Wherever teamwork, negotiation, training and development, and difference characterize both the dynamics and concerns of group and organizational behavior, all of these fields of study provide useful insight. As with the popular song about love and marriage, this book posits that *"we can't* [apparently] *have one without the other."*

What's new in the second edition?

The previous section discusses themes and focus areas that are continued in the new edition by popular request. What is new or refocused was included, in part, by readers' requests—both academicians and practitioners—but not entirely. Other topics were added from fieldwork within businesses of all sizes and ongoing research by the author over the last few years. What's new?

- a chapter (Chapter 4) focused on adult learning and generational differences that impact International Human Resource Development (IHRD)
- updated information regarding labor force trends and implications for workforce competencies needed in the future
- wider geographical focus of case studies and exemplar materials
- discussion of *universal* best practices in IHRD, vs. previous focus *only* on differences. In other words, an *etic* perspective is added to the book,[3] including but not limited to the following topic areas:

  ✓ the value of an organizational audit to IHRD practices
  ✓ best practices in job analysis, job design, and performance evaluation
  ✓ critical incident technique (CIT) and its value to best practices in job analysis, job design and performance evaluation

- additional relevant experiential exercises and cases
- references to organizations to consult for useful information relating to IHRD
- an expanded Glossary to include acronyms and their meaning
- updated information regarding the relationship of the book's content to leadership studies, and the importance of a leadership perspective to the book's contents
- a total of 10 chapters to facilitate use and application for varied educational delivery timelines. This new format allows for instructor flexibility to use the text as a stand-alone and/or to include supplementary materials, depending upon teaching style and preferences. As college programs and curriculums have become more "internationalized" due to globalization and its impact on accreditation requirements, readers are likely to appreciate the *etic* and *emic* perspective of this book. For example, the author has used this book as the stand-alone text in upper-level undergraduate courses, supplementing with articles on topics such as US and/or comparative employment law, labor relations and unionism. At the master's level, the text is very complementary with casebook dedicated approaches. It also lends itself well to executive training formats as grounding for simulations and role play as well as leadership studies
- the target audience: The focus shifts from "managers" and administrators or, from occupational "titles," to all those committed to workforce development, to include self-development in IHRD best practices. Note that *International Human Resource Development: A Leadership Perspective* is not intended to be an introduction to the study of human resource management. It is assumed that an "introduction" has already taken place through coursework or experience
- a chapter (Chapter 10) addressing "The Future of IHRD" and its intersection with the field of organizational development (OD). This discussion is based on ongoing fieldwork and interviews by the author with practitioners in both fields.

How is this book different from others?

Numerous publications address multicultural issues by focusing on awareness of "differences" at a macro level. As examples, there are those publications that target the expatriate or international assignee (IA) going to a foreign assignment for the first time, such as to Mexico or Japan. Their objective is to prepare IAs for adjustment within the host nation, and introduce them to culture-specific business practices. There is also extensive literature devoted to perceptual differences and orientations of groups of different ethnic and/or cultural backgrounds. These groups are generally characterized statically and relatively homogeneously. In others, communication tendencies are portrayed generically and are gender-specific—e.g., considerable emphasis is placed on gender difference; often gender is addressed in isolation from cultural and other constructs. All have their use and provide insight into issues relevant to communication. However, what do we do when all these variables such as job rotation, cultural difference, age, gender, etc. are in motion?

Renato Rosaldo stated that the idea of a homogeneous culture available for inspection was not possible. He argued three decades ago that "all of us inhabit an interdependent late-twentieth century world marked by borrowing and lending across porous national and cultural boundaries that are saturated with inequality, power, and domination."[4] This is still very true. *International Human Resource Development* recognizes that group composition may change *daily* in physical worlds, reassemble virtually, and/or reorganize in physical local, regional and international worlds. Therefore, what are individuals to *do* beyond recognition of and/or sensitivity to cultural and other differences? Herein lies the importance and uniqueness of this book; specifically:

a   It is grounded in the assumption that organizations and their environments are, indeed, *dynamic* and *changing*;
b   It moves beyond exhortations to be "sensitive" to difference, and [rather] introduces strategies and an eclectic toolbox for trainers and other student professionals that are results oriented;
c   It provides examples that are practitioner oriented, but grounded in multiple disciplines.

Topic coverage and organization

In **Chapter 1**, "Breaking the Code," the author explores the meaning of work in the Digital Age and how perceptions of work's meaning, leisure time, and time itself influence working styles. Also considered are culture's effects on individual and organizational perceptions of job roles and workplace relationships, and the impact of the intranet, extranet and e-commerce on workspace and home space boundaries, and job design.

Chapter 2, "The Limitations of Language," the relationships between culture and experience and between culture and language are discussed. This chapter clearly illustrates how and why language differences can be potential obstacles to understanding. It is important grounding for understanding the limitations of spoken and written discourse. The discussion also points to numerous issues with implications for organizational, group, and individual communication. Appendix 2A, "Transspecting Culture and Experience: An American in Paris," provides an application exercise to enrich chapter discussion and theoretical grounding of information. It is a useful exercise for soliciting heuristic analysis in varied settings.

Chapter 3, "Recognizing the 'Others' are Us: Demographic Trends in Countries around the World," characterizes the workforce of the twenty-first century and beyond, and projects a profile of the workforces of the future. The chapter points to globalization issues that influence workforce training and development around the world and competencies that will be required.

Chapter 4, "Learning: One Size Does Not Fit All," the author selectively addresses how adults learn, and generational differences that influence learning.

Chapter 5, "The Changing Face of Management," is an *intermezzo*, a pause that provides the reader with an opportunity to reflect on previous chapters. Included are integrative cases and vignettes that provide critical thinking opportunities for students to reach beyond theory to IHRD practice outside country borders.

Chapter 6, "Management's New Face," visits several classic and contemporary theorists for their perspectives regarding the functions of management. The discussion has implications for communication, ranging from communication tool choices to situational applications across disciplines and organizational levels of planning, and to challenges of effecting change within and across profit and not-for profit organizations. Appendix 6A provides additional application examples that are useful in academic and business settings.

Chapter 7, "Building Learning Organizations through Learning Landscapes," continues to address the need for broadened communication skills and language choices in order to maximize organizational and intercultural communication. In this chapter, individuals are challenged to create "learning landscapes"—to map and present developmental inventories to optimize understanding of agendas as well as complex, culturally diverse and polychromic environments. A case study provides an illustration of how this may be done, and why the learning landscapes serve to maximize organizational and intercultural communication.

Chapter 8, "Best Practices in IHRD," the author focuses on the universals that are tied directly or indirectly to human resource development wherever one goes. Special attention is given to the organizational audit and critical incident technique and their value to job design, performance evaluation, and ultimately to organizational effectiveness and learning.

Chapter 9, "Communications Design Issues of the Future," addresses how culture affects communication choices in the computer-based technology Information Age. The focus is on communication issues as they affect virtual workforce and human–computer interaction.

Chapter 10, "The Future of IHRD," the author discusses developments over the last few years that will impact practice of IHRD in the future, particularly the evolution and integration of organizational science and organizational development (OD) with IHRD. The information is based on fieldwork and interviews with practitioners in both fields. She intentionally does not define the practice of "international human resource" management until the closing chapter of the book, and explains why the preceding chapters are the reasons that important consideration was left to last.

The leadership perspective

Throughout this book, readers are urged to distinguish themselves in leadership roles. According to management and organizational behaviorist scholar, John Kotter, it is *leaders* who align people and set direction. Kotter illustrates and emphasizes the imperative for leadership through a military analogy: "A peacetime army can usually survive with good administration and management up and down the hierarchy, coupled with good leadership concentrated at the very top. A wartime army, however, needs competent leadership at all levels."[5] In *International Human Resource Development*, it is argued that competitive advantage depends on:

*   the ability to facilitate the interchange of thoughts and ideas through broadened communication design choices and skills
*   the ability to conceptualize complex individual, group, and/or organizational agendas
*   the ability to align diverse understandings of work and working styles with organizational goals and objectives.

Distinguishing features

In selected chapters, **Hallmarks of leadership** integrate prevalent thinking and principles of leadership with chapter information. **The leadership toolboxes** summarize important chapter points by providing working tools for problem-solving, decision-making, lifelong learning, and, ultimately, for competitive advantage. This book's position is that leadership skills can be *learned*.

The **Appendices** provide additional practitioner-based examples of how individuals may broaden their communication skills; the examples also serve to show how important it is to do so, given organizational and technological realities, workforce demographics, and working and learning styles.

The **Postscript** reiterates the importance of broad-based communication skills as organizations' physical, virtual, and demographic environments become more complex, dynamic, mobile, and unseen. It also points to design issues for computer-based technologies for transnational, virtually connected workplace environments of the present and future.

A **Glossary** is provided for clarification and instructional purposes, as well as a **Bibliography. Key terms and concepts** also follow chapter discussion.

Chapter notes and a useful **Bibliography** pull together a wide pool of resources for further reflection and study for both practitioners and student practitioners.

Student **Application exercises** are relevant to today's working environments. There are many opportunities for students from academic and work settings to integrate and apply theory to their real-life workplace experiences.

In retrospect . . . remembering important context to this edition

In the previous edition, I referred to the expression, "read my lips," popularized in August of 1988 during George Bush's Presidential nomination acceptance speech.[6] I did not recall if those words had any impact on me at all at that time. I do know that this book was not even a glimmer in my eye or mind in the late 1980s. Nevertheless, the implication of those words, as it turned out, proved as inspirational to the need for me to write the earlier edition as it is to this new sequel. The reasons why should become apparent to the reader as the book's chapters unfold.

In retrospect, the 1980s began as a crescendo of voices heralding the passing of traditional structure, roles and hierarchy in a variety of settings. On a "macro" level, the destruction of the Berlin Wall symbolized the disintegration of command economies. On a "micro" organizational level, the general external environment of business and industry continued to be increasingly dependent upon the ability to be effective and innovative in an international marketplace. The complexity and interdependency of workplace environments had brought about a redefinition of the workplace. R. Moss Kanter, as one example, focused on management and specifically on the "new manager," drawing attention to the workplace as a "collaborative forum" where managers must work across boundaries with peers and partners.[7] Participation was key. Rather than the traditional hierarchical or vertical chain of command, peer networking was deemed critical to effectiveness. With the advent of the 1990s, the concept of the "learning organization" became popularized: [an organization] "where people continually expand their capacity to create the results they truly desire, where new and expansive patterns of thinking are nurtured, where collective aspiration is set free, and where people are continually learning how to learn together."[8] Peter Senge argued that team learning starts with "dialogue" in a genuine "thinking together."[9] Enlightened organizations—whether they be the medical floor, the automobile assembly line, or governmental agencies—were apparently to rely increasingly upon cross-functional and channel member alliances, project and self-directed quality circles, and other teams. The practitioner literature urged the new managers to be "change agents," to empower their "associates," and to turn diversity into strength.

Through the interaction of academic pursuits—to include research at a large US manufacturing facility, fieldwork, long-time practical experience in strategic international management and marketing ventures, training, a Fulbright in Costa Rica in 2007, consultancy with organizations involved in radical change, and continued advisement and teaching—I recognize how challenging, indeed, "genuine thinking together" still is to achieve. Working and learning styles, work's meaning, communication styles, language and language usage, and words are not generally shared. This context continues to provide the urgency and inspiration for this book, and I sincerely hope it will be such for you, the readers, as well.

Instructor support materials

This book has **wide market reach**. There are numerous fields and applications for this book: Human Resource Management and Development, International Business, Applied Anthropology, Executive Training, Intercultural Communication, Management Education, Organizational Development, Human Computer Interaction Design, to name a few.

Acknowledgments

It's been said that personality is an outgrowth of one's culture and experiences; and, indeed, such is the case of this book and its author. While many acknowledgments begin with people, mine begin with the environment. I truly believe that my early childhood, "stoop-sitting" days in the inner city first introduced me to the polychronic world, and to what I later learned to call *perspectives consciousness*: the recognition or awareness on the part of the individual that he or she has a view of the world that is not universally shared, that this view of the world has been and continues to be shaped by influences that often escape conscious detection, and that others have views of the world that are profoundly different from one's own.[10]

Indeed, culture and experience shaped choices and the academic and business paths that led to this work.

The cross-disciplinary path I travel still often appears to be one "less traveled by" and understood, especially by those grounded in functional departmentalization. While many would agree that there is a need for inter-disciplinary and cross-functional collaboration in academic and business settings, respectively, the reality is that often perspectives continue to be siloed by structure, politics, and tradition. Therefore, I am grateful to those academic and business professionals who encouraged me to research and work through multiple lenses and across border zones. Those individuals include writers whom I've never met—e.g., the work in intercultural communication of Edward Hall (1976), and others whom, luckily, I did meet.

Dr. Erika Bourguignon—teacher, mentor, friend, and Professor Emeritus of Anthropology at The Ohio State University in Columbus, Ohio—continues to have an influence on my work. Meeting Dr. Bourguignon while at The Ohio State University was a very fortuitous encounter, indeed. She encouraged me to cross disciplinary lines and reach out to literatures that did not appear to speak to one another. And indeed I did, thanks to the extended hands of others—too numerous to mention—from The Ohio State University and earlier from the University of Chicago. Consulting through Interloqui® (http://www.interloqui.com) in international trade services and export management adds still another perspective to management across cultures. Along the way, special thanks go to the book's anonymous (but real) associates: AM, SVP, NN, Jim L., and C who crossed border zones to allow me to do research at their large Midwestern manufacturing facility.

International business travels in a management, sales, and marketing capacity during times of monetary and political crises, particularly in the early 1980s, through Latin America made me aware of the need for this book. Issues of diversity, to include literacy, gender, and economic attainment, had a significant influence on my professional business life, and now in my college teaching career. Additionally, the ongoing collaborative I have with students of all ages in international business, academic, and other organizational settings continues to enrich teaching, learning and writing endeavors.

Others along the way encouraged the application of anthropology, research and other of my interests to teaching International Organizational Development and Change. This advice, I believe, helps me place my own mark on the teaching of OB and HRM—now *International* Human Resource Management—at the Loeb-Sullivan School at Maine Maritime Academy.

Several years ago I attended a conference to investigate how anthropology, global education, international business, marketing management, organizational design, and systems theory might be applied to space (through the maritime analogies). The Fulbright Award I received for lecturing and research in Costa Rica in 2007 and the fieldwork done there for six months reconfirmed the content areas, old and new, that are foundational to this new edition. As I write this acknowledgment, I recognize that everything I write these days benefits from the value of "disciplines communicating." It is hoped that through this book, current and future business professionals will recognize the value of a multidisciplinary perspective to one's work.

Lastly, but surely not least, other significant inspiration for hallmarks of effective leadership presented in this book are derived from parenting my daughters, Kristen and Beth Anne. To the unseen reviewers, the feedback was most appreciated, and important to the development of the text.

Frankly, I am glad I chose the path less traveled, and thanks to those— seen and unseen—who have cheered me along the way and occasionally entertained a pause to refresh, including the team from Routledge UK, publishers of this book.

Elaine S. Potoker
April 24, 2010

1   Breaking the code

No definition of work will be complete since work is as complex as life itself.[1]

The word 'work,' like most words we use, seems simple enough. We all use it rather regularly, and its meaning seems obvious. But defining it—setting boundaries between what it is and what it is not—<u>is</u> difficult.[2]

The meaning of work

The Introduction to this book promises to navigate the reader through a self-discovery process of personal working and communication preferences. That process begins here. And, in that regard, no stone can remain unturned. Therefore, this chapter engages the reader to explore his/her personal understanding of the meaning of work itself.

Both of the above introductory quotes by different authors in different settings point to the complexity of defining and identifying what activities constitute "work"—no matter where we go. While work may be defined or understood the same way among two individuals from the same place and within the same industry, one can make no assumptions about "what constitutes work" in a particular locale based on personal, cultural, and/or previous local, national experiences. As an example, if one views "work" as only those activities that are job-*paid for*, he/she may miss a multitude of activities that are important to outputs such as the socialization that work often involves, the external organizational relationships that influence work, and much more. Defined herein, "work" refers to all those purposeful activities that contribute to achieving human, including organizational, community, and societal needs, and aimed to affect in whole or in part physical and/or virtual environments.[3] Therefore, even household work, and "women's work"[4] is "work." Yes, it may be "unseen," "unpaid-for," and arguably non-market oriented, but it is "work," nonetheless. Additionally,

Work supports all the other aspects of humans' lifeways. [It], consequently, is the pivotal concern and subject of conversation in all societies. Work relations, accordingly, touch almost all of our social interactions.[5]

Therefore, that which constitutes and influences "work"—its depth and breadth—is a phenomenon that must be discovered in every setting. Providing a rudimentary framework of what it may entail is what this chapter is, in part about—hence, the Chapter title, "Breaking the Code." The word "rudimentary" is emphasized here. This chapter's sole purpose is to heighten consciousness of the complexity of work's meaning, and to encourage trainers, managers, and other organizational stakeholders to explore work's influences and action chains in varied locations as they affect decision-making and design. The amount of research regarding work's meaning, e.g., its relationship to self, motivation, power and economic control, within industries, chronicled in industrialized, market-driven societies vs. subsistence societies, is voluminous.[6] Breaking the code is important, as work likely entails a complicated labyrinth of social relationships that influences events. Overlooking one or more might have a deleterious effect to desired outcomes. The reverse is true as well: recognizing their complexity is likely to optimize informed decision-making. For supportive illustrations, one only has to review the extensive stress- and creativity-related research being done in organizational settings addressing, e.g., how relative autonomy (vs. dependency), and feedback influence job role stress, creativity, and other job outcomes.

Cultural anthropologist Herbert Applebaum provided significant contributions to understanding the complexity of "work", i.e., work's activities, work's social relationships/networks, work's consequences, work and leisure, and more. In *Royal Blue* (1981), as one example of many by this author, he presents a case study of construction workers (and their work) in the United States. Inspired by this case, Figure 1.1 metaphorically compares the complexity of work's meaning to a piece of mica.

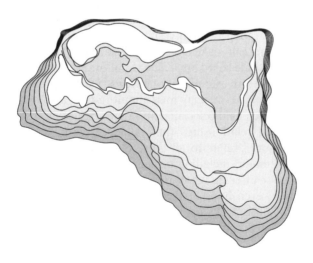

Figure 1.1 The meaning of work.

Why mica? It is argued that work and a mica crystal have many similar properties. Mica, as a generic term, generally refers to a group of aluminosilicate minerals that are shaped by environmental forces. Continuing with the analogy, although mica has the appearance of a whole crystal, it is really quite complex, indeed, in terms of its physical and chemical characteristics. It is also quite versatile in terms of its end-use applications—as is the potential of a society's human resources. While mica has a unique combination of strength, it can be separated easily into thin films that are quite resilient. Physically, the crystal appears transparent. Similarly, construction work for the laborer may seem readily observable. It involves particular knowledge (e.g., blueprint reading) and skills (e.g., mixing concrete, blasting). To delve deeper, however, involves peeling away of other related layers. Even though each layer is flexible and elastic to some degree, one layer, by itself, does not characterize the whole crystal. Its composite layers, if viewed as elements of work, include some of the following:

Work's meaning and complexity:

1 **The job itself.** This includes knowledge, skills, responsibilities.[7] This is, perhaps arguably, the layer that is most readily observable. Knowledge, skills, abilities and attitudes (KSAs) and job analysis are addressed further in Chapter 8.

2 **Degree of autonomy vs. dependence.** Does the worker control the process, and is he/she *expected* to act independently? This, in turn, is influenced by what the perceived roles of management are—often influenced by factors such as social class structure.

3 **Internal/external risk factors—i.e., degree of certainty or uncertainty.** Workplace autonomy vs. (inter)**dependence** is also related to the degree of danger job duties entail. Construction work involves a relatively high degree of danger; additionally, a skilled craftsperson relies upon himself/herself to fabricate the product. At the same time, the laborer is not completely independent. He/she relies upon other craftspeople to perform functions such as erecting the scaffold, mixing the mortar, and more. This sequencing of events that involve social relationships are referred to as "action chains." Action chains are very important to identify, as they cannot be assumed as universal in every setting.

4 **Social identity, self-concept, and prestige.** These elements are part and parcel of the complex silicate of work. Work is all wrapped up in one's real self,—i.e., the actual knowledge skills, and abilities one possesses; the ideal self—hopes and dreams for himself/herself (and/or others); and looking-glass self—how he/she is perceived by others. These factors are not entirely self-determined. Work, as well as its boundaries, is socially constructed. External influences play a significant role as illustrated by the following questions: Are equal opportunity in recruitment and upward mobility a social and cultural phenomenon? Are rights of entry

and rights of passage (upward mobility) determined by local, regional and/or national history, socio-economic status, or by qualifications, certifications, and democratic processes? Personal goals are, after all, contextually influenced by one or more of these factors to some extent. The same is true of action chains.

5   **Rewards/Punishments.** Rewards and punishments include pay, awards and other recognitions which, in turn, affect and are influenced by the previous items in this list.[8]

6   **Language/jargon.** Doing the work involves more than #1. Knowledge of the jargon is also key to socialization or feeling "in" vs. "out." Jargon can be quite thick, depending upon the industry and organization involved.

7   **Tools of the trade.** What are they, and are they available to everyone who needs them? In the twenty-first century, "tools" potentially may involve a great many instruments, to include, of course, computer-based technologies and equipment. Ownership is another factor here as resource allocations influence power flows, performance, achievement, recognition, productivity, and those who have vs. those who do not have access to knowledge.

8   **Labor relations.** Unions' role and power relationships with management are other work-related elements requiring analysis that probably have a direct or indirect effect on all of the items listed above. The differences can be quite remarkable, not only within countries, but also when comparing these relationships in one country against another.

9   **Values.** These refer to the "what matters here," and are embedded in all of work's elements; they are influenced by organizational, industry-related, cultural, historical, socio-economic and other factors. Orientation to time plays an important role as well: Religious grounding specific to the role of the individual in his/her universe may influence the degree of control the person may feel he/she has to effect change.

10   **Risk-taking.** One's relative disposition to take risks is related to all of the above, and also to the extent to which a society places a high value on reducing ambiguity and instability.[9]

Items 1–10 are not an exhaustive list of work's properties or meanings. Nor does the mica metaphor work in its entirety. In fact, (arguably) it fails, in part, since the elements of work often are *not* generally peeled away so easily. Indeed, they are generally dynamically intertwined. As an example, while item 1 may be easily identified in organizational life from review of a job description, the job description alone often does not encompass the many social relationships and responsibilities the position is likely to entail, for many reasons. Social protocols that are culturally influenced are other influencers. Further, designing the job *effectively* is a managerial challenge. As effective form *should* follow the role and function it is to perform, the effectiveness of the design involves careful consideration of items 1–10. These items are all elements of the *task environment* of work—factors related to the job itself. Reiterating, each layer is influenced by and influences others. None exists independently of the other's influence. However, those alone are not enough to break the code of the complexity of work. Let's return to those external forces, *the external environment*, that shape and influence the mica structure. Those include, but are not limited to resource availability (labor pool, financial capital), digital access (e.g., Internet technology and other technologies and processes that are not always compatible or standardized across borders), international communities, government entities (city, state, provincial, national), political processes, code of law, economic conditions, and socio-cultural characteristics such as age, values, education, social castes, religion, and history. Those forces are represented in Figure 1.2, "The context of work."

Resource availability

This concept refers those factors of production that are *basic*, such as land and natural resources, labor, and capital, and *advanced* factors, such as energy, skilled, educated and professional labor sources, R&D know-how, and communication infrastructure.[10] If these resources are not available, the "job itself" may be hampered in many ways, or simply not be done. It also may mean there are fewer *tools*, more job tasks to perform, more downtime, possibly more reason to outsource, which affects employment vs. displacement of workers.

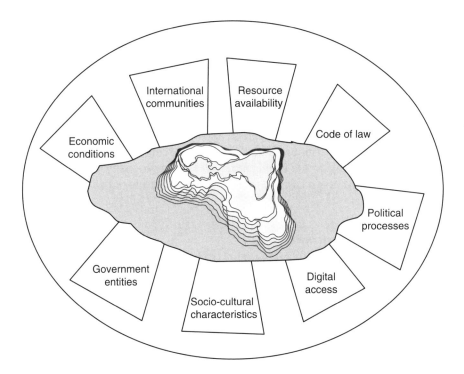

Figure 1.2 The context of work.

Code of law

This refers to the legal system that influences work practices. For example, employment law and employee rights specific to selection, hiring, promotion, disability, and compensation vary tremendously across countries with different legal traditions—e.g., code law countries and variations thereof, common law countries, and Islamic law which extends to all realms of life beyond just business practices.

Political processes

The origin of power flows and the degree to which government influences, and controls. For example, is government an *autocracy*, where "power is held by an individual or small group and supported by control of critical resources, property or ownership right, traditions, charisma, and other claims to personal privilege?" And/or, is it a *technocracy* where "rule [is also] exercised through use of knowledge, expert power, and the ability to solve relevant problems?"[11] External political processes often influence task environment preferences regarding risk tolerance, degree of centralization vs. decentralization, levels of hierarchy, priorities for allocating resources, decision-making and roles of decision-makers, leadership, and, ultimately, the degree of autonomy vs. dependence in the task environment.

Digital access

This refers to the availability of an advanced communications infrastructure that supports and enables the worker to get business done in a timely, efficient, and effective way. The world is still a long way from achieving harmonization of information management system technology across borders for customs control, logistics management, and new business formation. Harmonization or lack of harmonization of technology can be a barrier to getting work done, not only across borders, but within borders between municipalities, counties, and provinces, as applicable in both developed and developing countries.

Socio-cultural characteristics

These include, but are not limited to world views, religious tenets, language, and norms of behavior that have the potential to influence the way "things get done." As an example, in countries where Confucianism is ingrained in the cultural tapestry, respect for preservation of hierarchical relationships is likely to be a behavioral norm. These relationships are deemed valuable to preserve social order and often tend to influence organizational employee relationships.

Government entities

These are public organizations and agencies that provide services at the national, regional, and local levels. Government entities may have the right to sue, regulate, collect taxes, provide subsidies to enhance competitive advantage, and/or represent barriers to business activities. Those possessing semi-autonomous or autonomous authority are obviously both players and stakeholders having potential to influence a company's task environment.

Economic conditions

These are factors that impact activities relating to the production and distribution of goods and services in a particular geographic region. These include, but are not limited to unemployment, infrastructure development, GDP, GNI, and inflation.

International communities

In the context of international relations, these are groups of nations that often join together for a common cause. As an example, Article 23 of the United Nations Declaration of Human Rights does identify standards relating to respect of human dignity in the workplace. The UN, therefore, potentially influences and/or sets guidelines for employment best practices as companies expand beyond their borders.[12]

Work, technology, and leisure in the digital age

Earlier discussion aims to illustrate that a commercialized notion of work or, *what I do at my employment that is paid for*, would be narrow, indeed. Similarly narrow, would be to view "leisure" as the opposite of work—particularly in the twenty-first century. Internet technologies, portability of laptops, BlackBerries, cell phones, virtual communications and more have blurred the duality of work and leisure. Leisure—if defined as, *what I do in my own time*—may now also be one's work, and equally as self-fulfilling (or not), and pleasurable. In other words, if work and leisure in industrialized societies were once on opposite ends of a long continuum, today that continuum is disappearing, depending upon where one travels.

Additionally, one's work—whether at home, in physical organizational office spaces, en route, and/or during leisure—may often be interrupted by text-messaging and emails. Workspaces are, indeed, porous and penetrable, depending upon available technology. While many pundits attribute longer working days to effects of globalization and Internet access, or to tendencies toward workaholism, there are other explanations worthy of consideration. Could it be that the integration of work, leisure and penetration of sacrosanct work and home spaces by technology make the working day interminable? Time will tell.

This is not to suggest that work and leisure have necessarily ever been on opposite ends of a long continuum in industrialized societies. C. Davis (2000) describes just the opposite during the nineteenth century in the US Davis mentions that middle-class occupations—professionals, businessmen, and farm owners—saw little difference between their private life and their work. Each was intertwined in the other, often consuming them. A clear distinction between work and leisure is seen in twentieth-century US when the relationship between salaried employees and authority and job roles tends to be precisely defined. While not mentioned, this distinction may have been an effect of the rise of the Classical School of Management in the early 1900s. It appears, therefore, there can be no hard and fast view of the work–leisure continuum, or of the distinctions between the two, particularly as one travels to other workplace scenarios. A single constant is that both continue to be influenced by the contextual external and internal environmental factors mentioned earlier (Figures 1.1 and 1.2).

Case in point: Work or leisure—What is it?

During her business life, Nury Marshall used to have a policy about mixing work with home life. While she also worked at home, this was never gainful—paid-for work related to employment. Gainful work was done at work, and between the hours of 7:30 and 4:00. She never brought work home. Home was her refuge. In fact, if work had to be done after hours, it was accomplished in the appropriate workspace,— i.e., the office, on the weekends. None of her personal belongings were kept at work. Work-related phone calls reached home only in the case of emergencies. Personal calls, however, were received at work, and were somewhat regulated by company policy.

Today her home and work boundaries are very negotiable and fluid. Nury works at both her office and home. Both are integrated through Internet, cell phone, text-messaging, and email connections. The relative amount of access to her organization's intranet is regulated by certain rules of "law" such as firewalls and passwords, and other digital securities. Her office is an extension of her home—particularly in the summertime when she "moves in" to do the pleasurable writing she enjoys. Some signs of home life adorn walls and shelves. Not caring to do work at all is equated with turning off the computer or leaving the BlackBerry in the car. This is ironic, as for others, being on-line for one activity or another is a leisure activity. Leisure for Nury is fishing, dancing, and tennis; writing is questionable as one or the other. Apparently it is equally a leisure, work, and home activity. Her waiting times in airports, travel time on planes or by bus, and play with nieces and nephews are often computer- and Internet-technology-based. So who is to say which is which? Not even Nury could probably answer that question without hesitating to think.

In short, Nury negotiates (and manages) her working style every day. No one regulates that for her, excepting organizational policies, and indirectly, the forces depicted in Figures 1.1 and 1.2. Question: What does this all mean? Answer: *It depends.* Apparently, work is not only socially constructed, but today it is apparently *individually* shaped, deconstructed, negotiated, and constructed—in varying degrees. Question: Who's to say what the "right" way to work (as defined herein)? Answer: *Well . . . that depends too on the workplace and workspace.* As an example, in corporations concerned with digital sabotage and information safeguards, obviously, digital rights management (DRM) and policy will inevitably influence distinctions between work and leisure.[13] Law also influences these practices.[14] Policy (and trust), in turn, will be influenced by external factors—events such as the World Trade Center tragedy of September 11, 2001; and so the nature, meaning, and style of work. *The beat goes on, so to speak.*[15] It is a social construction in every society, i.e., influenced by the elements shown in Figure 1.2 and the complexity of the task environment with which these elements interact continuously. One needs to figure it out—break the code—and never take it for granted based on one's own experience.

Let's turn to technology: As technology generally refers to actions, techniques, machines, and systems used to transform inputs into outputs that contribute to satisfying human needs, it becomes obvious that both work and technology may be difficult to distinguish. Anthropologist Marietta Baba points to the difficulty of separating work and technology:

> If one observes the operation of a CAD (computer-aided design) workstation, for example, it is nearly impossible to untangle the being and actions of the CAD operator from the existence and performance of the machine. The CAD operator possesses within her body and mind the knowledge and skill that are needed to operate the CAD machine.[16]

While new technologies and applications continue to evolve in the Digital Age, the interrelationship between work and technology is not new. From early times humans have utilized tools to enhance and improve their efforts. This chapter does not attempt to provide theoretical discussion regarding the differences and interrelationships between work and technology.[17] Suffice it to say that work and technology are viewed as intertwined, but not the same. It is key to recognize that socio-cultural contexts continue to influence how and whether technology and other tools will be used to satisfy human needs. For that matter, the same is true of all of the constructs mentioned in Figure 1.2.

Additionally, technology's usage can be expected to have a ripple effect on other factors such as social relationships and action chains. Indeed, technology can potentially increase the autonomy or shared interdependence of individuals, or be an instrument of power to those in the chain of command. Technology may involve entirely new forms of activities, networks and actors. Reverting to the mica crystal metaphor, adding a layer of technology requires careful analysis of its fit with Items 1–10 listed earlier in the chapter (Figures 1.1 and 1.2). As intranet (private company-wide information systems), and extranet (the connection between company information systems and external users), and e-commerce blur borders between workspace and home space, managers need to know how design factors may positively or negatively influence the output of human resources—an important and increasingly mobile factor of production in integrated global economies.[18]

Recognizing ethnocentric tendencies

> Many of the deeper, more significant features that characterize a given culture may be experienced as threatening when first encountered. The action chain is no exception, because in a culture that prides itself on freedom and individuality, the AC [action chain] reveals that the actor, instead of being autonomous, is directly and intimately bound up in the behavior of others. . . . [People] stubbornly resist the notion that there is anything about themselves they don't know.[19]

F. Gamst discusses the importance of discovering the "web of rules" that guides each society's work. He emphasizes that "human work cannot be understood merely in terms of efficiency of exchanges in the market."[20] This echoes the thematic anthem, so to speak, of this chapter. Nevertheless, it is argued that researching a system of rules, the salient elements of Figures 1.1 and 1.2, requires systematic study that begins with *self*-assessment.

Ethnocentrism is defined herein in its broadest sense. The term generally refers to the expectations that one acquires over time as a member of a particular cultural or subcultural group. Alternatively stated, it is the expectation that work "happens"—meaning it is organized, has similar meanings, and is driven by the *same* web of rules as in one's own culture. The ethnocentric person generally sees the ways of "others" as not only unfamiliar, but possibly as inferior—to be rejected or "improved."

In actuality, seldom does the same "web of rules" apply across and within cultures.[21] Let's consider the following two scenarios, based on personal business experiences in the US vs. Latin America. These vignettes *only* address action chains. None of Figure 1.2 is addressed here.[22] Notice the difference in the action chains related to each situation.

Reflection on "action chains": United States versus Latin America

Borrowed from ethology, the action chain is closely linked conceptually to the situational frame. An action chain is a set sequence of events in which usually two or more individuals participate. It is reminiscent of a dance that is used as a means of reaching a common goal that can be reached only after, and not before, each link in the chain has been forged. . . . Every action within a frame has a beginning, a climax and an end, and comprises a number of intermediate stages.[23]

Case in Point 1a: An Appointment at a Water Municipality (US)

Research and case study support that in the US there is a preference to act as individuals (individualism) rather than as a group (collectivism).[24] This tendency toward individualism is rarely noticeable at a conscious level, yet it frequently invades one's working style and one's expectations of others. As an example, let's say I have a 10:00 a.m. appointment to meet with the Chief Engineer of a water municipality to discuss my company's interest in getting its pipe-cutting tools specified for future purchases with the water authority. I enter the office close to 10:00. I walk over to the appropriate reception area. I greet the secretary; state my name; perhaps hand her a card; I mention that I have an appointment with Mr. XXX at 10:00 a.m. The introductory portion of the action chain is completed.

Vs.

Case in Point 1b: An Appointment with a Water Municipality (Central America)

The US series of events as described would be ill-advised in Latin America. There, extended social relationships—to include family—potentially contextualize every workplace activity. Transactional thinking, i.e., concern with punctuality, time, and profits, generally does not overshadow long-term relationships in a list of priorities. The action chain in these parts of the world generally goes something like this:

I arrive at the municipality close enough to the appointed time. As I enter the door, I scan the room and acknowledge other individuals working there by nodding, smiling, and/or quietly uttering, "*buenos*" (short for *buenos días*, or "good day") as I make my way over to the appropriate reception area. The introductory part of the action chain is complete.

The US direct-to-the-counter approach does not acknowledge the human beings who are part of the work that gets done every day of the week. The interesting thing about the latter action chain is that if it is compromised in any way, the individual who skips over certain links in the chain generally doesn't notice that she/he has erred. The rudeness is accomplished, unknowingly. In the US example, adding links (e.g., a Latin American visiting the US) might be regarded as irritating and effusive. The North American in Costa Rica, as an example, might be put off by the greeting rituals, considering them "so unbusinesslike." Reiterating, action chains and social norms are learned from the time one is a small child. That does not mean, however, that they are die-cast in each individual forever. Individuals can learn to modify and/or adopt new working styles in varying degrees, as necessary.

Bridging border zones

In countries where there are historical roots of socio-economic disparity and lack of mobility between classes, often there is a tendency to see its effects in organizational life, in the form of power distance. Power distance refers to the extent to which status differences are emphasized between levels of authority.[25] Evidence of high power distance may be found in autocratic managerial practices, as opposed to the more democratic involvement of subordinates in decision-making and information sharing. In a high power distance setting, typically subordinates might wonder why an expatriate manager would be asking their opinion or be sharing information that traditionally was reserved for managers. Empowering subordinates to make or provide input on decisions would be atypical, and might be perceived as managerial incompetence if pursued without knowledge beforehand.

Yet, research supports that these border zones can be bridged when managers recognize what they are and why they exist, and define clear goals, roles, values, and (subsequently) design systems and structures that are supportive of these. Recalling earlier comments, form follows function. Companies such as Wal-Mart and Visa International are among those companies that have successfully negotiated border zones involving differing managerial styles. Apparently, negotiating a fit between one's own style of working with those of others reaps positive rewards if knowledge-based. Taking the time to assess similarities and distinctions in one's own environment compared with those of others is key.[26]

Summarizing, this chapter initiates the self-discovery process the reader is to perform throughout the book. The reader asks, *what are **my** expectations* for work and leisure? When participating in new workplace settings, *what influences work and leisure in those places? What action chains have I grown to expect? How might my template clash or complement in another setting?* The differences and similarities are vitally important to one's ongoing effectiveness in the workplace. Indeed, one size does not fit all. This type of analysis counts among the defining characteristics of leadership discussed in the following section.

Hallmarks of leadership

The subject of leadership has been addressed throughout history by many writers from many walks of life. The following selectively presents defining hallmarks of leadership as they apply to this chapter's discussion.

Contextual intelligence

Joseph Nye, Jr., acknowledged expert on the subject of leadership, and former assistant secretary of defense for International Security Affairs, the chair of the National Intelligence Council, and the deputy undersecretary of state for Security Assistance, Science, and Technology, points to the importance of "contextual intelligence" (CI) for those who aspire to leadership—and particularly to country presidents. CI is the essence of "smart power." Teddy Roosevelt obviously had it, as he knew how to balance soft and hard skills effectively according to the way in which he analyzed the context of the situation. The ability to see beyond agendas to extrapolate influential factors such as those illustrated in Figure 1.2 are vital in a world often polarized by war, terrorism, and economic turmoil.[27]

Knowing thyself [28]

Leaders uncover what informs their perceptions and perceptual screens—those walls through which all information must pass. However, this chapter argues for a much more expanded notion of self than one's personal moods, emotional intelligence, and idiosyncrasies. It also includes being a *knowledge-seeker*, discovering the web of elements that contextualizes and influences one's working environment (see Figures 1.1 and 1.2).

Transspection

Gen. Wm. Pagonis (1992), as one example, points to the importance of knowledge and empathy as essential traits of leadership. Anthropologist and global educator Robert Hanvey (1975)—when discussing qualities that are important to develop for cross-cultural awareness—prefers *transspection* to the term, "empathy." While "empathy . . . is the capacity to imagine oneself in another role in the context of *one's own* culture, transspection means the capacity to imagine onself in a role *within the context of a foreign* culture."[29] Learning to "transspect" complements the broadened view of the *know thyself* hallmark, particularly important in an age of global inter-connectivity. The transspection process involves placing oneself in the mind of another by learning their beliefs, assumptions, etc. The distinction is important (and preferable as an attainable trait) in the context of this discussion, as it supports the importance of knowledge-*seeking* as a quality of leadership.[30]

Principle of equifinality: knowing when to use it

As stated by Frederick Smith, Chairman and CEO of Federal Express, "the primary task of leadership is to communicate the vision and values of an organization."[31] The principle of equifinality embodies the idea that there may be *numerous* ways to achieve organizational goals. True, there may be one right way to work in circumstances where regulations, guidelines, and standard operating procedures (SOPs) are required to assure security, quality and/or privacy. In other situations, one needs to guard against ethnocentrism, and find ways to bridge the gap between preferred or traditional ways of doing work. Focusing on those activities that *really* matter is key.

 Leadership toolbox 1: The meaning of work

"Leadership does not reside in the routine activities of organizational work, [but rather] *in anticipation of* non-routine organizational events." Leaders are often involved in boundary management obligations. Therefore, leaders must ". . . be attuned to environmental events, interpreting and defining them for their followers. . . ."[32]

1   *When encountering unfamiliar workplace scenarios, analyze how work is understood in every setting. Research action chains and external influences. Develop a holistic understanding of work: Discover what influences the meaning of work, if and how technology is used (& why), and norms and border zones between work and leisure. Informed decision-making depends upon these activities to optimize satisfaction of human needs.*

2   *Guard against ethnocentrism in making choices and in managing diverse working styles. Bear in mind that there are many resources to assist with knowledge pursuit. Those include, but are not limited to library and on-line resources, and selectively seeking training: e.g., role-play opportunities, simulations, field experiences, and knowledgeable "informants."*[33]

Key terms and concepts

action chains, self-concept, work's meaning,
ethnocentrism, external environment, digital access,
extranet, external environment,
factors of production, socio-cultural characteristics,
power distance, task, environment

Exercises

It's time to begin *your* voyage of self-discovery.

1   Using Figure 1.2, analyze your own working environment. Draw a chart and describe. If you are not part of a workplace environment, consider others such as homelife, teamlife, and/or volunteer work you do or have done.

2   As your situation permits, compare your analysis from the previous step in discussion with a co-worker or another student, and evaluate why similarities and differences exist.

3   Transspect your environment further. Consider Items 1–10 in the list in pages 3 and 4, and describe how each relates to your work experience.

4   Relate the contents of this chapter to your experiences in other locations.

What preparation did you have for those experiences? In retrospect, were/are they adequate? Explain.

Appendix 1A
Case studies

Country snapshot: England[34]

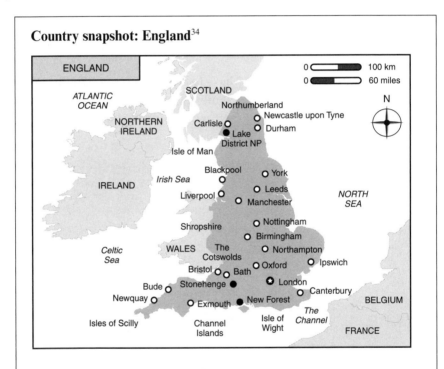

Area: 130,410 sq. km (50,352 sq. mile), 57 percent of the area of the island about the size of North Carolina.

Population: 50 million; projected to 68 million in 2056 (May 2008 est.)

Density: 1010/1.61 km (1 sq. mile); projected to 1349 in 2056

U.K. total: 60,943,912 (July 2008 est.)

Capital: London (population density, 12,377 sq. mile, May 2008, est.)

Religion (UK totals): 72 percent Christian, 3 percent Muslim (52 percent of the non-Christian population), 1 percent Hindu (18 percent of the non-Christian population), 0.6 percent Sikh (11 percent of the non-Christian population), 0.5 percent Jewish (8.7 percent of the non-Christian population), Buddhist 0.3 percent (4.9 percent of the non-Christian population).

Currency: Pound sterling (GBP) = £

HDI Index (UK): 21 out of 179 countries (2008 http://hdr.undp.or/en/statistics)[35]

System of law: common

Background: The kingdom of England is part of the island of Great Britain, which also includes the kingdom of Scotland and the principality of Wales. With Northern Ireland, together they are the United Kingdom of Great Britain and Northern Ireland—or the UK. From the sixteenth century to the peak of its power in the nineteenth century as a military and naval might, it was often said that the sun never set on the British Empire. Indeed, colonial expansion was fueled by interest in new markets, need for raw materials and more, with British colonial reach extending to an estimated one-quarter of the world's population.

Today, England is a significant player in international trade and finance, participates in the G-8 forum, and is a member of the European Union—although it remains outside of the monetary union which has adopted the euro. England's inhabitants generally represent 84 percent of the total of the UK population. The country is projected to be the most crowded in Europe due to large-scale immigration and higher birthrates among recent immigrants: Note population density figures above—almost twice that of Germany and four times that of France. Immigration not new to this area—dating back centuries; however, the scale of immigration, particularly from outside of the EU, amounts to two-thirds of the total; therefore, it is a subject of conversation due to its impact on the labor force, housing, and infrastructure.

Case 1A.1

Gareth Evans: The road to hell

John Baker, chief engineer of the Caribbean Bauxite Company of Barracania in the West Indies, was making his final preparations to leave the island. His promotion to production manager of Keso Mining Corporation near Winnipeg—one of Continental Ore's fast-expanding Canadian enterprises—had been announced a month before and now everything had been tidied up except the last vital interview with his successor—the able young Barracanian, Matthew Rennalls. It was vital that this interview be a success and that Rennalls should leave his office uplifted and encouraged to face the challenge of his new job. A touch on the bell would have brought Rennalls walking into the room but Baker delayed the moment and gazed thoughtfully through the window considering just exactly what he was going to say and, more particularly, how he was going to say it.

John Baker, an English expatriate, was 45 years old and had served his 23 years with Continental Ore in many different places: in the Far East; several countries of Africa; Europe; and, for the last two years, in the West Indies. He hadn't cared much for his previous assignment in Hamburg and was delighted when the West Indian appointment came through. Climate was not the only attraction. Baker had always preferred working overseas (in what were termed the developing countries) because he felt he had an innate knack—better than most other expatriates working for Continental Ore—of knowing just how to get on with regional staff. Twenty-four hours in Barracania, however, soon made him realize that he would need all of this "innate knack" if he was to deal effectively with the problems in this field that now awaited him.

At his first interview with Hutchins, the production manager, the whole problem of Rennalls and his future was discussed. There and then it was made quite clear to Baker that one of his most important tasks would be the "grooming" of Rennalls as his successor. Hutchins had pointed out that, not only was Rennalls one of the brightest Barracanian prospects on the staff of Caribbean Bauxite—at London University he had taken first-class honors in the B.Sc. Engineering Degree—but, being the son of the Minister of Finance and Economic Planning, he also had no small political pull.

The company had been particularly pleased when Rennalls decided to work for them rather than for the government in which his father had such a prominent post. They ascribed his action to the effect of their vigorous and liberal regionalization programme which, since the Second World War, had produced 18 Barracanians at mid-management level and given Caribbean Bauxite a good lead in this respect over all other international concerns operating in Barracania. The success of this timely regionalization policy had led to excellent relations with the government—a relationship which had been given an added importance when Barracania, three years later, became independent—an occasion which encouraged a critical and challenging attitude toward the role foreign interests would have to play in the new Barracania. Hutchins had therefore little difficulty in convincing Baker that the successful career development of Rennalls was of the first importance.

The interview with Hutchins was now two years ago and Baker, leaning back in his office chair, reviewed just how successful he had been in the "grooming" of Rennalls. What aspects of the latter's character had helped and what had hindered? What about his own personality? How had that helped or hindered? The first item to go on the credit side would, without question, be the ability of Rennalls to master the technical aspects of his job. From the start he had shown keenness and enthusiasm and had often impressed Baker with his ability in tackling new assignments and the constructive comments he invariably made in departmental discussions. He was popular with all ranks of Barracanian staff and had an ease of manner which stood him in good stead when dealing with his expatriate seniors. These were all assets, but what about the debit side?

First and foremost, there was his racial consciousness. His four years at London University had accentuated this feeling and made him sensitive to any sign of condescension on the part of the expatriates. It may have been to give expression to this sentiment that, as soon as he returned home from London, he threw himself into politics on behalf of the United Action Party which was later to win the pre-independence elections and provide the country with its first Prime Minister.

The ambitions of Rennalls—and he certainly was ambitious—did not, however, lie in politics for, staunch nationalist as he was, he saw that he could serve himself and his country best—for was not bauxite responsible for nearly half the value of Barracania's export trade?—by putting his engineering talent to the best use possible. On this account, Hutchins found that he had an unexpectedly easy task in persuading Rennalls to give up his political work before entering the production department as an assistant engineer.

It was, Baker knew, Rennalls' well-repressed sense of race consciousness that had prevented their relationship from being as close as it should have been. On the surface, nothing could have seemed more agreeable. Formality between the two men was at a minimum; Baker was delighted to find that his assistant shared his own peculiar "shaggy dog" sense of humor so that jokes were continually being exchanged; they entertained each other at their houses and often played tennis together—and yet the barrier remained invisible, indefinable, but ever present. The existence of this "screen" between them was a constant source of frustration to Baker since it indicated a weakness which he was loath to accept. If successful with all other nationalities, why not with Rennalls?

But at least he had managed to "break through" to Rennalls more successfully than any other expatriate. In fact, it was the young Barracanian's attitude—sometimes overbearing, sometimes cynical—toward other company expatriates that had been one of the subjects Baker had raised last year when he discussed Rennalls' staff report with him. He knew, too, that he would have to raise the same subject again in the forthcoming interview because Jackson, the senior draughtsman, had complained only yesterday about the rudeness of Rennalls. With this thought in mind, Baker leaned forward and spoke into the intercom. "Would you come in, Matt, please? I'd like a word with you."

Later, when Matt Rennalls entered John Baker's office, Baker greeted him, "Do sit down. Have a cigarette." Baker paused while he held out his lighter and then went on.

"As you know, Matt, I'll be off to Canada in a few days' time, and before I go, I thought it would be useful if we could have a final chat together. It is indeed with some deference that I suggest I can be of help. You will shortly be sitting in this chair doing the job I am now doing, but I, on the other hand, am 10 years older, so perhaps you can accept the idea that I may be able to give you the benefit of my longer experience."

Baker saw Rennalls stiffen slightly in his chair as he made this point so added in explanation, "You and I have attended enough company courses to remember those repeated requests by the personnel manager to tell people how they are getting on as often as the convenient moment arises and not just the automatic 'once a year' when, by regulation, staff reports have to be discussed."

Rennalls nodded his agreement so Baker went on, "I shall always remember the last job performance discussion I had with my previous boss back in Germany. He used what he called the 'plus and minus' technique. His firm belief was that when a senior, by discussion, seeks to improve the work performance of his staff, his prime objective should be to make sure that the latter leaves the interview encouraged and inspired to improve. Any criticism must, therefore, be constructive and helpful. He said that one very good way to encourage a man—and I fully agree with him—is to tell him about his good points—the plus factors—as well as his weak ones—the minus factors—so I thought, Matt, it would be a good idea to run our discussion along these lines."

Rennalls offered no comment, so Baker continued: "Let me say, therefore, right away, that, as far as your own work performance is concerned, the plus far outweighs the minus. I have, for instance, been most impressed with the way you have adapted your considerable theoretical knowledge to master the practical techniques of your job—that ingenious method you used to get air down to the fifth-shaft level is a sufficient case in point—and at departmental meetings. I have invariably found your comments well taken and helpful. In fact, you will be interested to know that only last week I reported to Mr. Hutchins that, from the technical point of view, he could not wish for a more able man to succeed to the position of chief engineer."

"That's very good indeed of you, John," cut in Rennalls with a smile of thanks. "My only worry now is how to live up to such a high recommendation."

"Of that I am quite sure," returned Baker, "especially if you can overcome the minus factor which I would like now to discuss with you. It is one which I have talked about before so I'll come straight to the point. I have noticed that you are more friendly and get on better with your fellow Barracanians than you do with Europeans. In point of fact, I had a complaint only yesterday from Mr. Jackson, who said you had been rude to him—and not for the first time either.

"There is, Matt, I am sure, no need for me to tell you how necessary it will be for you to get on well with expatriates because until the company has trained up sufficient men of your calibre, Europeans are bound to occupy senior positions here in Barracania. All this is vital to your future interests, so can I help you in any way?"

While Baker was speaking on this theme, Rennalls had sat tensed in his chair and it was some seconds before he replied. "It is quite extraordinary, isn't it, how one can convey an impression to others so at variance with what one intends? I can only assure you once again that my disputes with Jackson—and you may remember also Godson— have had nothing at all to do with the color of their skins. I promise you that if a Barracanian had behaved in an equally peremptory manner I would have reacted in precisely the same way. And again, if I may say it within these four walls, I am sure I am not the only one who has found Jackson and Godson difficult. I could mention the names of several expatriates who have felt the same. However, I am really sorry to have created this impression of not being able to get on with Europeans—it is an entirely false one—and I quite realize that I must do all I can to correct it as quickly as possible. On your last point, regarding Europeans holding senior positions in the company for some time to come, I quite accept the situation. I know that Caribbean Bauxite—as they have been doing for many years now—will promote Barracanians as soon as their experience warrants it. And, finally, I would like to assure you, John—and my father thinks the same too— that I am very happy in my work here and hope to stay with the company for many years to come."

Rennalls had spoken earnestly and, although not convinced by what he had heard, Baker did not think he could pursue the matter further except to say, "All right, Matt, my impression *may* be wrong, but I would like to remind you about the truth of that old saying, 'What is important is not what is true but what is believed.' Let it rest at that."

But suddenly Baker knew that he didn't want to "let it rest at that." He was disappointed once again at not being able to "break through" to Rennalls and having yet again to listen to his bland denial that there was any racial prejudice in his make-up. Baker, who had intended ending the interview at this point, decided to try another tack.

"To return for a moment to the 'plus and minus' technique I was telling you about just now, there is another plus factor I forgot to mention. I would like to congratulate you not only on the calibre of your work but also on the ability you have shown in overcoming a challenge which I, as a European, have never had to meet.

"Continental Ore is, as you know, a typical commercial enterprise—admittedly a big one—which is a product of the economic and social environment of the United States and Western Europe. My ancestors have all been brought up in this environment for the past two or three hundred years and I have, therefore, been able to live in a world in which commerce (as we know it today) has been part and parcel of my being. It has not been something revolutionary and new which has suddenly entered my life. In your case," went on Baker, "the situation is different because you and your forebears have only had some fifty or sixty years' experience of this commercial environment. You have had to face the challenge of bridging the gap between fifty and two or three hundred years. Again, Matt, let me congratulate you—and people like you—once again on having so successfully overcome this particular hurdle. It is for this very reason that I think the outlook for Barracania—and particularly Caribbean Bauxite—is so bright."

Rennalls had listened intently and when Baker finished, replied, "Well, once again, John, I have to thank you for what you have said, and, for my part, I can only say that it is gratifying to know that my own personal effort has been so much appreciated. I hope that more people will soon come to think as you do."

There was a pause and, for a moment, Baker thought hopefully that he was about to achieve his long-awaited "breakthrough," but Rennalls merely smiled back. The barrier remained unbreached. There remained some five minutes' cheerful conversation about the contrast between the Caribbean and Canadian climate and whether the West Indies had any hope of beating England in the Fifth Test before Baker drew the interview to a close. Although he was as far as ever from knowing the real Rennalls, he was nevertheless glad that the interview had run along in this friendly manner and, particularly, that it had ended on such a cheerful note.

The following morning, Baker had some farewells to make, so he arrived at the office considerably later than usual. He had no sooner sat down at his desk than his secretary walked into the room with a worried frown on her face. Her words came fast. "When I arrived this morning I found Mr. Rennalls already waiting at my door. He seemed very angry and told me in quite a peremptory manner that he had a vital letter to dictate which must be sent off without any delay. He was so worked up that he couldn't keep still and kept pacing about the room, which is most unlike him. He wouldn't even wait to read what he had dictated. Just signed the page where he thought the letter would end. It has been distributed and your copy is in your 'in tray'."

Puzzled and feeling vaguely uneasy, Baker opened the "Confidential" envelope and read the letter (see page 24).

Exercises: Breaking the code

This case is an excellent opportunity to explore factors that are addressed in Chapter 1. Appendix 2A provides an opportunity to analyze the root causes of conflict and discomfort through diagramming.

1   Discuss (a) Item 1 (**"The job itself"**) and (b) Item 2 (**"The degree of autonomy vs. independence"**) from page 3 as they relate to this case.

   a   In other words, irrespective of cultural issues, what are the knowledge, skills, and abilities that are required for chief engineer of the Caribbean Bauxite Company of Barracania—the position that Rennalls is to fill and Baker is about to leave?

   b   Consider all the direct and indirect stakeholders that will probably have a direct and/or indirect effect on decision making for this position.

2   Analyze the conversation between Rennalls and Baker. How might history explain Rennalls' feelings toward Baker and vice versa? Summarize and document your sources of information. Also consider any aspects of Figure 1.2 that require analysis in order to discover the "web of rules" that may influence protocol at the Caribbean Bauxite Company.

3   Critique the way in which Baker handled Rennalls' performance appraisal. Most importantly, support your views with wisdom from gurus in the field, as well as your own business experience. Return to this exercise after reading Chapter 8.

From: Assistant Engineer
To: The Chief Engineer, Caribbean Bauxite Limited

ASSESSMENT OF INTERVIEW BETWEEN MESSRS.
BAKER AND RENNALLS
[RENNALLS' LETTER TO BAKER]

14th August (year)

It has always been my practice to respect the advice given me by seniors, so after our interview, I decided to give careful thought once again to its main points and so make sure that I had understood all that had been said. As I promised you at the time, I had every intention of putting your advice to the best effect.

It was not, therefore, until I had sat down quietly in my home yesterday evening to consider the interview objectively that its main purport became clear. Only then did the full enormity of what you said dawn on me. The more I thought about it, the more convinced I was that I had hit upon the real truth—and the more furious I became. With a facility in the English language which I—a poor Barracanian—cannot hope to match, you had the audacity to insult me (and through me every Barracanian worth his salt) by claiming that our knowledge of modern living is only a paltry fifty years old whilst yours goes back 200–300 years. As if your materialistic commercial environment could possibly be compared with the spiritual values of our culture. I'll have you know that if much of what I saw in London is representative of your most boasted culture, I hope fervently that it will never come to Barracania. By what right do you have the effrontery to condescend to us? At heart, all you Europeans think us barbarians, or, as you say amongst yourselves, we are "just down from the trees."

Far into the night I discussed this matter with my father, and he is as disgusted as I. He agrees with me that any company whose senior staff think as you do is no place for any Barracanian proud of his culture and race—so much for all the company "clap-trap" and specious propaganda about regionalization and Barracania for the Barracanians.

I feel ashamed and betrayed. Please accept this letter as my resignation which I wish to become effective immediately.

c.c. Production Manager
        Managing Director

Source: Gareth Evans, "Road to Hell." Reprinted
(Parts A, B, C) by permission of the
Harvard Business School #8095-119757865-0351.

Country snapshot: India[36]

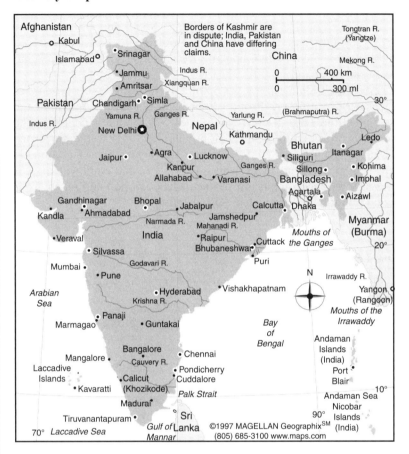

Area: 3,287,590 sq. km (1,269,219 sq. miles) slightly more than one third the size of US

Population: 1166 million (July, 2009 est.), projected to 1400 million by 2025

Population density: 354/ sq. km (918/sq. miles)

Capital: New Delhi (population density, 9340/sq. km)

Religion: Hinduism (80.5 percent), Muslims (13.4 percent), Christianity (2.3 percent), Sikhs (1.9 percent), Buddhist (0.8 percent), Jains (0.4 percent)

Currency: Indian rupees (INR)

HDI Index (India): 134 out of 177 countries

System of law: English common law

Background: The Republic of India is located in South Asia. It is the seventh largest country by geographical area. It is bordered by Pakistan to the West, People's Republic of China, Nepal and Bhutan to the North, and Bangladesh and Myanmar to the East. India was annexed by the British East India Company from the early 18th century and became an independent nation in 1947.

Today, the Indian economy is among the fastest growing economies in the world, with a GDP of $3.304 trillion (2008 est.). India has the world's second largest labor force, with 523.5 million people.[37] The country is projected to be the most populous country in the world surpassing China in year 2025.[38] Despite significant gains in economic growth, improvements in its healthcare system, and employment generation, India faces significant problems like overpopulation, environmental pollution, poverty, dense urbanization.

Case 1A.2

Suyog Dharmadhikari, Navneet Jain, and Elaine S. Potoker: Dark days at Sunlite

Mike Parker, a budding young engineer, was sitting in his office in Detroit, Michigan wondering:

> Why did his gradual effort to empower the employees of Sunlite to make their own decisions go wrong?. . .
> Why did the employees not seem to care about project completion; why the lax attitude? What would help them to facilitate faster completion of the project?

He recalled it had only been one year ago when his boss walked in his cubicle to ask him to manage a project in Pune, India, and now he was scratching his head trying to figure out what happened

Sunlite group is a Pune-based Indian company that manufactures various forged and machine components for the automotive and non-automotive sectors. Established in 1966, the company's core competency lies in providing end-to-end solutions from product conceptualization, development, to manufacturing, testing and delivery of the final product.

The company's product range consists of generic high-volume industrial components such as bearings and forgings and also specialized components for the automotive, aerospace, and energy industry. The company originally had 70 employees. However, with the company's expanding operations and diversification from a primary automotive ancillary to an engineering enterprise, the employee numbers increased to 6500 in 2007. Soon, the outstanding reputation for customer service, coupled with the management commitment to quality and technical research, made Sunlite group the preferred domestic and global supplier for a major original equipment manufacturer (OEM).

Being an Indian company, the work culture at Sunlite was deeply influenced by Indian social and political factors. The company is unionized and the company's labor union was strongly affiliated to a political group in India. The company is divided into hierarchies at different levels, with clear demarcation of responsibilities and authorities.

In 2007, Sunlite group was acquired by a US-based company called Greenfield Corporation, with Greenfield acquiring a 75 percent share in Sunlite in an all-cash transaction. Greenfield was a major OEM manufacturer and a preferred supplier for many top automakers in the US and around the world. The company had successfully expanded to some of the major automobile markets in Europe, Asia, and South America in recent years. Greenfield had a presence in many countries in Asia including China, but not in India. This recent acquisition not only gave it a foothold in India's growing automobile and auto-ancillary manufacturing sector, but also management control of Sunlite. It could now make decisions regarding the company's strategic and operational matters. As it turned out, the timing was right for such an acquisition, since the Indian new car market projections were quite positive. In fact, in 2008, the Indian new car market grew by 15.5 percent to reach a value of $28 billion; in volume terms, it grew by 11.3 percent to reach a volume of 1.7 million units.[39]

The management at Greenfield had never worked with an Indian company in the past, and, therefore, they were not familiar with the work culture in India. For this reason the management decided to let a local person manage the operations. The company also decided to set up a new magnetic particle inspection facility at Sunlite's Pune plant in India. The total duration for this project was estimated to be eight months and the project was to be headed by Rajeev Gupta, a 45-year-old civil engineer. Rajeev had extensive experience in the industrial construction industry, and he joined Sunlite as a supervisory engineer in 2001. He rose through the ranks quickly to become head of the engineering construction division.

The rationale behind the new installation was to improve the post-treatment heating operations such as shot blasting, magnetic particle inspection, finishing, and painting/rust prevention application. This was supposed to be a state-of-the-art processing facility and would be one of three in the world that Greenfield would operate. The project was scheduled to be completed in three phases:

- The first phase was completion of the machine foundation.
- The second phase was installation of the machine.
- The third and final phase was preliminary assessment of the machine to check for smooth functioning and any underlying defects of the machine.

On the US side, Michael Park, a young engineer with excellent project management skills, was assigned to manage the project at the financial and administrative level. A month into the project, his division head walked in and asked him if he would be interested in going to Pune to manage the project on-site as Rajeev had to quit because of some family issues. This was a major setback for the company, as no last-minute replacement was available for Rajeev, and the second phase had to be started within a few days, without any delays.

Mike had always wanted to travel outside the US, and upon hearing about this opportunity, he instantly signed up. Since Mike had already been handling the project, he had a good idea of the operations on a day-to-day basis. Based on his conversations and e-mail exchanges with Rajeev, he knew that Rajeev used to come in every morning at 8:30 am. He customarily would have a meeting with all the staff members and workers to review the progress of ongoing projects, redress workers' grievances pertaining to any resource constraints or the welfare issues of workers, and brief the workers about specific safety considerations for the day. In Rajeev's absence, the engineer and supervisor were responsible for conducting the meetings. Though the project engineer and supervisor were primarily responsible to oversee the field operations, Rajeev himself visited the project site regularly. He did so to maintain an effective control of the workers and guide them while performing risky operations. Rajeev headed the engineering division; subordinate to him was the project manager, the project engineers, site supervisor and site workers. Figure 1A.1 shows the reporting relationship pattern at the engineering division at Sunlite.

Greenfield sent Michael to India in order to ensure that the project would be completed in a timely manner. Soon after Mike's arrival, work started again at the facility. Initially, he was involved to a large extent in managing the day-to-day operations, but as time passed, he decided to let his colleagues take charge of the activities. However, in Mike's absence, the project engineer and the site staff portrayed a laid back attitude towards project completion. Often, the engineers would report to work late in the morning and leave before the scheduled time. Subsequently, the workers left immediately, leaving the site operations unattended. During work hours, the workers would be busy chatting with each other or doing other activities. Sometimes, the

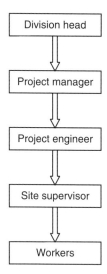

Figure 1A.1 Reporting relationships at Sunlite.

workers did not have enough resources to finish the daily planned activities.

The morning meetings were not organized regularly, as the field supervisor and engineer did not show keen interest in listening to workers' issues. There was no apparent central authority available to talk with the workers and resolve their issues. No one briefed the workers on safety issues either. There were frequent instances of workers' absenteeism such as a worker taking a half day without even informing the supervisor. After six weeks of Mike's taking charge of the project, the second phase was behind schedule.

Management at Greenfield was obviously concerned over missed deadlines, and frequently pressed Mike to expedite the project completion. Mike had an independent working style, and unlike Rajeev, he was neither comfortable with bureaucracy, nor with what he felt was micromanagement of the employees. Mike's approach towards managing employees was more like a facilitator, rather than being a boss.

One day, a new hire had a serious accident while working with a welding machine, and work came to a standstill at the facility. The unions were very upset with this incident and they decided to file a lawsuit against the company and threatened a strike. The local government ordered an inquiry into the whole incident, and the findings pointed that the workers were not briefed on safety issues by the concerned supervisor/manager. The matter worsened due to the absence of the project manager at the project site when the incident happened. All these developments further delayed the completion of the second phase. After learning about the incident, the management at Greenfield immediately offered a public apology, and offered compensation for the treatment of injured labor. Finally, the lawsuit was taken back and work resumed at the facility.

The management at Greenfield had enough troubles, and so they decided to send Rajeev Gupta back to the company. Fortunately for Greenfield, Rajeev agreed to join as a temporary substitute until project completion, and Michael was called back to the US. After 11 long months, the project was finally completed with a lot of time and financial resources wasted. Park was still trying to figure out what went wrong.

Exercise questions

1   Analyze the situation in the case; summarize the issues involved.
2   Research information specific to power distance and uncertainty avoidance specific to India vs. the United States. Search library articles that address management styles in India vs. the United States.
3   Summarize your findings.
4   How would you evaluate Michael's and Rajeev's management style?
5   What recommendations would you make to Michael in managing the situation in retrospect?

Case 1A.3A

Elaine S. Potoker: Subtle annoyances

Greg Daniels is a full professor at a college in the northeast United States. He is spending six months as part of a faculty exchange with a University in Montemayor.[40] Professor Daniels teaches an undergraduate senior-level strategic management course during the winter term. (Winter there is the rainy season.) There are 35 students in the class.

The class is apparently going well: The students actively participate in discussion. They turn in assignments when due. They express their appreciation for the opportunity to study with a distinguished faculty on exchange. Daniels, however, is bothered by the fact that as many as 5–10 students show up as much as half an hour late for class. From conversation with colleagues, this situation is apparently typical. To counter the tardiness, Daniels was advised to give a quiz each week at the beginning of the class. The situation improved. Other subtle annoyances involved the ten-minute break given half-way through the class. Some students did not return until one-half hour later, standing outside the classroom to socialize with friends in other classes or to phone friends on their cell phones. Daniels finds it uncomfortable to go out into the hall to shepherd students back to class.

The underlying causalities precipitating Daniel's subtle annoyances are complex. Heavy afternoon rains in winter are a fact of life and congested roads and spent infrastructure cause impossible delays. Additionally, neither Daniels nor other professors in the hosting University have the autonomy to require attendance: Attendance is not mandatory. Further, relationships take precedence over schedules. Many students are not in school during the day; evening is where they finally meet those they have been text messaging all day. Leaving extra early to assure prompt arrival to class may not happen if it means cutting short time with others during the day.

Daniels discovered that interesting application discussions pulled students back into class. Group work was a key motivator. While he never condoned the routine tardiness of some, he learned to place a higher premium on group interaction and active participation in group projects.

What would you do? Do you agree with Daniels? Explain.

Case 1A.3B

Elaine S. Potoker: The sound of silence

For the first few weeks, Professor Daniels specified that assignments be done individually. His pattern was to go around the room to solicit individual views and encourage commentary and reaction by other students. By week three, however, Daniels noticed a resistance to individual assignments: "Why do we have to do this by ourselves?" Daniels gave the standard answer, stressing that he wanted to get a sense of their individual grasp of the material and their ability to integrate relevant examples. The reaction was silence.

One day he received the following email. The students were asked to read a seminal article in the *Harvard Business Review* by Michael Porter (1996). The translation follows each line:

De: _____
From: _____

Enviado el: _____
Sent (date): _____

Para: _____
For: Professor Daniels

Asunto: Caso de Porter
Subject: Porter Case

Estimado profesor:
Dear Professor:

Deseo comunicarles mi disconformidad con la tarea asignada para la clase de hoy martes 18 de septiembre.
I am writing to inform you of my disagreement with the assigned homework for today, Tues., Sept. 18th.

El artículo "What is Strategy" by Michael E. Porter se encuentra en el idioma inglés
The article, "What is Strategy" by Michael Porter is written in English,

y como es de su conocimiento en nuestra carrera no llevamos ni un sólo curso de dicho
and as you know, in our program, we don't take even one course in that language, and

idioma y mucho menos con lenguaje técnico. Además, en la Carta al Estudiante discutida al inicio
much less with technical language. Also, in the Letter to Students discussed at the start

de clase; el sistema de evaluación es el siguiente:
of class, the evaluation system is as follows:

Participación en clase: 20%
Class participation:

Casos y actividades GRUPALES: 20%
GROUP activities:

Pruebas cortas individuales: 20%
Short quizzes

Trabajos de investigación: 20%
Research projects

Por lo que, las únicas asignaciones individuales son las pruebas cortas.
Therefore, the only individual assignments are short quizzes.

Debido a lo anterior no considero que este en el deber de realizar dicha tarea.
Due to the above, I don't feel that I have any obligation to do the assignment.

Realmente agradezco su deseo de enriquecer nuestro conocimiento.
I really appreciate your desire to enrich our knowledge.

Atentamente,
Sincerely,
Magdalena

What should Daniels do? What would you do?

Exercise

Through class discussion, identify the root causes of this situation and the effects they caused. Develop countermeasures to address the causes.

Country snapshot: Turkey

Area: 780,580 sq. km; 7200 km coastline; slightly larger than Texas

Population: 76,805,524 (July 2009 est.); projected to 100 million in 2020

Density: 158/1.61 km (1 sq. miles); projected to 206 in 2020

Capital: Ankara (population, 4,548,939; 2008—pop. density, 1233 sq. miles)

Religion: Turkey (Totals) Muslim 99.8 percent (mostly Sunni), other 0.2 percent (mostly Christians and Jews)

Currency: Turkish lira (TL)

HDI Index: 79 out of 179 countries (2009 http://hdr.undp.or/en/statistics)

System of law: civil law system derived from various European continental legal systems

Background: At the beginning of the twentieth century, the Ottoman Empire collapsed, and after the National War of Independence, today's Turkish Republic took its place among the independent and modern states of the contemporary world. When the Allied Powers occupied and partitioned Anatolia after World War I, Mustafa Kemal, later sur-named Atatürk (1881–1938), mobilized the Turks in Anatolia into a cohesive resistance force. After a victorious defense of the homeland for four years, the Treaty of Lausanne was signed with the Allies on July 23, 1923, which approved Mustafa Kemal's governmental sovereignty over Turkey's present borders.

Turkey's 783,562.38 sq. km of land is divided into seven geographic regions. The country is surrounded by four seas: the Mediterranean Sea, the Aegean Sea, the Sea of Marmara, and the Black Sea. Today, Turkey is an active member in the global world with its increasing international trade volume, participates in the G-20 forum, and is headed toward accession to the European Union. Geographically, Turkey is viewed as a land bridge between the East and West and North and South. Since the political economies of its neighbors vary tremendously in all directions, these factors present many challenges to the Turkish people and their government. Workforce mobility and migration are obviously huge factors that impact this country on an ongoing basis due to its strategic location.

With a total population of 70 million, of which 24.7 million people are active in the labor force, the country has the fourth largest labor force of the 27 countries of Europe. In addition to that, Turkey has a young, dynamic labor force with an average age of 28.3 years old.[41]

Case 1A.4

Okan Tuna and Elaine Potoker: My way or the highway . . .

Izmir, Turkey, January, 2006. Orhan Bakır, the head of the Board of Directors of Lo-Co Logistics (LCL) looked around at his audience—family members and the press—patiently awaiting his opening comments, and also introduced the head of the Board of Directors of Border Logistics, Patrick Brucher.

*"We are witnessing a historical moment for our company and Turkish Logistics market. After 6 months of negotiations with the managers of German Based **Border Logistics**, we finalized merger details that will increase the quality of our logistics operations and market share in Turkey. The new company will be named as **Border-Lo-Co Logistics (BLC,)** and **Border Logistics** will be represented by two members in the Board of Directors. One manager from Border Logistics will take over the CEO post of the new BLC venture for a 3-year-term. I believe that their experience in sophisticated logistics operations and our knowledge in the Turkish market will create an unprecedented synergy in the market."*

When Mr. Orhan Bakır finished his speech, his son, Ahmet Bakır, approached his father and hugged him very strongly; *"It is a really great moment for our family and company. You have done an amazing job."*

"Do not forget your effort, son," Mr. Orhan Bakır sighed and continued, *"You know, I have always wanted this company to be managed by the members of our family. Admittedly, you and your sister convinced me to do that. Your era has begun today."*

Although Mr. Bakır was in favor of this merger in terms of financial issues, he hid his upset from his son, Ahmet, about relinquishing half of the control to Border Logistics. Yet, as Ahmet walked away, he was not fooled. He knew his father well, and so did the family. His father had a very rigid management philosophy towards employees and suppliers. Organizational practices included long working hours and no overpay—a practice that was common in the Turkish logistics industry. Orhan was a little bit harsher than the other companies in the industry: He preferred to work with "outsiders" on a short-term basis. He always was reluctant to establish partnerships with anyone outside of the family. Ahmed didn't fault his father for this. The reasons were obvious: In Turkey, lack of trust in the legal process and the inflexibility of contracts were always reasons not to trust anyone but family members. Therefore, family companies in Turkey are the norm—an element of security for people looking for continuity and cohesion in an environment characterized by frequent crises and the loss of trust in state-run institutions. People need familiar institutions and traditions that they can hold on to as they try to adapt to change, because they essentially want stability and continuity.[42] Due to these facts, Mr. Bakır was inclined to increase the numbers of truck fleet instead of working suppliers. No . . . Ahmet had no illusions about the difficulty that was ahead of them. This merger was not going to be easy.

Mr. Bakır is 66 years old and has a deep knowledge of domestic land transportation in Turkey. Lo-Co Logistics was founded in 1981 by Orhan Bakır in Izmir to benefit the transportation activities generated by the Port of Izmir. The company invested heavily in land transportation both in domestic and international scope. Mr. Bakır also emphasized the investment in warehousing facilities all over Turkey in order to increase the coverage of LTL (Less-Truck-Load) services. Although the trade capital of Turkey is Istanbul, Mr. Bakır did not move the company's headquarters to Istanbul even though the Istanbul Branch of the company was generating more revenue than the other branches.

Orhan kept the General Manager post until 2004 and then he decided to pass this post to his son, but kept his daughter and son on the Board of Directors of the company since they both have a graduate degree on transport management from Germany and speak German very fluently.

First day in the office: a German in Turkey

February 2006. Mr. Brucher, Mr. Orhan, Ahmet Bakır, and Mr. Ralph Hemmerling met to discuss the immediate plans of the new merger. Mr. Brucher opened the session by introducing Mr. Hemmerling, CEO of the new merger in Turkey.

Mr. Hemmerling stood up and greeted all the participants: *"I am very humbled and proud for being promoted to this position. I will do my best. As you know, our immediate goal is to develop a domestic transportation service network in order to provide milk-run transportation services for the auto manufacturers in Turkey. In addition to that, we are also planning to give quality services to the FMCG (Fast Moving Consumer Goods) firms. While achieving those goals, we are planning to use Turkish truck transportation companies as suppliers instead of using our own fleet. This will cut costs considerably."*

Mr. Hemmerling had a transport management degree from a leading German University and was recently assigned as the Deputy Manager of Border Logistics (BL) in Logistics Operations. He started a new project to increase the capabilities of the company in terms of long term contracts. Since the first day of his transfer from a logistics department of an auto manufacturing company where he had spent 10 years in various positions, he brought his "in house" logistics expertise to BL. During his six years of tenure in the company, he was always in favor of contemporary management and human resource measures in order to achieve excellent logistics operations.

Hemmerling's talents also included development of a very successful supplier network for Border Logistics with small transportation companies. Partners of the company are small enterprises that have a fleet of 5–10 trucks. He started partner development programs with these suppliers in order to increase the communication and establish long-term relationships. Through commitment to Border Logistics, they achieved flexibility in their operations that they could not maintain on their own: In fact, BL now cooperates with over 150 carrier enterprises in Europe, thanks to Hemmerling's initial efforts. Thus, a fleet of over 1550 trucks is currently available to Border Logistics. Their state of the art supplier network enabled Border Logistics to create customer-integrated and contract logistics solutions.

The company increased its performance in milk-run operations especially for automotive companies. Milk-run is a delivery method for mixed loads from different suppliers. This term's origin is based on the dairy industry's practice—whereby one tanker collects milk every day from several dairy farmers for delivery to a milk processing firm. The milk-run method enables companies to decrease the inventory level and to increase the customer service level such as delivery on time. Border

Logistics collects the LTL (Less-Truck-Load) cargoes from suppliers and consolidates them in FTL (Full-Truck-Load) to deliver the point of manufacturing sites. However, delivery frequency is daily in most cases. This method requires a high level of sophistication and coordination in logistics operations. The success of Border Logistics is based on the efficient management model with its small partners. They use a common database to share the cargo and destination information among the main suppliers. In addition to that, they build their relationship on trust.

"I am in favor of milk-run operations as you know. However, I object to using truck transportation suppliers," boomed Orhan Bakır; *"Domestic transportation in Turkey is mainly done by trucks owned by very small companies. In most cases, a truck driver has only one truck and travels all over Turkey in order to find cargo. It is not very easy for Border-Lo-Co Logistics to manage such dispersed partners all over Turkey to give quality milk-run services."*

He then stopped, looked squarely at Hemmerling, and added, *"There are small and medium sized cargo intermediaries that match the truck drivers and the cargo owners. Those intermediaries are located in specific locations. For example, we have such a location in Izmir hosting more than 100 small intermediaries. Truck drivers visit these locations in order to find cargo for their trucks. Needless to say, we cannot avoid this reality and we need this system to manage efficiently to reach our objective. And it is not that easy to transform such suppliers to be our long term suppliers."*

Ahmet Bakır quickly intervened, *"The milk-run system requires sophisticated fleet management. It is a universal system. Needless to say, our potential customers' expectations are universal, too. It is inevitable that we will need to use such a proven system in Turkey."*

The meeting ended in a restaurant along the coast of Izmir Bay, where they had delicious Mediterranean fish and Turkish classical liquor raki. They all cheered for the success of the new merger. However, Mr. Hemmerling was thinking about the challenges awaiting him, while Orhan Bakır grabbed for his handkerchief to wipe the perspiration off his face.

Challenges for Mr. Hemmerling

The next day, Mr. Hemmerling arrived at the office very early and started to review information on Lo-Co Logistics while leaning back in his office chair. He first of all focused on the organizational and managerial environment of the company.

The company started to apply "Quality Management" practices within the title of ISO-9001 in 1999. They developed their first official organization chart, job descriptions and flow charts as a result of the quality management project.

Figure 1A.2 Organization chart of Lo-Co Logistics.

In addition to these developments, they made some improvements in strategic management such as application of SWOT analysis for long-term planning.

Mr. Hemmerling was very impressed by those achievements. However, after talking with some managers he realized that such practices within the name of the Quality Management project did not change the philosophy of the "family company." In other words, they had used such practices, not for the sake of the internal transformation within the company, but rather to "look good" for their customers and show they were progressive. He found the organization structure was quite traditional—divided into functional areas without many linkages, slow to respond to external changes (due to their traditional structure), and very centralized.

After finishing his review, Hemmerling entered Ahmet Bakır's office who greeted him: *"Turkish coffee?"*

Hemmerling nodded and added *"No sugar please,"* and then went on *"I do really appreciate your support in yesterday's meeting. I had much difficulty communicating with your father. However, I believe you appreciated the importance of working with suppliers by developing a long term program."*

"Partial support, I think," Mr. Ahmet Bakır replied. *"I do agree with my dad in some points. He started in business as a truck driver and he has a deep knowledge of the industry—and truck drivers' attitudes—in every detail. Truck drivers—and small truck owners—are not very easy persons to be managed by contemporary management techniques. We tried this before. During the Quality Management project, truck drivers received training. We also hired a consultant who tried to establish a supplier development program, including the small truck suppliers of the company. Such achievements did not yield measurable outputs."*

"I do appreciate your former effort; however, I do insist on overhauling your former system and improve it by using the know-how of Border Logistics," responded Mr. Hemmerling and he added: *"Border Logistics' organizational structure is horizontal and supports the empowered*

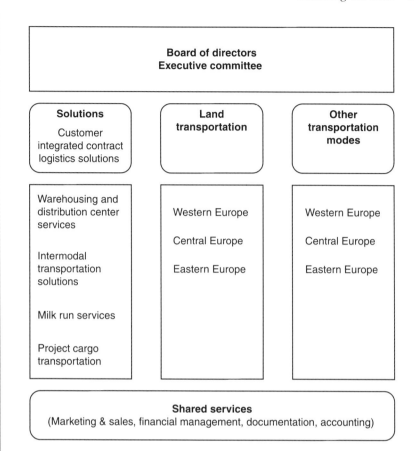

Figure 1A.3 Organization chart of Border Logistics.

roles within the organization. The company has three business segments: Solutions, Land Transportation and Other Transportation Modes. This structure creates the necessary flexibility and possibility to respond rapidly to changing customer and supplier demands. Rights and personality of individuals are respected. At the same time, every employee is given the opportunity and room for developing themselves and individual ideas are taken into consideration."

Mr. Hemmerling also described the importance of using suppliers in milk-run operations: *"You know, a milk-run system requires a very high fixed cost in terms of assets. We do not know the market potential yet. I think it is less costly to use truck transportation suppliers. I think we can start this system here in Turkey as soon as possible."*

Ahmet Bakır listened intently, peering at Hemmerling, yet with thoughts of the family traditions he knew so well. After Hemmerling finished, he replied: *"As you know, I am the one who convinced my family to make this merger. However, I really find your thoughts not very suitable for the Turkish market. Do not change the system right now. Keep it as it is, and maybe we can apply your strategy in the coming years!"*

Mr. Hemmerling was astonished; he was not expecting such a response from Ahmet. He replied: *"Mr. Bakır. Let me remind you I am representing Border Logistics here and we do appreciate the contemporary approaches in every process. So, it is inevitable to apply such principles here, in our new merger."*

Mr. Hemmerling left Mr. Bakır's office and sat down at his desk. He glimpsed the Bay of Izmir and smiled; *"How many more miles will I need to ride on this bumpy highway to find my way?"*

Questions

1   Why is this merger more complicated than it seems? Explain the factors—both seen and unseen—that each of the parties in the merger faces.
2   How do you understand the role of "logistics" in strategic business management? For assistance, go to the Council of Supply Chain Management web-site, http://cscmp.org/aboutcscmp/definitions.asp. Why are relationships so important in the field of logistics?
3   Based on the case, how may cultural differences interfere with creation of "efficiencies?" Or, explain why are "best practices" not always achievable due to cultural effects? Or *are* they? (See Chapter 8!).
4   What "web of rules" applies in making management decisions at LCL vs. Borders. How can these be resolved?
5   Analyze the conversation between Mr. Hemmerling and Ahmet Bakır. Considering the trust issue in Turkish family companies, how can this hurdle be overcome?

2   The limitations of language

The nuances of culture are complex and seem infinitely variable. These nuances are communicated by means of language[1]—itself complex and constantly changing. In any given instance, language and culture are intimately interwoven. Therefore, both are primary focal points of this chapter. A search on the Internet displays millions of definitions and conceptual illustrations of culture. Several are identified herein to effectively frame this chapter. Additionally, "culture and experience" are illustrated through a visual, rather than through words alone. Could one picture be worth 1,000 words?

Defining culture

It is a challenge to learn the elements of culture and their relationship to experience. Figure 2.1, "Culture and experience" is an artistic translation of the complexity of culture. The drawing is the result of a six-month collaboration with a Columbus, Ohio art teacher, Charles Gambill. The author identified three writers whose work seemed to capture culture's complexity, and Gambill generated his drawings based on these authors. The drawing aims to illustrate: (a) that culture is influenced by one's environment; (b) that it is *learned*, and that it has many elements (i.e., pieces); and (c) that discovering all of its elements might not be attainable in one's lifetime.

Minchihiro Matsumoto

He equates culture to a "metacommunication system [where] not only [do] words have meaning, but everything else has meaning."[2] The everything else to which Matsumoto refers includes nonverbal communication (NVC).[3] And so, in one society, one cultural element, e.g., use of words and language, might be much more evident than in another where symbols, NVC, and/or visuals might be more valued as a vehicle to record and describe events and experiences.

Erika Bourguignon

Her definition of culture points to the challenge involved in attempting to achieve understanding of culture and cultural differences. Bourguignon also views culture as a system, equating it to a puzzle with many interlocking pieces. She argues that one can start anywhere, but in order to see the whole "thing," we will have worked ourselves through the entire puzzle.[4] She also describes culture "as a matter of shared (or agreed upon) cognition."[5] This view is particularly important to the discussion presented in Chapter 4.

(It is important to note that in an interview with Bourguignon, she argues that seldom does anyone see the whole "thing"; no one can *ever* expect to accomplish that; but the idea is to do the best we can—whatever is realistically attainable within the course of one's lifetime or career.)

Irving Hallowell

Reading Hallowell also enriches our understanding of culture's complexity.[6] Hallowell emphasizes the interrelationship between one's uniquely individual context and experience as the "culturally constituted behavior environment".[7] In other words, culture is not to be regarded as an environment external to the individual, but rather a complex system shared by a group. The core and expressive representation of culture cannot be compartmentalized as they are so very intertwined. The context in which individuals develop and adapt as an inseparable biological and psychosocial unit affects their interpretations of the environment. Plants, animals, space, time, as only a few examples, all acquire meaning according to context. Context influences the individual from the time he or she is born. As an example, if one is a member of a high-tech, computerized society, one's view of the natural world may be far different than that of the *mestizo* Quiché people of Guatemala,[8] the Ojibwa of Manitoba, Canada, or the Amish of Lancaster, Pennsylvania. Conversely, if one is a member of a non-hunting and fishing society (e.g., a high-tech computerized society), plants and animals are likely to be regarded as part of the natural world, separate from one's daily existence and subject to society's control. To hear of individuals such as the Ojibwa who regard animals as "beings"—some having great power to determine one's fate—may seem weird or eccentric to someone raised in a very different environment. Yet, if a society's existence/survival has depended upon its relationship with the so-called natural world, the Ojibwa point of view appears perfectly logical. In a work setting—whether overseas or in the US—what may be weird or a novelty to one person has perfect logic to others and vice versa.

All of the aforementioned views of culture are integral to understanding culture's meaning, and are incorporated into the Figure 2.1 illustration, "Culture and experience."

The "culturally constituted behavioral environment" of the individual is graphically represented in the background as a topographical map without boundaries. That environment and the socialization process influence the puzzle pieces that comprise the complexity of cultures and experiences. The following sections provide examples of why the relative importance and size of certain puzzle pieces vary across cultures and societies. Figure 2.2, the

C. H. Gambill
Artist/ "Translator"

Figure 2.1 Culture and experience.
Source: Potoker (1994).

transspection process, illustrates that culture must be discovered from the inside.

The impact of experience on culture is expanded in the following section.

Culture and experience

For a long time anthropologists have studied the relationship between culture and experience. However, for (also) a long time their work, applied beyond

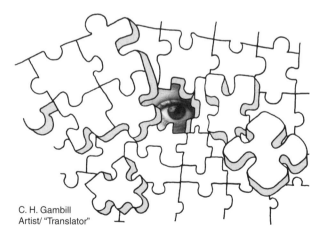

C. H. Gambill
Artist/ "Translator"

Figure 2.2 The transspection process.
Source: Potoker (1994).

the study of isolated populations, was seldom noticeable in business and related fields, and vice versa. Indeed, the interrelationship of culture to experience and culture to language has two very important implications to management, defined here as planning, organizing, leading and controlling human and material resources to accomplish specific goals and objectives. According to J. Higgins, the primary function of a manager is to "creatively solve problems and/or facilitate the creative problem-solving efforts of others".[9] Recalling the words of anthropologists, Hallowell, Sapir, and Whorf, it is therefore critically important for managers to identify *how and why peoples attach value to their resources*—i.e., land, labor, capital—in certain ways, as resources are *always* culture specific. Failure to do so may cause misunderstandings that lead to conflict, disinterest, and/or confusion. As examples, perceptions of time, orientation to resource protection or destruction, development and display of material culture such as dress and status symbols, and punishment are not represented in the same way across cultures. In today's complex globally interfaced workplace environment, managers must recognize that culture is not "available" for discovery; neither is it static or unidimensional. Rather, it is, as Sapir suggested, "gropingly discovered." Human resource training and development efforts must guard against reductionism, or the simplification of issues involving cultural and other diversities.

Training specific to the culture and experience of others should evaluate: What language symbols relate to certain concepts? What is socially acceptable or what are the social norms attached to certain situations? Why do certain cultures have longer tolerance for the passage of time? What amount of space is too little or too much for social interactions? Hallowell and others would ask us to discover culture from the "inside" rather than the outside, and with a historical perspective.

Complementing the perspective of Hallowell, Edward Hall points to the importance of cultural insight that "springs from within" when he argues that "there are many roads to the truth and no culture has a corner on the path or is better equipped than others to search for it."[10] That's good advice to the reader in his/her self-discovery voyage through this book. Looking at cultures from the inside recalls the "transspection" process discussed in Chapter 1.

In my business experience, I am often reminded of the writings of Hallowell and Hall. As an example, on several occasions I traveled to La Paz, Bolivia to attempt to effect specification of certain products within the mining and municipal water sectors in that country. The company for whom I worked had just introduced two new products that were viewed (from a US corporate perspective) to be much more time-effective and efficient than what we previously sold; additionally, the products were guaranteed to be non-sparking. Sparking from an electrical current traveling on metal was often the cause of eye loss and injuries among construction workers. I arranged to do numerous product field demonstrations that were apparently well received by the specification engineers. They acknowledged the apparent need for use of these products. Nevertheless, during my first visits I was surprised to see how little interest there was in purchasing products offering value-added time-based improvements in efficiency. Had I effectively researched the geography and history of the area, I would have realized that *time*, in a city thousands of miles above sea level, is a more a matter of pacing oneself with the conditions of the external environment. While an aluminum product is safer than metal from a non-sparking perspective, a far more effective selling point might be its lighter weight, given the effects of the altitude. Yet, it turned out that even this feature was not an effective selling point. "Light-in-weight" to these workers was viewed as "less male"—a tool for a "sissy," perhaps even more so because a female was discussing its virtues in a society where masculinism predominates. A wrench had to be heavy to be worthwhile. And further, so what if the heavy tool might spark? Risk avoidance was also not a handmaiden of masculinity.[11] Recalling Sapir, indeed, culture is "gropingly discovered." The Chapter 1 mica metaphor is also applicable to this situation, as the nature of one's "work" may be influenced by gender roles, caste systems and race (e.g., white, mestizo, Indian), education, and respective notions regarding the value of human life.

In *Silent Language* (1973), Edward Hall provides a graphic of dimensions of human activity that characterize a society's "way of doing things" consciously or frequently unknowingly. Admittedly, Hall's categories relating to culture are arguably debatable. Nevertheless, while more than three decades have transpired since the book's publication, the adapted Figure 2.3 still endures as a comprehensive display of cultural dimensions to be deciphered in the context of working environments. The illustration also may be used as a training tool to deepen awareness of the defining elements of one's own culture. Referring to Figure 2.3:

- **"Core"-related** aspects of human activity are those that engulf the participant in observable or passive experiences. As an example, class structure and castes impact associations in all aspects of life—to include internal and external business relationships, family, and government.
- **"Expressive"-related** aspects involve the web of rules that apply to behavior of individuals and groups. The conceptual drawing illustrates that there are norms and expectations for many aspects of human activity such as play, leisure, technology use and more. The earlier discussion of the culturally constituted behavioral environment applies here. Specific to Figure 2.3, the Bolivian case exemplifies the temporal orientation to technology usage, concepts of comfort (or ease of product—the aluminum wrench—usage), time sequences and the roles of men and women.[12] These **formal (F), informal (I) and technical (T)** aspects of human activity are among the unseen dimensions of culture that are "gropingly discovered" in unfamiliar settings.[13] Yet, frequently they are unrecognizable *even in familiar ones*, as "culture hides much more than it reveals, and strangely enough what it hides, it hides most effectively from its own participants.[14]

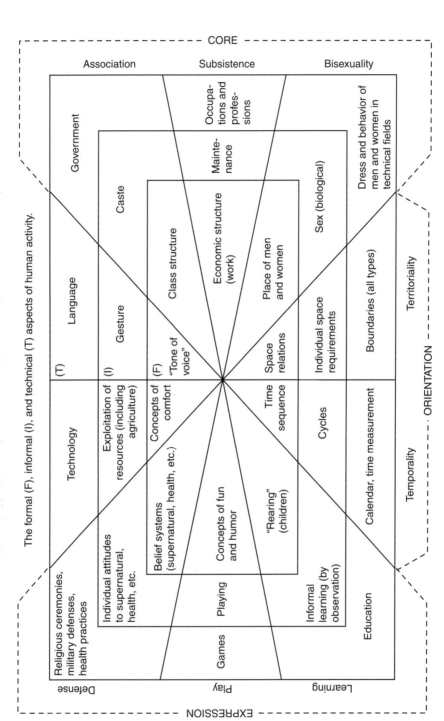

Figure 2.3 Transspecting culture's elements.

Source: Adapted from Hall (1973), p. 95.

We turn our attention now to "language"—a puzzle piece that does not translate in importance or meaning universally across cultures.

Culture and language

> One day that I missed a meeting, and then I met a department member in the elevator. And he asked, you know, I told him about, ohh, I feel so sorry I did not arrive at the meeting, then he asked me, '*how come?*'. And I was so confused. I didn't know '*how come*' means, cause I thought, you know, '*how come?*' is: '*how you are coming here?*' [Interview with a Taiwanese computer programmer].

The linguistic literature, particularly the writings of Edward Sapir and Benjamin Whorf, and the anthropological literature provide considerable insight into issues of cultural diversity. Both argue that language differences can be potential obstacles to understanding. It is through language that we construct our social reality; and clearly, no two languages do it in quite the same way.[15] Different cultures are outgrowths of *distinct worlds*—not the same worlds with different labels upon them. Additionally, communication between different cultures is, more than anything, communication between different systems of logic. A well-known interpreter for several US presidents once cautioned against assuming that everything would fall into place with the proper interpreters and translators. Bridge-building efforts are frequently doomed to failure if interpretation is done on a linguistic level alone. The biggest hurdles are generally on a different level—that of logic and thought.[16]

In a speech before the American Anthropological Association in 1911, Sapir read: "it is the vocabulary of a language that most clearly reflects the physical and social environment of its speakers. The complete vocabulary of a language may indeed be looked upon as a complex inventory of all the ideas, interests, and occupations that take up the attention of the community . . ."[17] Sapir emphasized, however, that language not be naively regarded as merely a systematic inventory of items that may seem relevant to the individual.[18] As individuals develop and adapt, language also records their experiences. In this sense, each language becomes an elaborate conceptual system, and each is likely to be different from others in some respect as regards fundamental concepts and orientations to the world.[19] Indeed, the orientations inherent in language as an outgrowth of culture, experience, and the socialization process are cited as reasons certain groups may attend or fail to attend to entirely different things in nature.[20] Unique patterns of cognition, perception, and logic embodied in language and mode of language usage are often underlying reasons for many difficulties in cross-cultural encounters.[21] If we base communication on verbal and written discourse alone, we may run into trouble.

Masao Kunihiro points to the complexity involved when people of different cultures meet; he views the result as "a complex fabric of differences in linguistic expressions compounded by the deeper conflicts in patterns of perception and logic."[22] While it may be generally acknowledged that genuine thinking together is achieved through dialogue, that's not so easy to achieve. Let's return to the Taiwanese programmer, and add another vignette to illustrate Kunihiro's comments.[23]

Interview with a Taiwanese computer programmer

One day that I missed a meeting, and then I met a department member in the elevator. And he asked, you know, I told him about, ohh, I feel so sorry I did not arrive at the meeting, then he asked me, "*how come?*". And I was soo confused. I didn't know "how come" means, cause I thought, you know, "*how come?*" is: "*how you are coming here?*"

The expression, "how come?" totally stopped this woman—communications ceased—and who can tell how much time went by until she was back into the conversation again, just from the standpoint of basic understanding. Words and patterns of logic apparently were not shared in this two-person exchange.

While Waiting on Line at the Post Office

(a hot afternoon in August . . .)

It was close to 3 p.m.; the line of people waiting for the one postal clerk wrapped around a 12ft. × 12ft. store front on three sides blocking the door exiting to the parking lot. "*Next please.*"

A man who appears to be in his 30s approaches the counter. Judging from his speech pattern, he appears to be from a country other than the US. He requires a money order for $20.00, and pays in cash.

Patron: "Excuse me, I want to be sure this goes to New York City."
Clerk: [without looking up] "Well, you need to write that on the envelope."
Patron: [He shows a crumpled piece of paper to the Clerk.]

"I [pause] you see, I need to send this to New York *City.*"

Clerk: [looking up] "New York, New York. That's how you write it."
Patron: [silent; then in a soft voice] "but [pause] it's New York *City.*"
Clerk: [louder, emphasizing each letter] "*NY . . .* wait. Where's the envelope? [even louder] "*NY . . . NY!.*"

The patron's whole demeanor begins to change. He looks around at the people waiting on line; his shoulders slump.
[I wondered what N.Y. meant to him?—*en* (*and? N?*) *why?*][24]

Both of the above field situations are chosen for their apparent simplicity, and because each involved communication between only two individuals.

Both involve commonly understood expressions in US English language discourse. We can only imagine how understanding might be jeopardized if we were to transpose these individuals to a team in an organizational setting.

The following subsection addresses the relative weight or ratio of importance that certain cultures place upon context versus content. It also illustrates why perceptions of communication, language and language use are not shared among all individuals due to culture and experience.[25] Additionally, it points to the inherent diversity that may characterize group members' individual preferences as regard modes of communication. It is a strong rationale for consideration of other communication strategies to support and facilitate the work of the workplace.

Country snapshot: Japan[26]

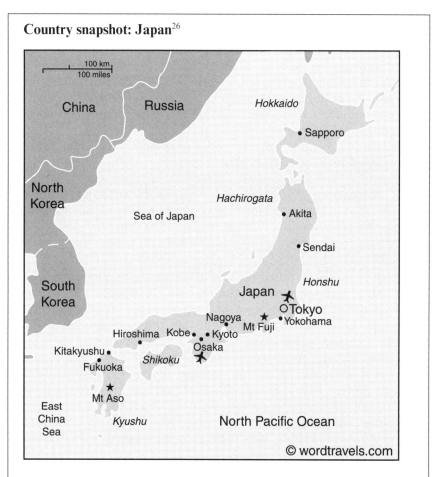

Area: 377, 835 sq. km. (145,902 sq. mi.); slightly smaller than California.
    Population: 127.3 million (2008 est.), and declining.
    Density: 873 (sq. mi.); 337 (sq. km) (2007 est.)
    Capital: Tokyo

Population: 12.7 million

Density: 5,847 persons/sq.km (est. 2007)—almost 17 times the national average.

Government: Parliamentary constitutional monarchy

Religion: Shinto and Buddhist 84%, other 16% (including Christian 0.7%)

Ethnicity: Japanese 98.5%, Koreans 0.5%, Chinese 0.4%, other 0.6% (2007 est)

Currency yen (¥ International Symbol)

HDI Index 8 out of 179 countries (2008 http://hdr.undp.or/en/statistics)

System of Law Civil Law—mostly influenced by German and French Civil Code Law

Background: Japan's land mass is an archipelago whose occupation is reported to date from 30,000 BC. Therefore, it is no wonder that history, in part, explains the Japanese tendency to view events from a long-term and high-context (HC) perspective. While Japan is a member of the G-8, and an economic power in Asia and the world, it has limited natural resources, relying heavily on imports in the agriculture, energy, and raw material sectors.

Eastern vs. Western Perceptions of Communication, Language and Language Use: Selected Examples

. . . language . . . is by nature . . . too linear, not comprehensive enough, too slow, too limited, too constrained, too unnatural, too much a product of its own evolution, and too artificial[27]

Much has been written about cultures that place more value upon context versus written and oral discourse. For example, the Japanese tend to place a great deal of importance on constant inter- and intra-group interaction of production, sales, research and design. In fact, it is generally acknowledged that the Japanese utilize many interactive group processes to improve managerial actions. Additionally, diagramming is used in conjunction with verbal discourse for problem-solving efforts. Planning continuous improvements, or *kaizen*, in organizational practices is facilitated through use of visual tools such as pareto diagrams,[28] cause-and-effect diagrams, histograms, charts, graphs and others.[29] However, it is important to explore why the Japanese generally view these techniques as important vehicles of communication.

Visual cues

A. Yamamoto, a Chief Researcher of the Industrial Property Cooperation Center in Tokyo, mentions the use of "visual information" as key to delivering technical education across cultures. Verbal language by itself makes understanding difficult enough in varied cultures. He considers explanations, whether they be written or spoken, one-dimensional. Yet, visual information has the potential to achieve understanding at a glance, as its essence is two-dimensional. Yamamoto believes illustrations and cartoons should be used as much as possible, rejecting the notion that the latter may not be considered by some as suited to the more "lofty" concept of education.[30]

It is not surprising that illustrations and cartoons are recommended for serious consideration as a tool for training across cultures. Comic-strip books and magazines are deeply rooted in Japanese popular culture, and are an important medium for many objectives, including the transmission of knowledge and values. In one comic book it would not be uncommon to see educationally oriented cartoons interspersed with charts and graphs, the idea being to bombard the reader with key information to be understood at a glance.[31]

It is well documented that in the early grades, Japanese teachers emphasize the use of posters rather than verbal instructional time to train students in procedural skills. As examples, posters may depict appropriate hand-washing techniques, proper arrangement of desk contents, etc.[32] Repetitive practices, or *tenarai*, are also vital to teaching to task.

Historical precedent for distrust of words by the Japanese is said to date back to the seventh or eighth centuries as documented in the *Kojiki*, the oldest collection of history and myth, and in the *Manyoshu*, the ancient book of poetry and song. Within these works is the concept of *Kotodama*: Words have spirits; or *Kotoage*: Speaking boldly was discouraged. There are also many Japanese proverbs that suggest speaking is not of primary value for communication of meanings.[33] Indeed, "to the Japanese, [verbal] language is **a** means of communication, whereas to the people of many other cultures it is **the** means,"[34] hence, the attention of the Japanese to visual cues. An analogy to the Japanese experience can be derived from India. In India, the mandala, a multidimensional map, was developed to enable people to see and understand the secrets of esoteric Buddhism. Although in existence 2,000 years ago, it is still in use today.[35]

Another dimension of graphs, posters and cartoons as a powerful training tool is the potential they offer to extend one's capacity to handle information in a system that already may be suffering from information overload. E. Hall describes the "'contexting' process" people perform when demands on their system, or inputs, exceed capacity.[36] It is generally agreed that the complexity of the workplace requires the need for increased information-handling capabilities. Visual cues, therefore, offer potential as a valuable aid to managing in culturally diverse settings.

The Ishikawa Diagram

A form of visual mapping applied to production as well as training and development is the "Cause-and-Effect Diagram," Figure 2.4. Kaoru Ishikawa

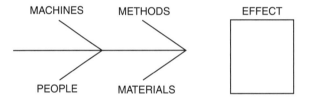

Figure 2.4 Cause-and-effect diagram.

created this visual tool to show the relationship between characteristics and cause factors influencing total quality control (TQC). He considered TQC vital to corporate health and character, to society, and to market share within a global economy. Yet, in Ishikawa's view, quality control (QC) could never come about simply by telling people to work hard. He argued that "one must understand the meaning of process control, take hold of the process, which is a collection of cause factors, and build within that process ways of making better product, establishing better goals, and achieving effects."[37] In order to facilitate the thought process and understanding of the process itself, he created the Cause-and-Effect diagram. In 1952 Kawasaki Iron Fukiai Works began to utilize this type of diagram to effect control and standardization. It is a visual aid that is utilized in many companies throughout the world—known by some as the Ishikawa Diagram, but now generally referred to as the Fishbone Diagram due to its shape.

As Figure 2.4 shows, the effect is found at the right-hand side of the diagram. Using TQC as an organizational example, achieving quality characteristics is the effect and the goal of the system. The branches are the causes. The branches may also be viewed as the process by which the effect is created or the process by which a goal may be achieved. The most popular causes include *machines, methods, humans, materials*, and more recently, *the environment*. The Fishbone is generally well known wherever quality control is practiced and in business and management circles, as it can be used not only for understanding processes, but also for analyzing root causes of problems and generating solutions.

A further use of this diagram is for purposes of strategic plan development. As an example, in one Northwestern Pennsylvania community a number of business leaders wished to set up an International Trade Development Committee through the Chamber of Commerce and the Erie Excellence Council. TQC is a standard for development of the Chamber for both the private and public sectors. The Fishbone process was utilized to generate a strategic plan to accomplish the mission statement of the International Trade Development Committee. The mission statement was the effect side of the diagram; the branches were the steps identified by the group for obtaining funding, building networks, etc.

One primary limitation in using the Fishbone is its linear orientation. Subsequent chapters address inherent problems with "line worship" from a cross-cultural and adult learning perspective. "Line worship" refers to the tendency to see situations in a compartmentalized, step-by-step, sequential fashion. The opposite is a tendency to view relationship and networks rather than details.

Despite its limitations, the Fishbone Diagram can be modified and utilized with non-linear models such as affinity diagrams and relations diagrams, and loops rather than lines, to maximize intercultural and organizational communication. These other visual tools are addressed in Chapter 6 and Appendix 6A.

"Face-to-face" (kao wo tsunagu)

It is generally accepted that both written policy and human relationships are important tools of organizational control. Both are used by Westerners and Japanese as a tool of management. However, according to many writers and researchers, the Japanese are characterized as having a preference for the human relationship, while the West depends primarily on the written word.[38]

Edward Hall and others discuss "syncing," or "being in sync" as a form of communication in itself.[39] People in interactions either move together or do not—i.e., they are either "in sync" or "out of sync." In societies where understanding is considered to evolve out of analysis and argument, words are key. As discussed, this does not characterize all cultures. As an example, to the Japanese, understanding is thought to evolve from an intuitive sensitivity to total behavior rather than through verbal analysis and argument.[40]

"Face interaction," "management by wandering around," and "interfacing" are terms that have been used to describe preference by the Japanese for "face-time," defined as person-to-person contact.[41] A case in point refers to Nemoto Masao, president of Toyota Gosai—one of the Toyota group companies that produces car parts, plastic and rubber products, and related products for the home. Nemoto prefers to be "close" to his workers, meaning "able to converse with them as time permits, as it is an effective way to alter procedures and teach and train through personal contact. Face-time reduces the need for paperwork and facilitates quicker decision-making.[42]

Face-time is grounded in the NVC side of the Japanese communication itself. Back-channeling or *aizuchi* is different in Japanese than in English. Nodding appears after almost every phrase, sentence, or groups of sentences uttered by the other participant. Even short words such as *hai* ("yes"-polite), *ee* ("yeah"-casual), *sou desu ne* ("that's so, isn't it?"), are a form of *aizuchi*.[43] The habit of bowing and nodding is so ingrained in the Japanese that it has been observed that secretaries nod and bow even when speaking to their bosses over the telephone.[44]

Nodding: A Gesture That Is Not Universally Understood

Nodding is a form of NVC that sometimes replaces the need for verbal expression. The gesture usually means "yes" in many parts of the world. However, nods can be as varied as their meaning. Some examples follow.

India. In India a nod up and down could mean "yes." From side to side it could mean "no." However, often the head movement can be a slight bobble of the head from side to side or movement of the head up and down—like a movement in the pattern of a figure eight—starting up and down and then going side to side. In this case, the nod can be a gesture of agreement, acknowledgment, or simply of recognition.

Bulgaria. It is reported that, particularly after World War II, the people of Bulgaria received training in how to mislead spies within the country. They were taught to nod in order to confuse their infiltrators. To this day a nod may have dual meanings, and may actually mean "no" when it appears to be an NVC strategy to communicate agreement. This is also said to be the case in parts of Greece, Turkey, and Iran. In the Byzantine era in Greece, nodding generally meant "no."[45]

---

*Learning through observation (*Minarai*)*

Each of the nonverbal forms of communication (NVC) discussed thus far should not be viewed as operational separate entities. Various forms of NVC, given a particular setting, are woven together as colors and texture are in a tapestry. Face-time and being in sync are likely to be concurrent in the Japanese preferred practice of learning through observation, or *minarai*. *Minarai* is key to understanding the prevalence of apprenticeships as a vehicle for learning, which in turn are inherent in the *sempai–kohai* relationships ingrained in Japanese culture. "*Sempai*" refers to workers who joined a company before other workers (i.e., senior workers) having more experience than junior workers. The junior worker is expected to learn from his/her superior. The senior worker is a mentor to his/her subordinate. *Sempai–kohai* is ingrained in Japanese culture and involves fictive kinship relationships that entail obligations and status hierarchy—e.g., teacher–student, master–apprentice, parent–child, supervisor–employee, etc.

Liza Dalby's fieldwork in Japan illustrates the rooting of *minarai* within geisha society.[46] An older "sister" is a model for the younger, apprentice geisha. Her *minarai-jaya* is a model, generally a teahouse, for learning by observation. Although in contemporary times the *minarai* period of new geisha in Akasaka, Japan is only six months, geisha who are now in their 50s or older are likely to have had a very different apprenticeship than their modern-day counterparts. Years ago, a young woman would likely have lived in a geisha house from as early as 11–12 years of age, and not become a full geisha until age 18.

In a context of business and industry, face-time, *minarai* and *tenarai*, learning by doing, or literally, learning with one's hands, are elements of NVC at work. The Japanese would obviously consider practice more valuable than words. "Technologies are systematic structures of techniques. Students cannot acquire new technical skills using only their brains. They also must learn them with their bodies."[47] All of the aforementioned has vast implications for management communication, including computer-based technology choices. These issues are discussed further in subsequent chapters.

High-context vs. low-context cultures

A high-context message (HC) communication or message is one in which most of the information is either in the *physical context*, . . . while very little is in the coded, explicit, transmitted part of the message. A low-context (LC) communication is just the opposite; i.e., the mass of the information is vested in the explicit code.[48]

Referring again to Figure 2.1, imagine that the large puzzle piece, the one shown in relief, represents the role of nonverbal communication in a particular culture— in this case the Japanese. Discussion heretofore supports that this particular puzzle piece will not necessarily be the same size across cultures. Indeed, its size will be much smaller in cultures that place more emphasis on verbal and written language use. These types of cultures are generally referred to in the intercultural communications literature as low-context (LC) cultures. The Japanese are considered to be a high-context (HC) culture as they emphasize the "everything else" mentioned in Matsumoto's definition of culture, or the nonverbal side of communication. The Japanese tendency to see context and relationships are in part derived from culture and experience: the extended kinship systems, history, geography, and other factors of the physical world surrounding individuals. In contrast, those from the US tend to be a low-context culture.

Chinese culture, as with Japanese, also tends toward an HC orientation. "The need for context is experienced when looking up words in the Chinese dictionary. To use a Chinese dictionary, the reader must know the significance of 214 radicals. . . . For example, to find the word for star one must know that it appears under the sun radical."[49] One character alone in the Chinese language might convey one meaning. Yet, adding other characters creates new words. As an example, the word "woman" is represented with one character. "Child" is another character. Putting both characters together for mother and child creates the word "good." The characters that are used to create the word "good" in the Chinese language convey much about the significance of both in Chinese culture. Indeed, there are many relationships to know, to include knowledge of history, in order to be conversant.

If viewed as a continuum, HC might be at one end with LC on the opposite end. Chinese, Japanese, Koreans, Thais, and Vietnamese, while they may not share similar views of life, certainly tend to be on the HC side of the continuum. The French and Latin Americans also tend to favor the HC side of the continuum.

Individualism, attention to detail as opposed to relationships,[50] and tendency toward linear thinking are part of the profile of a low-context orientation. In the US there is a tendency to view language as *the* primary means of transferring thought from one brain to another. Oral discourse as *the* vehicle for communication is not shared among peoples, as discussed earlier.

Hall captures the essence of the HC/LC dichotomy characterizing communication modes as follows: "What man chooses to take in, either consciously or unconsciously, is what gives structure and meaning to his world."[51] In other words, in cultures tending toward HC communication, the experiences of the physical world of the individual and/or individuals involved are extremely important to the interpretation of meaning. Meaning and context are inextricably intertwined with one another.[52]

Legal practices provide excellent examples of HC or LC preferences. US and Common Law systems typically look to precedent often at the expense of context and the physical world of relationships. In contrast, HC-type systems tend to allow great leeway into the testimony admitted as evidence. "The court wants to find out as much as possible about the circumstances behind the surface acts that brought people before the bench. Everything is heard: facts, hearsay, and gossip. The court wants to know what kind of human beings were involved. These aspects are normally irrelevant prior to determination of guilt in an American [US] court."[53]

Hall cautions that no one culture exists exclusively at the high end or the low end. We can speak only of tendencies toward high or low. Yet, tendencies are very important to understand when planning communication strategies. They are also extremely important to understand in the communication design choices of computer-based technologies, which is a subject addressed in Chapter 9.

Additionally, high attention to context also has implications for how a particular culture views the role of space or the role of "proxemics," defined as "man's use of space as an aspect of his culture, i.e., conversational distance, planning, use of interior spaces . . ."[54] Proxemics is another piece of the culture "puzzle" with important implications for cross-cultural training, communications design planning, and creativity. Recalling Matsumoto's definition of culture, this NVC dimension is illustrated in the Chapter 7 case study of Duromark, where not only words have meaning but also everything else. At Duromark, *by design*, culture and experience shape expectations for all workplace activities.

The following selectively presents defining hallmarks of leadership as they apply to this chapter's discussion.

Hallmarks of leadership

Communication as an essential people skill

In J. Dunnigan, and D. Masterson's (1997) *The Way of the Warrior: Business Tactics and Techniques from History's Twelve Greatest Generals*, the authors evaluate the tactics and techniques from among history's greatest generals. Making communication choices skillfully is a talent that distinguishes great leaders. Managing change, managing technology, managing teams in virtual and physical spaces, managing alliances, and managing talent all involve communication choices. Companies of the future apparently will rely upon those who have this talent as well.[55] Yet, it is not enough to simply advocate for effective communication without considering the puzzle pieces of the context to which it is directed. The leadership competitive advantage will depend on knowledge-seekers who transspect those contexts for important implications for communication design choices. Striving to see the unseen and hear the unheard is a necessary discipline for effective leadership.[56]

Effective tools

Having the most effective tools for the job is another characterizing element of the leader's profile. Dunnigan and Masterson (1997) also describe the importance of adaptability and insight in choice of tools through the example of Mongolian ruler, Genghis Khan, or Temujin. Temujin realized that an army of archers alone would not be sufficient against diverse opponents and terrains. He varied his methods and technology in accordance with these variables.[57] And so with communication choices, one must always blend HC and LC styles regularly to bridge border zones of preferences. Equally important is to recognize that one cannot assume that individuals share meanings or communication styles, no matter what the setting. "[A]ll organizations depend on the existence of shared meanings and interpretations of reality, which facilitate coordinated action. . . . [Leaders] invent images, metaphors, and models that provide a focus for new attention. . . . [A]n *essential* factor in leadership is the ability to influence and *organize meaning* for the members of the organization."[58] The leader channels *e pluribus pluribus* into *e pluribus unum*.

 Leadership toolbox 2: The limitations of language

1   *Be wary of "word worship." Managers must heighten self-awareness of their own discourse in interpersonal exchanges. Recognize the limitations of language; look beyond "read my lips" mentality.*

2   *"Genuine thinking-together" is not a naturally occurring phenomenon. Recognize that patterns of logic and perception are not created equally in all individuals. Supply visual cues to illustrate multidimensional realities. This will help to bridge the border zones between HC and LC orientations.*

The next chapter addresses how and why the internal and external environments of organizations have changed along with the roles of managers. Additionally, it points to the need to understand what is to be learned in order to facilitate integration of diverse perspectives into the change process.

Key terms and concepts

culture, *kaizen,* gestalts, Generation N,
culturally constituted, behavioral, environment, Generation X,
high-context, proxemics, Millenniums, Generation Y,
low-context, transspection, Baby Boomers, monochronic,
polychronic, syncing, *sempai–kohai*

Exercises

In this chapter the reader identifies and evaluates ingrained communication habits of the past and present. Subsequent chapters encourage the reader to reflect on other modes that may facilitate more optimal results. Reflect on *your* communications style, e.g., HC, LC, both?

1   Identify and/or assemble a portfolio of recent examples of communication or presentations you have made recently.

   a   Evaluate if your preferred communication modes tend to be more HC, LC or both. Explain.
   b   Provide an example of how you could transform an LC orientation to an HC orientation and vice versa. Incorporate a drawing or drawings that might enhance understanding.

2   Consider how *your* preferred modes of communication influence what you expect from others, e.g., teachers, trainers, mentors, business associates.
3   Prepare a visual that synthesizes a primary goal or goals you would like to achieve either independently or with co-workers. It should capture at a glance the vision you have of the future.
4   What types of communication do you receive within your workplace environment?

Which types do you prefer?

Plan to revisit this exercise as the discovery voyage continues into further chapters. Subsequently, the reader will evaluate how he/she might optimize personal communication styles and develop broadened communication skills in others.

Appendix 2A

Broadening analytic and communication skills through diagramming

Introduction

Chapter 2 addresses the limitations of language in human interactions. Visual cues, learning by observation, the way in which individuals are placed and occupy office spaces, and the design choice for organizational structure are also important to consider for maximizing organizational and intercultural communication. This appendix and the vignette and case included herein aim to illustrate that just talking about culture and experience also has its limitations. In other words, reliance upon language alone does not optimize transspection of culturally constituted behavioral environments (see Figure 2.1). In this section, potential other applications of visuals and graphic representations are explored.[59]

Their uses are illustrated in the following ways:

a   As problem-solving tools; and,
b   As elements of a learning landscape to developmentally track competencies that may be important to training and development of the expatriate (the IA) for his/her overseas assignment.

In "a" above, the Cause–and–Effect/Fishbone Diagram (Chapter 2, Figure 2.4) is used as a heuristic tool of analysis. The individual—the IA, the "associate", or group—attempts to identify and articulate what she/he/they experienced during an overseas assignment, and then analyze the culturally constituted factors—the interlocking puzzle pieces (Figures 2.1 and 2.2)—that might account for the reasons. When the puzzle is deciphered (as best as possible), many diagrams together constitute a "learning landscape" to be addressed in continued training and development of the IA: "b" (above). The idea is to facilitate the transspection process of the "intentional worlds" of others,[60] or worlds formed by culture and experience, and identify important "whats" (Chapter 3) to be learned.

The incident that is related in the vignette is based on a real experience. The name of the organization has been changed because there is no doubt that if this incident were to take place in other countries there would likely be a whole new interplay of dynamics involved due to reasons related to Figure 2.3 in Chapter 2. There is only one thing that organizations can count upon, and that is change. Therefore, the ongoing analysis of culture's effects and the applicable "web of rules" governing human interactions is clearly an imperative. The vignette aims only to illustrate how those effects may be discovered through an expanded communication toolbox and training.

An American (IA) in Paris

The effects (the symptoms)

First, refresh your memory of cause and effect by reviewing Figure 2.4, reproduced here as Figure 2A.1, the Fishbone Diagram. Now let us pretend we are viewing a clip from a film. As the film begins to roll, we see an individual who has traveled to France. This person has been there before, and frankly admits that it is not a favorite place. The individual remarks about the "coldness" of the French, saying, "*They simply are not as 'warm' as people from the US; if I start a conversation, often they do not respond. They just do not seem friendly as we are here [in the States]; sometimes they do not even look up when you are talking to them.*"

Now let us assign a gender to the individual in the film clip.[61] The individual is a woman, traveling alone on business. She is also a member of an international business organization devoted to service. Several of the businessmen she visits also happen to belong to this organization, so she is invited to a dinner sponsored by the organization. Prior to going to the dinner, there will be an afternoon pastry and cocktails party to which she is invited. She arrives at the designated hotel and is surprised to find that none of the men she saw earlier is there. This afternoon get-together is an event for the wives. The IA does not speak much French; she does speak English and Spanish and manages to communicate, albeit haltingly. The IA finds the women "cold." When questions are addressed to her, she perceives that there are subtleties involved. It appears the women are curious to know if she is married; they question, "*Are you traveling with your husband?*" The IA finds these questions particularly irritating, although she attempts not to show her "discomfort."

Next scene: A waiter approaches them to take an order for cocktails; she orders an extra dry martini. The women seem surprised—yet, they all exclaim,

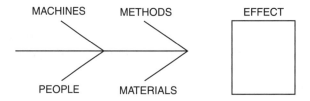

Figure 2A.1 The Fishbone Diagram.

how "good" martinis are. Nevertheless, no one orders an alcoholic beverage. They all choose *jus de pamplemousse* (grapefruit juice).

Next scene: finally, the men arrive. The men, the wives, and the IA leave to go to dinner. The IA is seated at the head table. In her view, there seems to be much more pomp and ceremony to the occasion than she is accustomed to. On the way over to dinner, several remark, some jokingly, that in this particular community there are no women who belong to this organization; "*some day*," they say, "*perhaps there will be.*" (A Scottish gentleman takes her aside and mentions, in English, that day will probably not happen for a while.) During dinner the IA and the Scottish gentleman chat a while. They are joined by his friend, a gentleman from Galicia (Spain), who speaks Spanish. The IA feels at "home." Conversation is exchanged in both English and Spanish. She wishes to query these men about the absence of women in their organization, and feels comfortable to do so. The Scotsman replies that he personally feels women would be a good idea; yet, he believes the men are afraid to allow women members because their wives might not like the idea of "their men" being with women on meeting days. She translates for the Galician gentleman, who laughs and agrees. (There is a business service club for company wives. However, these women primarily assist the men with charitable events.) Several men join in the conversation—a few women (who did not offer to speak English before) try to do so; all seem interested in discussing their experiences at club events in other countries and particularly those countries where women members are more the exception than the rule.

Let's stop the film projector now and appreciate the complexity of the scenes we watched. The dynamics going on here are immense in scope. It is simplistic to believe one could ever diagram them in entirety. Nevertheless, there is a great amount of instruction that can be derived from some analysis. How do we discover it? And then, once it is interpreted to some extent, how do we train the same individual and/or others to be effective in a comparable situation? Of course, the training and the trainer(s) should always footnote that no organizational situation is comparable across cultures.

Transspecting the causes of discomfort

R. Carroll, in *Cultural Misunderstandings: The French-American Experience*, emphasizes the importance of listening to one's own discourse. As soon as we introduce value words, e.g., "good", "bad", "cold" (as in disposition), "the French are . . .", the "Japanese do . . .", etc., it is time to recognize that these are our perceptions and not necessarily accurate in terms of the cultural text. Carroll suggests it is wise to: (a) listen to one's own discourse; and (b) discover the different cultural premises that inform relationships.[62] This is likely to require some study; it may also require the discovery of a knowledgeable informant such as the Scottish gentleman and the wife who spoke Spanish. In a larger frame, we are reminded of the writings of Hallowell and Shweder, referenced in earlier and subsequent chapters, or the need to look for explanations within the culturally constituted behavioral environments or the intentional worlds of others.

Working backwards from the total puzzle grounding "An American in Paris," we try to understand the pieces. Once the pieces are discovered, there is an understanding of the "effect." The whole puzzle—or as much as is possible to know—becomes a dynamic "learning landscape" for the future.

As Edward and Mildred Hall explain, while there is a great variation in personality, character and temperament among the French, "a Frenchman enjoys the extravagance of rhetorical flourish, and other French people do not find this foolish."[63] What may have seemed pompous and perhaps odd or foolish to the IA is quite comfortable to the French. Monuments and ceremony are quite normal to the French, as both demonstrate love of French history and a glorious past.

Carroll explains that (from his [French] perspective), American (US) conversation is an "informal verbal exchange of thoughts"; others have said that Americans do not like gaps in conversation. Although Carroll's perspective may suggest a tendency toward the stereotypical—in describing the French vs. the Americans, his insight is helpful. The French *converser* (centuries ago) meant, "'to live with someone,' 'to frequent,' a meaning which is still alive today."[64] To participate in conversation involves commitment, or, engagement in the sense of involvement, rather than the informality to which an American may be accustomed.

Carroll emphasizes, it is *not* the value judgments that matter, but rather it is the cultural analysis. He argues, "What interests me here is not to compare 'American culture' to 'French culture' which is an immense, if not impossible task, but to identify areas of contact, meeting points between the two cultures where there is, so to speak, a *hitch* [emphasis added]; that is to identify the context in which cultural misunderstandings can arise".[65]

Returning to the Fishbone Diagram, through group brainstorming the trainer/facilitator asks the group to describe the noticeable effect or the feelings the IA is experiencing. Those feelings are summarized as discomfort in Figure 2A.2. This figure is Figure 2A.1 developed to reflect the experiences of the IA.

The facilitator asks for potential causes of discomfort. Initially, individuals are asked to list words that characterize the value judgments that caused discomfort in the IA. Those include, but are not limited to, words describing relationships and events such as "warm," "cold," "unfriendly," "insensitive," "pompous," etc. Working backwards, the trainer explores the world views that might be causal factors for the witnessed effect. Herein some cross-cultural training ensues, and fishbones are labeled that represent some of the significant "hitches"—admittedly not all—which are the root causes of the IA's discomfort. The trainer engages the group in the process of collecting the real potential causes of discomfort. The word "process" is emphasized as all these intervening factors are interrelated and contribute to the effect. Examples are in the following categories.

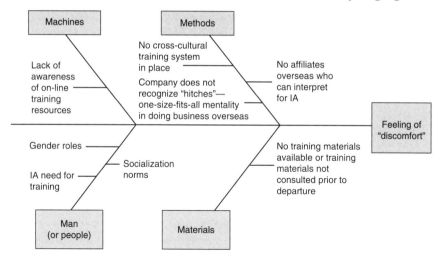

Figure 2A.2 Cause-and-effect diagram: IA in Paris.

"Man" or people

These are characteristics and/or expectations of the individual(s) involved. In the case of the IA, she obviously needs training and has certain expectations regarding gender roles and socialization in a business setting. Her hosts obviously have other expectations.

Materials

One might ask what training materials were available to her; and if they were available, did she utilize them?

Machines

How might Internet resources be of assistance to the IA?

Methods

Refer to the manner in which individuals, groups and organizations set out to accomplish their goals. The IA could read about doing business in France. She could also view a film; or, perhaps she could be engaged in a role-play opportunity prior to departure.

Carroll's explanation of conversation is only one microcosm of possible interpretations of the discomfort exhibited in the film clip. Figure 2A.1 illustrates how, through training, the facilitator can illustrate that the initial thoughts regarding discomfort of the IA—the French are "cold"—were only value judgments or expressions of discomfort. The real causes stemmed from expectations that were driven by the IA's culture and experience. There are many other "hitches" that are potentials for fishbone analysis—for example:

- Why does the IA from the US expect that the French should be speaking English? Is that attitude a reasonable expectation, or rather, is it a very ethnocentric view?
- What other implications does an ethnocentric attitude pose in terms of preparation for going overseas?
- Why is the IA irritated by questions about her marital status? How should she respond in this cultural context?
- How might her experience be comparable to foreign IAs visiting the States?

What other potential "hitches" could be anticipated? The key is to try to describe the scene objectively, and then enter into its translation through the world view of others.

What does one do then? As only one instructional example, assuming one recognizes the cultural differences in the first place, it would not be a good idea to engage in a debate over why there are no women in this organization. Herein lies the importance of transspecting the environment of the individuals from the host country in an effort to develop perspectives consciousness.

Returning to the Fishbone Diagram as a training and development tool, the bones of the fish also may be viewed as competencies to be identified and developed in order to optimize one's effectiveness in a context such as the one described earlier. Developing these competencies enables the IA to cross over the hitches—or the border zones. The management science literature and TQM refer to these "little bones" as the "countermeasures" to be developed to remedy a problem. The diagram is a visual for charting competencies as they evolve; or it can be used to document current—already existing— attributes of the individual. The use of a knowledgeable informant and/or trainer and/or facilitator is also valuable to develop the ability to transspect. After identifying root causes of discomfort, possible countermeasures could include cross-cultural training and development in language skills, and role play through utilization of authentic case studies.

Teaching the IA to recognize that culture is not just out there to be discovered at a glance is key. The transspection process is a lifelong one; gropingly discovering culture is optimized through an expanded communication toolbox. Caution is advised, however. It is not suggested that transspection will be achieved through diagramming and developmental agendas alone, as that would be a simplistic notion at best. It is suggested as an assistance to the process—nothing more.

In short, the diversity characterizing organizational environments makes it increasingly important to facilitate the transspection process through development of perspectives consciousness. This is a complex task indeed, as organizational environments are dynamic entities that construct and deconstruct on a daily basis. In turning diversity into strength, managers allow workers opportunity to provide input through group brainstorming and problem-solving. One world view is not necessarily the solution to a problem or the proper approach to an opportunity. The utilization of the Fishbone Diagram is suggested as a diagnostic tool for analysis of effects, causes, and possible solutions; employees are participants in the process. The subtleties of culture are often hidden, even from those who live and learn within it. The IA obviously needs all the assistance she can get to help with decision-making and socialization.

3   Recognizing the "others" are us

Demographic trends in countries around the world

The world stands on the threshold of a social transformation—even a revolution—with few parallels in humanity's past.[1] The ageing of OECD societies over coming decades will require comprehensive reform addressing the fiscal, financial and labour market implications of ageing. . . .[2]

The above quotes, written a decade ago, stand as a prophecy regarding the demographic kaleidoscope—aka the patterns of migration and diversities—that characterize the future of the labor force around the world. While previous chapters aim, in part, to heighten the reader's awareness of one's personal working and communication style(s), this chapter identifies existing and future trends in workforce demographics and the challenges and implications they pose for management, leadership, and, ultimately, design. Once again, the reader is urged to reflect on his/her assumptions. The chapter title, "Recognizing the 'Others' Are Us," suggests that migration, aging, and labor shortages in the developed world are changing the face of the global human resource landscape. "Otherness," or the ethnocentric way a majority group may have once viewed "others" (those of varied nationalities, ethnicities, age) entering their workforce, are discovering that "otherness" is the norm, and hence, the chapter title, "Recognizing the 'Others' Are Us."

Selected global population and migration trends[3]

More people live outside their country of birth today than at any time in history, and the numbers of people who move across international borders are expected to continue to rise in the future.[4]

Europe and Japan face a future of hyper-aging and gathering population decline. Between 2005 and 2050, the proportion of the population that is aged 65 and over will jump from 16 to 28 percent in Europe and from 20 to 38 percent in Japan. Middle age is one thing, but old age is quite another.[5]

Research framing this chapter reveals that there are a great many governmental and non-governmental organizations involved with compiling similar data about percentages of participation of the labor force by sex, age, nationality, and more. According to the Center for Strategic and International Studies in Washington (CSIS), the four major agencies that produce population projections are the World Bank, the International Program Center in the United States, the Census Bureau, and the International Institute for Applied Systems Analysis in Austria.[6] International migration is also followed by the Population Division of the Department of Economic and Social Affairs of the United Nations Secretariat, and the Organization of Economic Cooperation and Development's (OECD) Continuous Reporting System on Migration, also known by its French acronym (SOPEMI). The following quote from a UN Populations Division report points to the accelerated importance of migration to governments internationally:

> The implementation of national policies to affect levels and patterns of international migration has also intensified, spreading to all regions of the world. Discussions on issues such as sustained low fertility and population ageing, unemployment, brain-drain and brain-gain,[7] worker remittances, human rights, social integration, xenophobia, human trafficking and national security have led to a re-examination of migration policies and the potential benefits and disadvantages accruing to sending, receiving and transit countries. Over the past decades, the number of Governments adopting new measures to influence migration has grown rapidly.[8]

One only has to review the *XXVI 2009 International Population Conference Program* agenda of the International Union of the Scientific Study of Population (IUSSP) to see that population studies and their implications for policy and resources are of keen interest to the international community as globalization and mobility of resources intensify. Conference topics include, but are not limited to:

- Population aging and intergenerational relations
- Internal migration and urbanization
- Transnational communities, social networks and international migration
- Demography of minority and migrant cultural groups
- Using demography in business and public sectors
- Women's empowerment: Measurements and determinants
- The international migration of highly skilled workers
- Trends in disability and their implications
- Low fertility: Present and future.[9]

Labor force participation rates by age vary widely among countries and may be comparable or not depending upon government reporting policies, grouping categories, and other variables.[10] Despite these statistical shortcomings— and there are many[11]—it is clear that by the year 2050, population age structures and growth rates will have changed remarkably due to downward trends in fertility rates and upward trends in longevity. At the start of the 1900s, a median age higher than 30 did not exist, and even as of 1950, it had risen to only age 36. Figure 3.1 lists countries projected to have medians of age 50 and over by 2050. This phenomenon, anticipated to drive a rise in the full-benefit retirement age two decades ago,[12] is now a workforce reality.

Additionally, as shown in Figure 3.2, another first-time phenomenon involves countries experiencing declining populations by 2050 due to these reduced birth rates—as many as 44 countries, with most located in Europe. As businesses scan the world for factors of production, *the implications for human resources are significant.* Questions being asked already include, but are not limited to:

- Should we consider more outsourcing of labor across borders?
- How can we maximize the value of the older worker?
- What are the implications for training and development going forward?
- How will economies support health benefits for retained older workers and pensions for a larger pool of retirees, particularly as government contributions dwindle?[13]

Then there is the balancing act, so to speak, that organizations and societies will have to perform: How to provide opportunities for the youngest of our labor force while recycling and/or integrating older populations?

The following section aims to build awareness of the diverse and mobile demographic international landscape of the twenty-first century. Individuals who anticipate working in areas other than their host countries would be well advised to examine labor force characteristics through any of the resources listed above and others referenced in the notes to the chapter. The reader is also encouraged to review information regarding the literacy profile of the

Taiwan	56.3	Hong Kong, SAR	54.0	Armenia	52.3
Japan	56.2	Ukraine	54.0	Croatia	52.1
Bulgaria	55.9	Romania	53.9	Cuba	52.0
South Korea	55.5	Slovakia	53.9	Germany	51.8
Slovenia	55.3	Latvia	53.8	Belarus	51.7
Czech Republic	55.0	Italy	53.5	Hungary	51.2
Poland	54.4	Greece	53.3	Portugal	51.1
Singapore	54.3	Lithuania	52.8	Austria	50.9
Spain	54.2	Bosnia & Herzegovina	52.7	Georgia	50.2

Figure 3.1 Countries where median age is projected to be 50 or over in 2050.

Source: C. Jackson and N. Howe (2008). *The Graying of the Great Powers*, p. 2.*

Note: *The authors compiled information from UN sources and from the Council for Economic Planning and Development, Taiwan. Countries with less than 1 million inhabitants were not included.

Already Declining		Beginning 2009-2029		Beginning 2030-2050	
Hungary	1981	Italy	2010	Azerbaijan	2030
Bulgaria	1986	Slovakia	2011	Denmark	2031
Estonia	1990	Bosnia &		Belgium	2031
Georgia	1990	Herzegovina	2011	Thailand	2033
Latvia	1990	Greece	2014	North Korea	2035
Armenia	1991	Serbia	2014	Singapore	2035
Romania	1991	Portugal	2016	Netherlands	2037
Lithuania	1992	Cuba	2018	Switzerland	2040
Ukraine	1992	Macedonia	2018	UK	2044
Moldova	1993	Spain	2019	Hong Kong, SAR	2044
Belarus	1994	Taiwan	2019	Puerto Rico	2044
Russian Federation	1994	South Korea	2020	Kazakhstan	2045
Czech Republic	1995	Finland	2027		
Poland	1997	China	2029		
Germany	2006				
Japan	2008				
Croatia	2008				
Slovenia	2008				

Figure 3.2 Countries with declining populations by onset date.

Source: C. Jackson and N. Howe (2008). *The Graying of the Great Powers*, p. 3.*

Note: *The authors compiled information from UN sources and from the Council for Economic Planning and Development, Taiwan. Countries with less than 1 million inhabitants were not included.

workforce along with information from the Human Development Index (HDI), an index that rates countries based on human outcomes as measured by a combination of literacy, educational attainment, and GDP per capita.[14]

Snapshots[15]

Migrant stocks and flows

Migrant stock generally refers to the number of non-nationals residing in a specific location at a particular point in time. Figure 3.3 shows countries hosting the highest share of international migrants as a percentage of their population in 2005. In 2005, foreign migrant stock in the U.K. was only 3 percent, which explains why it is not on the list. However, as of 2008, it grew to 11 percent. Over the period from 2010 to 2050, the US is projected to lead the list with Canada, the U.K. and Australia among the top eight. It is anticipated that Australia will be the UK's largest source of migrants.

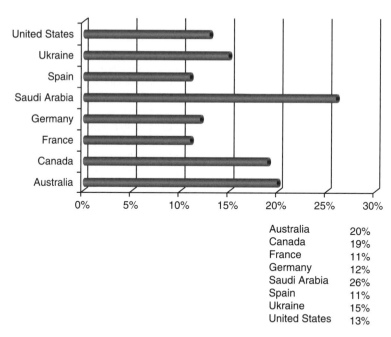

Australia	20%
Canada	19%
France	11%
Germany	12%
Saudi Arabia	26%
Spain	11%
Ukraine	15%
United States	13%

Figure 3.3 Countries hosting a high share of foreign immigrants as a percentage of their own population (2005).

Source: United Nations Population Division[16]

In Northern America, Europe, Oceania, and in Latin America and the Caribbean, female migrants represented more than 53 percent of migrant stock in 2005; this trend is not the case in Asia and Africa—with decline evident in Asia.

European Union

From 2004 to 2050, the median age of the EU will increase from 39 to 49 years. There is no doubt that all regions of the world, excepting sub-Saharan Africa, will see significant graying of their populations. Nevertheless, only the EU will experience decline of population over the next 40 years.[17] Therefore, in the EU, the "balancing act," as described in the earlier section, is real.

A 2008 conference report by P. Ester and H. Krieger, *Labour Mobility in a Transatlantic Perspective*, summarized conclusions by leading researchers from the US and Europe regarding demographic trends and their impact. It pointed to the need to significantly reconcile the insufficient supply side of labor against demand in the EU. Encouragement of cross-border mobility of labor was deemed key to achieving improved market efficiencies. Efficiencies include, but are not limited to, better distribution of skills, and fewer excessive concentrations of labor and unemployment in identified geographical areas. These were among the EU labor market weaknesses identified at the March 2000 Special European Council, "Toward a Europe of Innovation and Knowledge." Plans to address these weaknesses became the Lisbon Strategy and an EU social model committed to creating the most "competitive knowledge-based economy in the world and overall increased participation of older people."[18] Subsequent to a forum in 2008 in Brussels, the Commission of the European Communities announced it would hold a European forum every two years to review how EU policies are responding to demographic change.

Realization of cross-border EU mobility is apparently easier said than done. The Ester and Krieger report also found that Europeans prefer to stay at home. Overall, only 1 percent of those of working age change country residence in a given year (compared to 3 percent in the US). One reason cited involved the aversion to leaving one's home country social networks. Further,

> Moving from New York on the east coast of the US to Los Angeles on the west coast, for example, represents a move within one nation, with one common language, under the same labour market legislation. However, if a European worker moves from Helsinki in Finland to Barcelona in Spain, this represents a move between countries, which have different languages, cultures, labour market systems, fiscal regimes and institutional arrangements.[19]

The report also suggested concern with potential of a loss of youth and brain-power to other regions.

Figures 3.4a–d clearly illustrate why infusions of labor are *inevitable* to supplement respective labor forces. For example, the sheer number of people in Germany, Sweden, Italy and Greece would be declining if it were not for population gains due to migration. It is reported that net migration to the EU tripled to 1.6–2 million people per year, with Spain, Italy and the UK receiving about 75 percent of net migration into the EU from 2002 to 2007. At the start of 2007, 4 percent of those living in the EU were not EU citizens;[20] in 2006, 68 percent of foreign immigration was from non-EU countries.[21]

Non-EU migration to the region is a subject of considerable debate. A 2009 Internet search of "balanced migration" yields over 100,000 sites that address the subject. Migration Watch UK states that almost 750,000 individuals have left the UK, and almost 2.5 million migrated there between 1998 and 2008—a wave of immigration that is 25 times higher than any point in the history of immigration since the 1066 Norman Conquest.[22] By 2050, the population in Germany would decrease by 25 percent if it were not for immigration, while in the UK and France it would still increase.[23] It is anticipated that foreigners will comprise 30 percent of Germany's population by 2030.[24] Almost one-half of the 7 million migrants born in Africa and residing in OECD countries are living in France, Belgium, Spain, and the Netherlands. France is residence to the largest population of Moroccans internationally.[25] No matter how one turns the kaleidoscope, it is clear that an expatriate

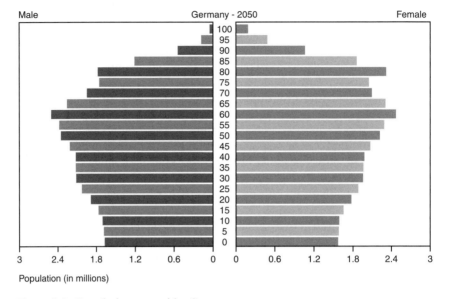

Figure 3.4a Population pyramid—Germany.

Source: http://www.census.gov/ipc/www/idb/country.php

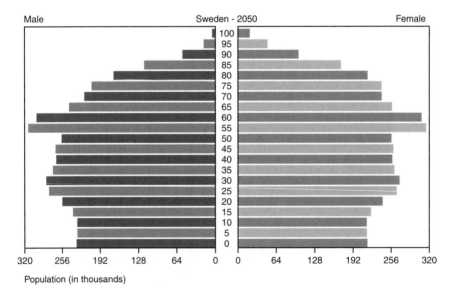

Figure 3.4b Population pyramid—Sweden.

Source: http://www.census.gov/ipc/www/idb/country.php

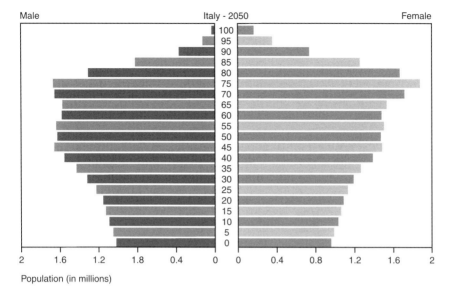

Figure 3.4c Population pyramid—Italy.

Source: http://www.census.gov/ipc/www/idb/country.php

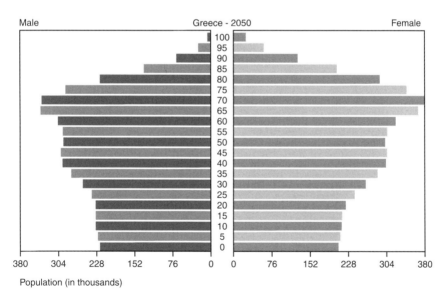

Figure 3.4d Population pyramid—Greece.

Source: http://www.census.gov/ipc/www/idb/country.php

working in the EU will see demographic transformations requiring skill sets that go far beyond technical skills.

Asia

Over 60 percent of the world's population is in Asia, with two countries—China and India—the most populous nations in the world. The Asian Population Association (APA) was organized in Bangkok from 2007 to 2009 to address the need for demographic study in the region. The APA hosted a session for the first time at the XXVI IUSSP 2009 conference (mentioned earlier) on the topic of "The Demographic Landscape in Asia." That landscape includes a dramatic and continuing fertility decline—steeper than in the EU, and an aging population. While earlier discussion indicates that the EU will be unable to replace its populace organically, this is even more notable in East Asia—particularly Japan, South Korea, Taiwan, and urban China. All will experience decline below replacement levels, as Figures 3.5a–d illustrate dramatically.

Projections for China show that by 2040, 100 million of China's 400 million elderly will be over 80 years of age, a demographic transformation deemed to be nothing less than "staggering."[26] Figure 3.6 shows that by 2030 the percentage of the elderly in China will surpass that in the United States. Obviously, this has implications for labor supplies, shortages, and migratory patterns.

China's population structure projected to 2050 is a stark contrast from that of India—Figure 3.7. High birth rates in India versus the one child policy of China is a reason that explains why India's population stayed comparatively

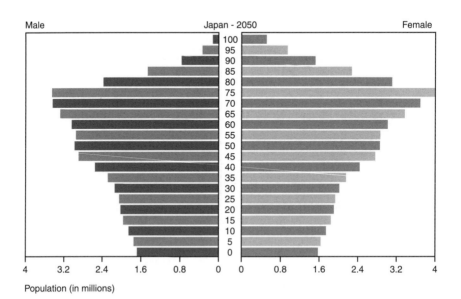

Figure 3.5a Population pyramid—Japan.

Source: http://www.census.gov/ipc/www/idb/country.php

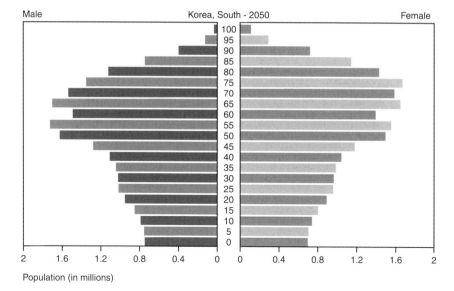

Figure 3.5b Population pyramid—South Korea.

Source: http://www.census.gov/ipc/www/idb/country.php

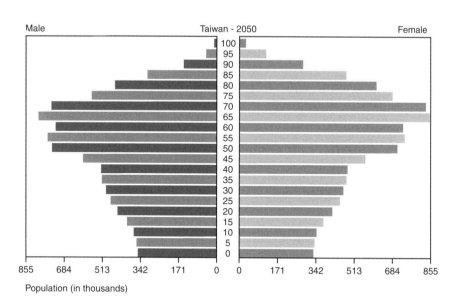

Figure 3.5c Population pyramid—Taiwan.

Source: http://www.census.gov/ipc/www/idb/country.php

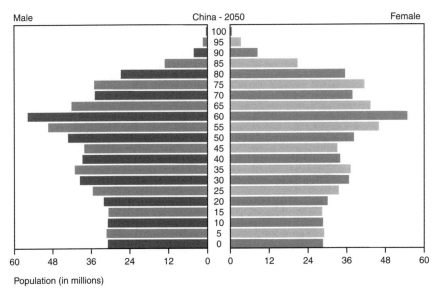

Figure 3.5d Population pyramid—China.

Source: http://www.census.gov/ipc/www/idb/country.php

young.[27] In 2005, the median age of the population was around 29 years old. Nevertheless, as Figure 3.8 shows, India too will be feeling the effects of aging by 2050. Additionally, while reports generally show that India ranks among the top population emigration nations for the past 30 years, there are

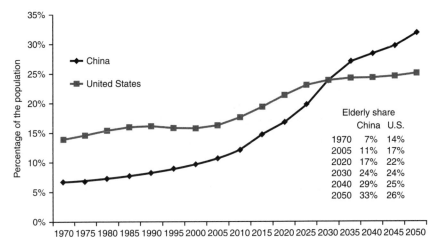

Figure 3.6 Within a generation, China will have an older population than the United States.

Source: R. Jackson, K. Nakashima, and N. Howe, *China's Long March to Retirement Reform: The Graying of the Middle Kingdom Revisited* (Center for Strategic and International Studies, 2009).

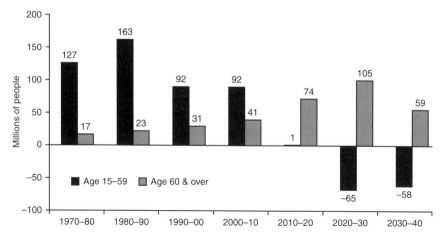

Figure 3.7 China's working-age population will shrink even as its elderly population explodes.

Source: R. Jackson, K. Nakashima, and N. Howe, *China's Long March to Retirement Reform: The Graying of the Middle Kingdom Revisited* (Center for Strategic and International Studies, 2009).

projections that the former "brain drain" may evolve into "brain gain" as India's economic growth lures its people back to their homeland.[28]

Data for 2005 show that major source countries of migrants in Asia are Bangladesh, India, Nepal and Sri Lanka, with Singapore, Malaysia and Thailand depending considerably upon foreign labor. Of all the countries in Southeast

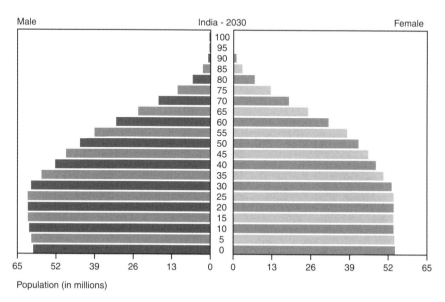

Figure 3.8 Population pyramid—India.

Source: http://www.census.gov/ipc/www/idb/country.php

Asia supplying labor elsewhere, the Philippines have the highest share of migrant stock in foreign locations.[29] Reports that speak of an Asian diaspora in terms of migrant stocks generally point to China, India, and the Philippines as the source countries. Most of the migrant flows in the Middle East are from Asia.[30]

Latin America

For those who think of Latin America as a place of burgeoning populations and large family sizes, accelerated birth rates, and excess of labor, think in this way no more. This image may have characterized the region in the 1980s, but no longer. Latin America is apparently another area that is experiencing a demographic transformation. While fertility rates have declined "precipitously" for most countries, other significant news is that life-expectancy "has soared" and is approaching the levels of the developed nations.[31]

By 2050, the median age in Latin America will be 40 years; in 2005 it was 26 years. The 65–year-old and older population will have tripled in size representing more than 18.5 percent of the population.[32] This by no means parallels the profile of the rapidly aging countries of the EU and East Asia shown in Figure 3.1. Nevertheless, as Figure 3.9 shows in the case of Mexico, Brazil, and Chile, the projected numbers of elderly may surpass that of the United States.

Since the US is the primary destination country in the Americas and the world for migration, the following section zeros in on labor force projections for the country as a whole, and then turns to selected States and cities to illustrate what that demographic landscape is and is projected to be regarding migrant stocks.

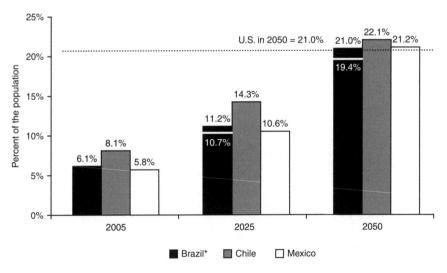

Figure 3.9 Latin America's population will age dramatically.*

Source: R. Jackson, R. Strauss, and N. Howe, *Latin America's Aging Challenge: Demographics and Retirement Policy in Brazil, Chile, and Mexico* (Center for Strategic and International Studies, 2009).

Note: *The lower projection for Brazil is the UN medium variant; the higher projection is by CSIS and assumes a constant 1.8 fertility rate.

North America: focus on the United States

There is extensive statistical information from many agencies regarding the demographic profile of the United States workforce, with projections available up to the year 2050. Information herein is captured mainly from the Census Bureau (www.census.gov), the Department of Homeland Security (www.dhs.gov) and the Bureau of Labor Statistics (www.bls.gov)—all useful resources for many reasons, e.g., to predict and verify available labor force characteristics and to determine market viability for creation of goods and services. Selected data will hopefully dismantle possible perceptual screens and/or stereotypes that may exist in the mind of the reader regarding the population and workforce of a particular locale. As the opening chapter comments suggest, if one's *modus operandi* is to approach human interactions from a particular tradition—e.g., white and Anglo-Saxon-Protestant, Japanese Shinto and Buddhist, Malaysian and Islam or Buddhist—and regard everyone else as "others" or about, "otherness," it is probably time to delve deeper. Indeed, others characterize many national workforce profiles, to include the US. A profile of corporate life in Los Angeles at the turn of the twentieth century, as an example, might have been white and male, but not now.[33] Management of diversity is more important now than ever before.

Selected US workforce characteristics: older and demographically diverse

More than two decades ago, many predicted that a significant portion of the workforce would be between the ages of 45 and 54 by the turn of the twenty-first century.[35] Figure 3.10 illustrates quite convincingly that this prediction has come true. The median age of the workforce continues to rise, with the median age expected to be around 42 years by 2020.[36] The generation following the median group into the workforce will be significantly smaller. By mid century, 23 percent of the workforce will be in the 55 years and older group,[37] and only those representing the top two bars of the 2050 pyramid are likely to have a personal memory of typewriter usage, work *before* the Internet, e-based and Internet technologies, search engines, and work–leisure time flexibility.

Referring to Table 3.1, women will represent 47 percent of the total civilian labor force by 2010. Hispanics will surpass the representative percentage of Blacks by 2050 by more than ten percentage points at 24.3 percent. This comparison is arguably useful since Hispanics are an "ethnic group," while "Blacks" are a race. Said another way, Hispanics are *not* a race.

An ethnic group refers to a social group that distinguish themselves from others by race, religion and/or national origin, while race—e.g., Negroid, Caucasian, Malayan, Native American, Mongoloid—refers to genetically transmitted and inherited traits of physical appearance.[39] The US Census disclaimer is as follows,

> **Hispanics or Latinos** are those people who classified themselves in one of the specific Spanish, Hispanic, or Latino categories listed on the Census

2000 questionnaire—"Mexican, Mexican Am., Chicano," "Puerto Rican", or "Cuban"—as well as those who indicate that they are "other Spanish/Hispanic/Latino." Persons who indicated that they are "other Spanish/Hispanic/Latino" include those whose origins are from Spain, the Spanish-speaking countries of Central or South America, the

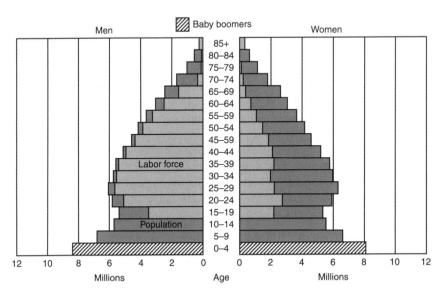

Figure 3.10 US pyramid summaries of population and labor force, 1950, 2000, and projected, 2050.

Source: M. Toossi (2006): A new look at long-term labor force projections to 2050. *Monthly Labor Review*. Retrieved April 24, 2009 from <http://www.bls.gov/opub/mlr/2006/11/art3full.pdf>

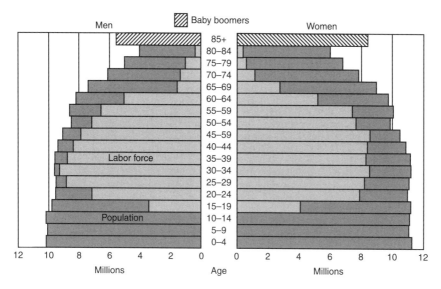

Figure 3.10 Continued.

Dominican Republic or people identifying themselves generally as Spanish, Spanish-American, Hispanic, Hispano, Latino, and so on.

Origin can be viewed as the heritage, nationality group, lineage, or country of birth of the person or the person's parents or ancestors before their arrival in the United States.[40]

The next excerpt is particularly important to interpretation and application of these statistics:

People who identify their origin as Spanish, Hispanic, or Latino may be of any race. **Thus, the percent Hispanic should not be added to percentages for racial categories.**[41]

While Table 3.1 does not address projections for Asian minority groupings, it is expected that this very diverse group will increase annually at 2 percent and represent 8.3 percent of the labor force by 2050.[42] Migrant stock data is addressed in the following section.

Immigration: the "main engine" of US population growth[43]

According to M. Toossi (2006), Senior Economist of the Bureau of Labor Statistics, immigration will be the "main engine" of population growth and future diversity of the US workforce for years to come. Figure 3.11, "US Demographic Diversity Snapshot: Make No Assumptions about Your Workforce and Your Customers," was meant to open people's eyes to the

Table 3.1 US civilian labor force by age, sex, race, and Hispanic origin, 2000, 2005, and projected, 2050[38]
[Numbers in thousands]

	Level			Change		Percentage change		Percentage distribution			Annual growth rate	
	2000	2005	2050	2000–05	2005–50	2000–05	2005–50	2000	2005	2050	2000–05	2005–50
Total, 16 years and older.	142,583	149,320	194,757	6,737	45,437	4.7	30.4	100.0	100.0	100.0	0.9	0.6
Age, years:												
16 to 24	22,520	22,290	25,808	–230	3,518	–1.0	15.8	15.8	14.9	13.3	–.2	.3
25 to 54	101,394	102,773	124,392	1,379	21,619	1.4	21.0	71.1	68.8	63.9	.3	.4
55 and older	18,669	24,257	44,556	5,588	20,299	29.9	83.7	13.1	16.2	22.9	5.4	1.4
Sex:												
Men	76,280	80,033	103,183	3,753	23,150	4.9	28.9	53.5	53.6	53.0	1.0	.6
Women	66,303	69,288	91,574	2,985	22,286	4.5	32.2	46.5	46.4	47.0	.9	.6
Race:												
White	118,545	122,299	142,371	3,754	20,072	3.2	16.4	83.1	81.9	73.1	.6	.3
Black	16,397	17,013	26,809	616	9,796	3.8	57.6	11.5	11.4	13.8	.7	1.0
Asian	6,270	6,503	16,124	233	9,621	3.7	147.9	4.4	4.4	8.3	.7	2.0
All other groups*	1,371	3,505	9,453	2,134	5,948	155.7	169.6	1.0	2.3	4.9	20.7	2.2
Ethnicity:												
Hispanic origin	16,689	19,824	47,317	3,135	27,493	18.8	138.7	11.7	13.3	24.3	3.5	2.0
Other than Hispanic origin	125,894	129,496	147,440	3,602	17,944	2.9	13.9	88.3	86.7	75.7	.6	.3
White non-Hispanic	102,729	103,891	100,189	1,162	–3,702	1.1	–3.6	72.0	69.6	51.4	.2	–.1

Age, sex, race, and ethnicity

Source: M. Toossi (2006) p.20. http://www.bls.gov/opub/mlr/2006/11/art3full.pdf

Note: *The "all other groups" category includes (1) those classified as being of multiple racial origin and (2) the race categories of (2a) American Indian and Alaska Native and (2b) Native Hawaiian and other Pacific Islanders. For this group, all 2000 numbers are estimates.

The Newest Markets

Asian Indians in Detroit? Cubans in New Jersey? All across America, new immigrants are changing cities in dramatic and unexpected ways.

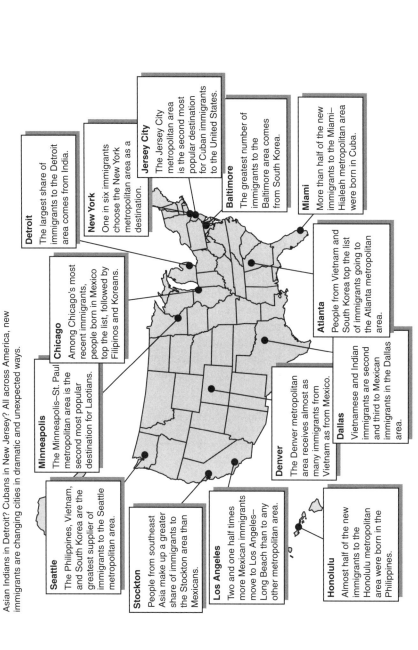

Seattle
The Philippines, Vietnam, and South Korea are the greatest supplier of immigrants to the Seattle metropolitan area.

Minneapolis
The Minneapolis–St. Paul metropolitan area is the second most popular destination for Laotians.

Detroit
The largest share of immigrants to the Detroit area comes from India.

New York
One in six immigrants choose the New York metropolitan area as a destination.

Jersey City
The Jersey City metropolitan area is the second most popular destination for Cuban immigrants to the United States.

Baltimore
The greatest number of immigrants to the Baltimore area comes from South Korea.

Miami
More than half of the new immigrants to the Miami–Hialeah metropolitan area were born in Cuba.

Chicago
Among Chicago's most recent immigrants, people born in Mexico top the list, followed by Filipinos and Koreans.

Atlanta
People from Vietnam and South Korea top the list of immigrants going to the Atlanta metropolitan area.

Stockton
People from southeast Asia make up a greater share of immigrants to the Stockton area than Mexicans.

Los Angeles
Two and one half times more Mexican immigrants move to Los Angeles–Long Beach than to any other metropolitan area.

Honolulu
Almost half of the new immigrants to the Honolulu metropolitan area were born in the Philippines.

Denver
The Denver metropolitan area receives almost as many immigrants from Vietnam as from Mexico.

Dallas
Vietnamese and Indian immigrants are second and third to Mexican immigrants in the Dallas area.

Figure 3.11 US demographic diversity snapshot: make no assumptions about your workforce and your customers.[44]

Source: Allen, James, and Eugene Turner 1988. p.27. Based on information from the US Immigration and Naturalization Service.

so-called "new wave" of immigrants to the US in 1988 and to the impact they would have on the social fabric of the country.

Fast-forwarding two decades later and toward more detail, Table 3.2 shows the top 10 States in the United States in which immigrants established legal permanent residency during fiscal year 2008. These States are host to 22 percent of those who acquired LPR status. This status is defined as follows:

> A legal permanent resident (LPR) or 'green card' recipient is defined by immigration law as a person who has been granted lawful permanent residence in the United States. Permanent resident status confers certain rights and responsibilities. For example, LPRs may live and work permanently anywhere in the United States, own property, and attend public schools, colleges, and universities. They may also join certain branches of the Armed Forces, and apply to become US citizens if they meet certain eligibility requirements.[45]

Figure 3.12 examines the LPRs of these States more closely using available 2007 data from the Department of Homeland Security, and lists the largest populations of LPRs in these 10 top hosting States. An interesting factor, also shown on the map, is the fact that in most cases, LPR women outnumber males as a portion of the population in every State. Yet, review of employment data shows that the percentage of males versus females and their respective employment and job status varies.[47]

Data show that in 2008 the major countries representing the new LPRs were Mexico, 17 percent, China, 7 percent, and India, 6 percent.[48] While the

Table 3.2 Top 10 states hosting legal permanent resident flows in 2008

State of residence (Ranked by 2008 LPR flow)	Number	%
Total	1,107,126	100.0
California	238,444	21.5
New York	143,679	13.0
Florida	133,445	12.1
Texas	89,811	8.1
New Jersey	53,997	4.9
Illinois	42,723	3.9
Massachusetts	30,369	2.7
Virginia	30,257	2.7
Georgia	27,769	2.5
Maryland	27,062	2.4
Other	289,570	26.2

Source: Adapted from the Office of Immigration Statistics, Department of Homeland Security[46]

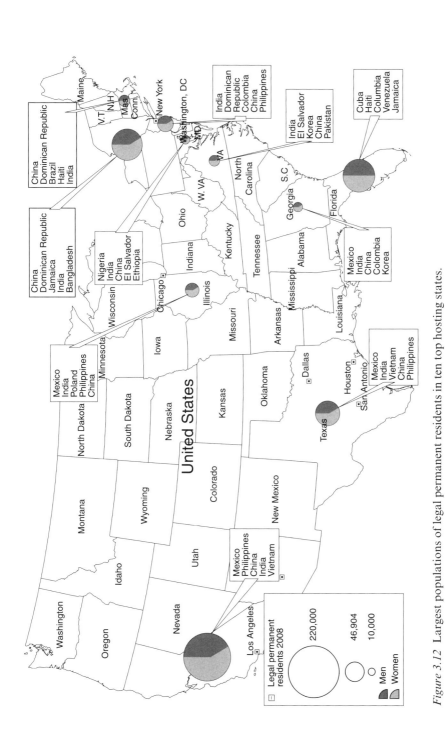

Figure 3.12 Largest populations of legal permanent residents in ten top hosting states.

Source: Compiled from data provided by the Office of Immigration Statistics, Dept. of Homeland Security.

information captured is from 2008, these individuals may have already been living in the US prior to this year.

In short, new immigrants have been arriving in the US for quite a long time. Recalling the Leadership Toolbox items of Chapters 1 and 2, consider the manager who might visit his or her plant in Jersey City, New Jersey, versus a hypothetical plant or subsidiary in Seattle, Washington. Each location is a new experience—each with its own dynamics and developmental requirements. Could we ever assume that one communication strategy— words alone, and a Western perspective—might be appropriate for both of these locations, or any others?—perhaps not. Indeed, organizations are already complex and dynamic social systems and this is the reason why all of the above discussion poses immense challenges to the development of human resources. Underlying these challenges is the need to know more about how adult learning may be facilitated. Demographic diversity is the rationale that takes us further on our journey to Chapter 4, "Learning: One Size Does Not Fit All."

Hallmarks of leadership

There is only one hallmark for this chapter. In light of the aforementioned, it deserves its place as a stand-alone.

Contextual intelligence (Chapter 1), yet with "granular understanding"

M. Baghai, S. Smit, and P. Viguerie argue the importance of knowing markets granularly to gain insight into how organizations should deploy their resources, to include their people.[49] Knowing the details of your demographic landscape is to grow opportunity identification.

Key terms and concepts

demographics, Hispanics, migrant stock,
diversity, LPRs, race,
ethnicity, nationality, HDI

Exercise: Test your assumptions regarding a particular locale. Get "granular."

1   Visit the "World Fact Book" link of the Central Intelligence Agency at <http://www.cia.gov/cia/publications/factbook/index.html>. Choose a country in which you have not worked/visited as yet, or one in which you expect to work or visit. Check (a) age structure, (b) life expectancy at birth, (c) literacy, (d) fertility rates, (e) ethnic

---

groups, (f) primary religions, (g) population density per sq. km.—
Compute this number yourself if it is not listed. Compare these
data to those of your home country. What differences and similarities do you notice? Illustrate in a table and explain.

2 Visit the US Census web-site at <http://www.census.gov>.
Compare the demographic profile of two hypothetical or real
working locations. As an example, choose the respective countries
of two capital cities and compare (a) age percentages; (b) representative percentages of nationalities, race, Hispanics; (3) literacy
(and/or educational attainment); (4) gender. What differences and
similarities do you notice?
(Illustrate in a table and explain.)

3 What implications do the findings of Numbers 1 and 2 have to
"human resource planning" and communications? See Glossary
for key terms.

4 Based on chapter discussion regarding race, ethnic groups, and
nationality, how would you recommend that the Census categories
be improved in order to accurately represent the population characteristics of a particular country? What are the challenges to
implementing your suggestions?

5 Research on the Internet for the current country members of the
European Union.

4 Learning
One size does not fit all

> I have been involved in a number of projects which brought me into contact with businessmen, lawyers, physicians (mostly psychoanalysts and psychiatrists), diplomats, artists, architects, engineers, designers and laborers. All have been concerned with the solution of real-life problems. These experiences, particularly those having to do with teaching and educating, convinced me that people, even within the confines of a single culture, learn in many different ways.[1]

Chapter 2 navigates the reader through aspects of the complexity of culture. Chapter 3 aims to build awareness of the diverse and mobile demographic landscape of the twenty-first century: "New demographic" profiles show that birth rates are generally declining and/or falling below replacement levels, while adult populations continue to grow in selected Asian countries, European and American populations. Additionally, it clearly illustrates that immigration (foreign born) will inevitably fuel labor growth in varied degrees throughout the world. What does an aging workforce mean to design of effective communication, not only within organizations, but also with customers and other stakeholders? How do generational differences impact orientation to work, training, and more? In terms of communication and working styles, could one ever assume that one "size" fits all? These questions and others are the focus of this chapter, and involve knowledge pieces with implications for the leadership toolbox.

Workforce dynamics and adult learning

The amount of information from education, psychology, and related literatures addressing the subject of "adult learning" is endless, indeed, and well beyond the focus of this book. Topic areas include: the aging process and its effect on learning, educational attainment as it affects learning, motivational research regarding willingness to participate in learning activities, demographics as they relate to participation in education programs, self-directed learning vs. formal classroom learning, analyses of adult learning environments, the learning process and split-brain studies, intelligence and age, adult developmental theory, and many others. There is also an extensive body of literature relating to the nature and dimension of "learning styles", for example (a person's) characteristic ways of processing information, feeling and behaving in certain situations.[2]

Regrettably, frequently writing on adult learning neglects the socio-cultural perspective in favor of the predominant psychological orientation.[3] Additionally, scientific studies of learning styles, to include the Kolb Learning Style Inventory (LSI) model, have limitations since, frequently, the effects of workplace dynamics on the individual are not considered. Workplace dynamics include, but are not limited to, the concurrent effects of workforce turnover and job rotation on the nature of work, individuals' and teams' preferences for learning delivery formats and methodologies, and the effects of virtual environments on physical worlds and vice versa on both teams and individuals. Alternatively stated, "styles" are assessed in isolation, rather than in dynamic social constructs.[4] Nevertheless, it is generally agreed that learning in adulthood is an intensely personal activity. In addition, finding an appropriate match between adult learning styles and the form of instruction is important in learning environments.[5] Some individuals may prefer to learn by listening, others by observing, others by reading; some work better in groups; others do not.[6]

Albert Einstein is an interesting example of the implications of differences in learning styles for managing and training development efforts. He recalls: "my principal weakness [as a pupil] was a poor memory, and especially a poor memory for words and texts."[7] In trying to describe his method of thought, Einstein said, the essential part was a "rather vague" nonlogical playing with "visual" and "muscular" signs, after which explanatory words had to be "sought for laboriously."[8] Indeed, Einstein claimed he did not think in words. Physical images and visual images worked far better for him. The agony he experienced in translating imagery into words (rather than vice versa) is understandable, recognizing that even when words are used, no two people—even from the same culture—may use the same word in exactly the same way. Additionally, "if we bring in psychological factors such as feelings and emotions, as well as metaphors and delicate nuances, we know even less about the process by which meaning is assigned and transmitted through speech."[9] Adding to the dynamics reflected above are the "action chains" mentioned in Chapter 1 (Hall, 1976). Action chains are very culturally constituted, and an important puzzle piece of Figure 2.1 in Chapter 2.

Recalling the Chapter 2 discussion regarding high-context (HC) and low-context (LC) cultures, Hall further observed that high-context people tend to be polychronic—that is, involved in doing many things at one time. Conversely, monochronic peoples tend to be one-thing-at-a-time oriented. In fact, they often tend to be disoriented when confronted with polychronic individuals.[10] Indeed, there are many different orientations to learning within the internal and external environments of organizations.

As subsequent discussion will show, cognition, or the way in which the brain perceives and processes information and the pathways and schemata established therein, is very influenced by experience. HC orientations and polychronic tendencies vs. low-context orientations and monochronic tendencies also have implications for how individuals will attend or listen to their logic and to their approach to problem solving.[11]

Alternatively stated, HC orientations might intentionally or unconsciously shut out ("turn off") an LC, monochronic approach, to a situation and vice versa. Many examples of this phenomenon are available from personal career experiences in university teaching and business/management training. Frequently, if I approach a subject from a contextual perspective in audiences comprising primarily Westerners, or those having roots in European and Anglo-Saxon cultures, often I find impatience with the approach. Invariably, this audience will prefer a bullet by bullet approach, e.g.,

- xxx
- xxx

a list of factors that are functionally related to the issue at hand. They become frustrated with approaches that focus on relationships and "big picture" considerations.

On the other hand, in classes and workshops that include Malaysians, Japanese, Chinese, and others from Asia, frequently individuals express confusion caused by a linear approach to problem-solving. In conversation and interviews they often mention that Western logic is *so* different. One US student wrote on a teaching evaluation form—in an international human resource course that addressed "cognitive processing across cultures":

"Dr. P., I never did get used to:

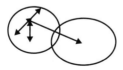

I still prefer:

———

———

——— "

The comment is wonderfully instructive as this student recognized that her preferred mode of communication and logic was LC and monochronic by nature.

Managers are also advised to be wary of EEO (US equal opportunity-oriented) workforce descriptions. Race and gender are not even close to a sufficient profile for assessing relative workforce homogeneity vs. non-homogeneity. As an example, I am reminded of fieldwork I did over a two-year period within one division of an organization in the mid 1990s. There was a great deal of dysfunction and in-fighting within this division. Working in teams was essential for future success in order to be responsive to market needs. The EEO workforce profile of these 724 employees would lead one to believe that this was a relatively homogeneous group of individuals: 80 percent Caucasian, 13 percent Asian American (from China, India and Japan in order of largest to smallest group). Other smaller percentages were 5 percent Black, 1 percent Hispanic and 0.2 percent Native American. Male and female distributions were about equal. After looking further, I learned that a significant percentage of the Caucasian group was from Eastern Europe. For the Japanese, the group experience was quite enjoyable; for the Eastern Europeans the idea of being collectivized was totally abhorrent. The Eastern Europeans expressed that they fled socialized life to have the opportunity to work individually!

What does all this mean to trainers and employees at all levels? It means that one needs to strike a balance when targeting any audience. How to do that is addressed in subsequent discussion and in Appendix 6A through practitioner examples. Additionally, knowing how *adults* learn must be factored into training formats. Too much focus on difference can also be risky. Again, a balance needs to be struck. This is a focus area of Chapter 8, "Best Practices in IHRD."

Mental modeling

Portraying workforces as follows:

- comprising adults, and growing older;
- growth-fueled by foreign born;
- each with culturally constituted learning styles;
- performing increasingly complex tasks within and across (increasingly) participative and dynamic organizational environments;
- influenced in varied degrees by the availability of digital access and technology-based infrastructures.[12]

What theoretical base informs training design?

There is extensive research specific to how people receive, store, retrieve and transform information. However, an inherent limitation is the fact that many studies have been done with children primarily in formal educational settings and with computer learning. Work with adults often focuses primarily on aging and its effect on memory.[13] Within this research it is noted that as adults age, they are found to be less effective in organizing new material for learning. Yet when older subjects are given clues in advance of what will have to be remembered later on, age differences tend to decline.[14] This is an important consideration in training design, given the profile of the future workforce.

Research on mental modeling and use of advance organizers provide further rationale for the need for management skills beyond spoken communication. It is generally agreed across several disciplines (e.g., educational psychology, human factors, and training and development) that individuals interact effectively with their environment by organizing knowledge into meaningful patterns stored in memory. These knowledge structures are given a variety of labels called schemata, cognitive maps, and/or mental models.[15] Effective training design should present an explicit conceptual model of the material to be trained through "advance organizers" or "scaffolding" to assist with retention of targeted materials.[16] These models improve learning as they help the trainee focus attention on relationships and components within a system. Additionally they assist the trainee in organizing and connecting information. Frequently, conceptual models and advance organizers tend to be highly language-dependent,—i.e., they are outlines or overviews of information comprising words and written statements. Other limitations include that they may focus on a single task or activity to be learned in a formal setting where context is not a primary concern and/or is relatively static. Additionally, the orientation to learning is very linear path-oriented. Even the term "scaffolding" presumes a linear progression.

Cross-cultural studies, such as Dorothy Lee's (1950) discussion of the Trobrianders, indicate that experience does not necessarily follow a linear pattern. According to Lee, "our own insistence on the line, such as lineal causality, for example, is also often based on unquestioned belief or value."[17] She found that Trobrianders, as evidenced in their discourse and actions, showed no concern for chronological sequence or causal relationships,—i.e., there was no developmental line sequence. Lee wondered if it was appropriate, therefore, to accept without question the presence of the line in everyone's reality.[18]

S. Biesheuvel (1949) also pointed to the importance of appreciating differences in how people view spatial relationships: "In our European culture, orientation with reference to the four main points of the compass, or to the vertical–horizontal axes of the body [i.e., rectangularity], is an accepted feature of daily life."[19] In discussion of testing, he posits that cultures that do not have this habit of mind are at a distinct disadvantage.[20] Cross-cultural research further supports that the physical world may also cause an individual to be more susceptible to certain types of visual illusions. "Carpentered" worlds, or those characterized by right-angled physical environments, are likely to influence individual habits for making perceptual judgments.[21]

The writings of Hall (1976) and Kolb (1984) provide further valuable insight into the multidimensional and dynamic nature of learning. Hall argues, "we have been taught to think linearly rather than comprehensively."[22] An example illustrating Hall's argument involves the learning of penmanship skills in early childhood education. Figures 4.1a and 4.1b depict a totally different orientation to space of the young Japanese child versus the US child. In the US, orientation to cursive writing generally begins in the second grade. A child practices writing skills following the lines and strokes from left to right (write!). Penmanship exercises generally continue through fifth grade at school and as a homework activity. The Japanese experience, however, is very different from US (and Western) training. Calligraphy lessons orient the child to placing *kanji* in a grid (see Figure 4.1b). Achieving balance is key. While good posture during writing is generally emphasized in both cultures as appropriate physical orientation to the writing activity, the Japanese teacher encourages total body control through summoning of energy from the abdomen. Mastery is sought as early as first grade. There-fore, while one culture is training to look at a line from left to write (right)—

Figure 4.1a Linear orientation to writing and space (US).

Source: Handwriting: A Way to Self-Expression (1993). Columbus, OH: Zaner-Bloser, Inc. Reproduced by permission (inside cover).

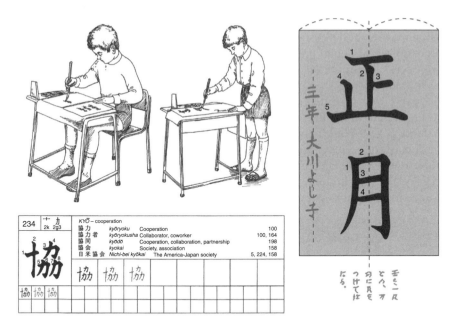

Figure 4.1b Holistic orientation to writing and space (Japan).

Source: Hadamitsky, W., & Spahn, M. (1991) *A Guide to Writing Kanji and Kana*, Book I, Charles E. Tuttle Co., of Boston, MA and Tokyo, Japan.

for *years*—another is visualizing balance of the self and writing holistically within a space. These are *very* different orientations considering the early age and the amount of lifetime experience the practice is likely to involve.[23]

The discussion heretofore provides insight into why individuals may prefer certain modes of communication versus others. This potential for ethnocentrism in communication has huge implications for many aspects of organizational life, to planning, and even to the design of information technologies—to be explored further in subsequent chapters. Trainers and others must examine their own culture and experiences in order to discover what preferences may lie in their own unconscious, and then strive to bridge the way to others. This is notably true if we add another level of complexity to the training design and learning equation—specifically, that of how to bridge facilitation of learning across generations.

Bridging left brain/right brain border zones

Human brain and art education research provides further insight into why individual culture and experience influence preferred communication modes, and may, perhaps, be roots of potential barriers to development of others.

Research supports that there are numerous ways to tap and expand the potential of the human brain. Betty Edwards credits the earlier research of psychobiologist Roger Sperry—winner of the Nobel prize in 1981—for insight into the dual nature of human thinking. According to Edwards,

> the corroborating research since Sperry's original work is overwhelming. Moreover, even in the midst of the argument about location, most scientists agree that for a majority of individuals, information-processing based primarily on linear, sequential data is mainly located in the left hemisphere, while global, perceptual data is mainly processed in the right hemisphere.[24]

While culture and experience undoubtedly influence preferred modes of communication, both also potentially influence informal and formal education modes and learning in many ways. Figure 4.2 compares left-mode and right-mode characteristics of the brain. The left brain is more logical and linear, while the right is holistically oriented; the left is more analytic while the right synthesizes the parts into a whole.

Edwards' work points to possible ways to expand human brain potential through self-analysis, training and effective training design.[25] While Edwards argues for the power of drawing, Gareth Morgan advocates the use of metaphor. Others advocate expanded use of tropes, but these, of course, must be used carefully due to language differences. From personal experience and

L-Mode

Verbal: Using words to name, describe, define.
Analytic: Figuring things out step-by-step and part-by-part.
Symbolic: Using a symbol to *stand for* something. For example, the drawn form ☜ stands for eye, the sign + stands for the process of addition.
Abstract: Taking out a small bit of information and using it to represent the whole thing.
Temporal: Keeping track of time, sequencing one thing
After another: Doing first things first, second things second, etc.
Rational: Drawing conclusions based on *reason* and *facts*.
Digital: Using numbers as in counting.
Logical: Drawing conclusions based on logic: one thing following another in logical order—for example, a mathematical theorem or a well-stated argument.
Linear: Thinking in terms of linked ideas, one thought directly following another, often leading to a convergent conclusion.

R-Mode

Nonverbal: Awareness of things, but minimal connection with words.
Synthetic: Putting things together to form wholes.
Concrete: Relating to things as they are, at the present moment.
Analogic: Seeing likenesses between things; understanding metaphoric relationships.
Nontemporal: Without a sense of time.
Nonrational: Not requiring a basis of reason or facts; willingness to suspend judgment.
Spatial: Seeing where things are in relation to other things, and how parts go together to form a whole.
Intuitive: Making leaps of insight, often based on incomplete patterns, hunches, feelings, or visual images.
Holistic: Seeing whole things all at once; perceiving the overall patterns and structures, often leading to divergent conclusions.

Figure 4.2 Developing the potential of the human brain.
Source: Betty Edwards, *Drawing on the Right Side of the Brain.* Penguin Putnam (1989).

research, I am convinced of three things: (1) that creativity can be learned; (2) that there are many paths to creativity, and none are mutually exclusive; and (3) that these paths facilitate the arduous process of bridging and crossing border zones, not only between right and left brain tendencies, but also between working and communication styles. As examples, I have used drawing and metaphor rather intuitively for years in (international) management training and development endeavors.

Recall the student who said, "Dr. P., I still prefer:

———

———

———."

In workshops and executive training seminars, individuals who begin a course frequently are urged to embark on a developmental journey aimed to bridge high-context, polychronic orientations—i.e., blending relationships

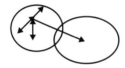

with their low-context, monochronic orientations and vice versa through drawing and use of metaphor.[26] Individuals who have never drawn in their life, or exclaim that they are not creative, gradually recognize that these are capabilities that are dormant—awaiting permission to be released.

Generational differences

Earlier discussion addresses approaches aimed to facilitate adult learning. These approaches and techniques are important to bear in mind as the Baby Boom generation, generally referring to those born in the mid-twentieth century or around the end of World War II, continue to be a significant percentage of the workforce. Yet, whether it be "Boomers," Generation Xers—those following the boomers or about from 1965 to 1980, the Yers—those following the Xers and often referred to by (too) many names as the offspring of the Boomers, or the Millenniums, the Dot.Coms and Generation N—these are all *adults* of varied ages in the workforce. The Zers, born in the mid nineties and after, are still too young for attention herein; yet, as with the other generations before them, already much is being proliferated prophesying their likes, dislikes, primary influences, their expectations of management, work attitudes and values, and personality traits. This section does not reproduce that already prolific generational literature.[27] Rather, it captures select information with implications for training, working styles, and organizational development. Specifically:

a **Establish and nurture a common purpose**. Research suggests that obstacles to adult learning may be reduced by instilling a unity of purpose within the organization and its stakeholders.[28]
b **Avoid stereotyping individual or group needs based on generational (or other) labels or traits**. Studies show that there is a great deal of overlap between these generations. For example, not all Millennials are advanced in technology usage. Further, different generations are also recycling and retooling themselves at varied life stages. Analysis of factors such as "a" (above) as an element of organizational culture, Figure 1.2 discussion of Chapter 1, socio-economic characteristics within the labor force, and degree of labor force mobility is imperative to optimally influence learning styles and potential instructional and communication design choices. Personal biases must be kept in check as well.[29]
c **Build a "blended infrastructure" that supports diverse learning styles, and training and development goals**.[30] Bear in mind that blogs, Facebook and hosts of other social networking venues are now part and parcel of all generations. How to leverage those experiences to advantage in recruiting and retaining employees can only be a competitive advantage to HR professionals and others.

For example, a great deal of attention in business and industry has been given to "gaming," not only as a learning and instructional tool, but also as a recruitment tool. For examples, the Entertainment Software Association reports that American Express Company, Bank of America Corporation, International Business Machines Corporation, JPMorgan Chase & Co., and Nokia Group utilize training games for employees developed through Games 2Train. Advertisements for recruitment for the British intelligence surveillance branch (Government Communications Headquarters—GCHQ) are run in varied on-line video games.[31]

Why is there so much interest in recruiting "gamers," particularly those who grew up with gaming?

An answer is that research suggests cognitive processing of individuals who have grown up on video games have been influenced profoundly in a number of ways: They appear to be more willing to take risks and are competitive, and view winning and competition as the norm. Therefore, since the Ners also apparently value hands-on and interactive learning, the curriculums of trainers face more challenges going forward: *How to make training more interactive?*[32] *How to provide more trial and error?*—aka, the replays they enjoy in gaming experiences. *How to integrate andragogy principles*, which are student-centered, versus pedagogical principles, which are teacher-centered and lecture-oriented? "In the pedagogical model, teachers assume responsibility for making decisions about what will be learned, how it will be learned, and when it will be learned. Teachers direct learning."[33] Therefore, the traditional pedagogical approach is being challenged. These students "want to have a say in their education, contribute toward the discussion of how they will learn, participate in hands-on activities, and collaborate with their colleagues."[34]

These gamers are also "Generation Ners." The following quote supports the discussion heretofore:

> Basic andragogy principles offer more to Generation N than the common pedagogical approach. . . . Calling upon the gaming side of modern technology as well as the hypertext mindset . . . Generation N's learning style is hands-on and not necessarily linear in fashion. Forget instruction manuals, tech tips and lecture-based lessons; this is the generation that plays to learn.[35]

While research shows that lifelong gamers tend to dislike formal learning and authority, it is unclear, at least to this author, that this tendency translates equally across socio-cultural groups everywhere, or in countries where gaming has grown up with gamers and vice versa. The same is true regarding data that show that gamers' attitudes toward teams and team-building tend to be superior to non-gamers. In short, caution should be exercised in making generalizations about this generation or others, particularly in cross-cultural and national communities, since this literature is still evolving.

As J. Beck and M. Wade (2004) state in their seminal book, *Got Game: How the Gamer Generation Is Reshaping Business Forever*, gaming is, indeed, a "social phenomenon."[36] They point to the US, Europe and Asia in particular, where its influence has been felt. While gaming data show that the average gamer is 35 years old (US), the Entertainment Software Association research supports that 26 percent of gamers are over the age of 50.[37] Chapter 9 addresses "Communication Design Issues of the Future," taking into account how culture affects communication choices in the computer-based technology Information Age.

The above considerations, along with Chapter 2 issues regarding "The Limitations of Language," have many implications for those who are charged with effecting change within contemporary and future organizations, and, therefore, this issue is addressed in the section to follow.

Producing change in organizations

Ford (1992) and Ford and Ford (1995) emphasize the importance of conversations with production partners to establish common understanding and performance measures for change. Their argument is that production of change occurs in the process of communication: "When we speak of producing a change, we are talking about bringing into existence some . . . result, product, or outcome that did not exist [before]. . . . Communication necessarily involves *'speech acts'* [emphasis added], and . . . speech acts are actions in language."[38] These acts of communication may serve to clarify interpretation of events, plan for the change, establish new (cross-functional and departmental) relationships with peers, and set mutually agreeable expectations and performance measures. The change process apparently relies on the power of verbal discourse,[39] and that emphasis is understandable, recognizing that proponents of this process may evolve from a low-context cultural perspective. However, those charged with human resource management and development must recognize how mixed a pot of ingredients we may derive when constructing a hypothetical workplace team in virtual and physical spaces. The ingredients could include varied cultures and experience, representing differing perceptions of communication and logic, and adult learning styles.

Recalling the discussion of high-context cultures, planning improvements in organizational practices (*kaizen*) is facilitated through the use of visual tools such as pareto diagrams and others that are described later on. To turn diversity into strength implies the ability to access the process. Subsequent chapters point to strategies that enhance the opportunity to participate in the process of change, thereby turning diversity into strength. The visual cue, as one example, augments the communication of the spoken word. Nevertheless, this section does not suggest that these strategies will be effective for all individuals. It does suggest that they should not be overlooked.

Based on business and teaching experience, case study,[40] and continued research, attention to mental modeling, cognitive mapping, and creativity training appear vital to managers and trainers and others.[41] According to E. Hall, helping with "information overload,"—i.e., coping with increased demands and complexity, involves helping with the contexting process.[42] Spatial relationships and the use of space in training also appear important considerations for facilitators of adult learning. As it is generally agreed that people learn in gestalts, or, complete units, managers and trainers should be asking: How might I/we map and present developmental inventories to optimize understanding of complex, culturally diverse and polychronic environments? How might learning be facilitated? These questions led to a dissertation, completed in 1994, and to further attention to the creation of "learning landscapes." This expression is a proprietary term that expands the concept of mental modeling and cognitive mapping, and is discussed in a chapter to follow. But first there follows a caution to the reader.

What is to be learned?[43]

[A]s Aristotle, Cicero, and Quintilian realized many centuries ago, she or he who would speak or become interactively involved in intercultural efforts must know many things, and must not be satisfied with merely learning a set of techniques or gathering a bag of rhetorical tricks.[44]

Earlier discussion points to the diverse demographic and psychographic (life-style) profiles of the current and projected workforce. The term *diversity*, in itself, is laden with numerous possible meanings. Working definitions include people of different cultures, and/or national affiliations, and/or gender, and/or age, and/or power and authority, and/or ethnic orientations, learning styles, disability, and more. There is not enough space herein to debate or review its numerous interpretations. Nevertheless, despite some conventional wisdom, we can probably agree that diversity is not a phenomenon that recently descended upon us; nor is it a phenomenon of the twenty-first century. It has been here a while. Additionally, there can be no doubt that:

1   there is a great deal to know about all groups;
2   no one could ever hope to know everything; and
3   that techniques must be compatible with and nurtured by an organizational philosophy and common purpose.

A senior vice president of a large Midwestern manufacturing facility conveys the points in the list above by using the analogy of a chemical reaction. In an interview questioning him about training techniques that have been success-ful within his organization,[45] the SVP cautioned against overemphasis on "techniques" to the exclusion of atmosphere; his comments recall this section's beginning quotation.

> I think one of the problems which we face constantly is that we talk about the training—the people tend to think more about the technique of the trainer—how to teach people. But before you think about how to, you have to think about the supportive atmosphere. And I think we are finding that as far as people feel secure, people feel comfortable, people are motivated, people have a chance to think that this is their company, or feel the ownership of a job, then almost 80 percent [are] successful. On the contrary, you don't create an atmosphere and you emphasize on the training itself—know-how, technique—then that's the 20 percent chance of success . . . *Like a chemistry [chemical]; you know you put the chemis-try in cold water, it doesn't react. But you have a certain temperature of the atmosphere, then we can expect a much better reaction.* [Emphasis is added to illustrate techniques will fall flat without a nurturing organizational culture.]

This author does not suggest that those charged with labor force develop-ment simply learn a bag of techniques to manage and develop demographi-cally diverse individuals. As the profile of the workforces becomes more demographically diverse, organizations will need to provide an environment where training audits and enables individuals and groups with diverse working styles. Learning organizations evolve; they are not born. The Hallmarks of Leadership that follow will help you reach beyond techniques to a higher calling. The following section identifies several defining ones related to the discussion in this chapter.

Hallmarks of leadership

Chief "honcho" of organizational learning

"In a learning organization, leaders are designers, stewards, and teachers. They are responsible for *building organizations* where people continually expand their capabilities to understand complexity, clarify vision . . .—that is, they are responsible for learning."[46]

Continuous learning

Leaders are role models for those who follow. They demonstrate a commitment to expanding capabilities—not only personally, but also in others. Leaders of learning organizations give individuals "permission" to be creative. They nurture creativity and learning through a "bottom line" and policies that reward both.

Creative designer and systems thinker

"The neglected leadership role is the *designer* of the ship."[47] Management is, after all, an *intensely* creative activity. Multiple methodologies and designs may be necessary to optimize organizational learning.

 Leadership toolbox 4: Learning – One size does not fit all

1   *Research the demographic profile of your workforce, community, and your stakeholders—near and far. Develop and expand your own capabilities to convey past, current, and future complexities.*
2   *Techniques are likely to fall flat without a nurturing organizational culture that values and commits to learning. Assure that individuals have permission to be creative, and provide them with training and implementation opportunities to do so.*
3   *Integrate principles of andragogy into instructional design. Recognize you are working with **adult** learners of varied ages.*
4   *Given a nurturing atmosphere, pay attention to context; additionally, continue to assess your own culture, experience, and preferred working communication modes to watch out that personal preferences do not become a barrier to others.*

Key terms and concepts

andragogy, pedagogy, mental modeling,
monochronic time, gaming,
polychronic time, texting

Exercises

1   Read a journal article (not a Googled summary) that addresses the generation to which you supposedly belong regarding learning preferences. Evaluate if you fit with the group that is described.

2   Recall a formal or informal classroom or training experience that was particularly enjoyable for you. Explain why it was enjoyable.

3   Read the article by Jeff Feiertag and Zane Berg (2008). Choose two points addressed in the article and discuss their strengths and limitations.

4   Regarding a training exercise, Dean Foster (1992, p. 80) describes an event that happened when individuals from other countries were asked to fill in the blank regarding the following US proverb: "God helps those who___." US individuals and especially white Anglo-Saxon-Protestants usually get the answer right, and fill in the blank with *help themselves*. Asians, on the other hand, usually fill in the blank with *help others*. How do you explain this? And what implications does this have on training design and learning preferences?

5   Intermezzo

The changing face of management

In this chapter, the changing environment of organizations is viewed from a socio-historical perspective. It is meant to be an *intermezzo*—an opportunity for the reader to pause and reflect on the rationale and need for the book. The chapter clearly illustrates why a "read my lips" mentality may not have "worked" as the US entered the 1980s and the workplace became more mobile, more complex, and more competitive. While its focus centers on the United States experience, the reader should regard the US (only) as an example. While historical context differs regarding immigration flows on a country-by-country basis, there are striking similarities across countries regarding the attitudes and debates surrounding immigration of foreign born people and their impact on respective labor forces, infrastructure, policy and much more.[1] Uncovering the unseen—i.e., the socio-historical perspective that shapes a diverse workforce in *any* locale, is recalled as a hallmark of leadership. Multi-local and multi-global managers and HR developers and trainers are and will, undoubtedly, be challenged to facilitate integration of diversity and participation in change and development processes in many locations.[2]

Management vs. integration of diversity in the US—a sociological historical perspective

During the late nineteenth and twentieth centuries, newcomers to America were generally expected to take on the behavior and attitudes of the dominant Anglo-Saxon mold of their adopted country and give up the cultural forms of their native land.[3] Once the immigrant had acquired the social ritual and language of the native community, she/he was considered "assimilated." The terms "assimilation" and "acculturation" are used interchangeably in this discussion, and generally refer to the meeting of individuals and/or groups of different cultures that result in changes in the original cultural patterns of either or both. English, of course, was the language of the predominant culture to be acquired; subsequently and simultaneously it was believed that identification with social behaviors occurred. Definitions of assimilation suggest a belief that as cultural differences disappeared, so too would rivalries and conflict.[4]

A decade prior to the Civil War, John Quincy Adams wrote in a letter [regarding immigrants in the US],

> They come . . . [not] to a life of independence, but to a life of labor—and, if they cannot accommodate themselves to the character, moral, political and physical, of this country with all of its compensating balances of good and evil, the Atlantic is always open to them, and they can return to the land of their nativity and their fathers . . . They must cast off their European skin never to resume it.[5]

There was a tendency to place people in social categories. Indeed, life would be difficult for someone who would wear none of the labels that the dominant society provided—whether it be in the workplace or the school setting.

Anglo conformity was in full force during the Americanization movement during World War I. Milton Gordon points to the flush of patriotic fever that predominated during this time, referring to the "pressure-cooking" assimilation that prevailed.[6] Both Federal agencies, such as the Bureau of Education, and private organizations were dedicated to persuading the immigrant to learn English and to revere American institutions. Underlying this assumption was that after all this was done, "differences" would disappear, or at least be neutralized. The idea of the US as a "melting pot" became idealized.

Sociologists were already studying and recording the effects of immigration on urban America—very visibly in this country's literature from the time of the Industrial Revolution. Anthropologists recognized and studied diversity long ago, many urging that each culture be understood in its own terms.[7] Yet, while noted individuals in these fields were addressing issues of cultural diversity,[8] their work apparently went unnoticed in the training and development (T&D) literature, as only one business-related example.

In a frequently cited and first review of personnel training and development, John Campbell remarked that the T&D "world" had only recently discovered cultural differences. Campbell comments, "what has proven noteworthy is the sudden discovery of discrimination and cultural/ethnic differences."[9] His review pointed to the need for new methods, and cross-cultural studies of organizations.[10]

Interest in the field of comparative management paralleled the internationalization of firms (e.g., the rise of the multinational corporation [MNC]), and the recognition that organizational theory had not yet come to grips with culture and the environments in which organizations were based. According to Nancy Adler, *et al.*,

> Research in developmental psychology, sociology, and anthropology shows that there are major differences among the cognitive processes of people from different cultures. In the era of the global corporation, cultural diversity has to be recognized, understood, and appropriately used in organizations. It is suggested that cross-cultural management would

greatly benefit from comparative studies considering the impact of cognitive aspects of culture on managerial practice.[11]

Twenty years after Campbell's review, Raymond Noe and Kevin Ford identified cross-cultural training and diversity training in organizational settings as *emerging* (emphasis added) issues deserving of further research under a subheading entitled: "Training for Success within a Diverse Workforce and Culture."[12]

As illustrated in Figure 5.1, concern with cultural difference and diversity in T&D in the US evolved as two separate domains. Even post-twenty-first century, *cross-cultural* studies of training in business and industry generally address issues of expatriation, repatriation, and adjustment to and from the overseas environment.[13] Additionally, although not universally, they often aim to develop skills and attitudes important to successful interactions with those of different cultural backgrounds.[14]

Diversity training, however, evolved from general concern with issues of discrimination and misunderstandings that arise in the domestic workplace due to age, ethnicity, gender, and/or disability, as examples, with emphasis on black–white relations. Thousands of studies have dealt with diversity training.[15] The majority of these studies target prevention of misunderstandings and/or conflict resolution that might bear upon productivity and job satisfaction. In practice, training program objectives frequently involve modification of behaviors, attitudes and/or practices to create a work environment conducive to productivity and job satisfaction through "sensitivity" toward others. How to turn diversity into strength *vis-à-vis* strategies for integration

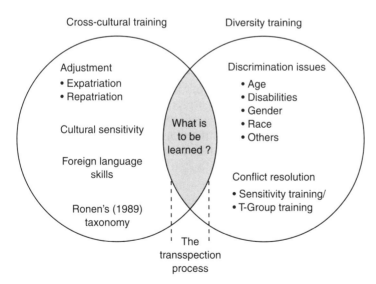

Figure 5.1 Cross-cultural training vs. diversity training.

are generally not apparent. In short, management of diversity was far from pluralistic well into the late 1970s; rather, control, hierarchy, and uniformity were the name of the game. Many businesses have yet to recognize and address both realms within a *holistic* diversity picture in accordance with the demographic realities mentioned in Chapter 3.

Management theory and education

Critical to the fabric of American life during the late nineteenth and early twentieth centuries was the nature of business involvement in education. The first half of the twentieth century is generally characterized as a time when industry was a key driver behind vocational education. This was undoubtedly influenced by post-wartime remobilization efforts.[16] During this era the "scientific" approach to management predominated within the Classical School of management theory. There was overriding concern with the job task—i.e., how to do the job most efficiently and how to increase worker productivity.[17]

Management theory that focused on the human element of organizations and addressed group and individual interactions became known as the "behavioral approach" to management. Nevertheless, its primary concern was to reveal the effect of behavioral factors *on productivity*. The behavioral approach focused on the social factors that would motivate workers to be more productive, while the scientific approach was concerned with the organization of the task to be performed. Neither was mutually exclusive; both influenced management.

Managers were trained in interpersonal skills for "handling" human situations so that productivity would not be interrupted. Indeed, while not provable, it could be argued that diversity training is more a factor of US thought and practice regarding a perceived need to assimilate or melt away cultural differences than a conscious effort to integrate diversity as part of a decision-making process within the workplace.[18]

Why were efforts aimed at assimilation not successful? According to Gordon (1964), it was due to the not-so-simple fact that (the immigrant) "had a positive need for the comfort of his own communal institutions."[19] As long as Americans, albeit hyphenated—e.g., Japanese-Americans, Afro-Americans, etc.—continued to organize themselves into subsocieties based upon religious, racial and quasi-racial and nationality groupings, the "melting pot" idea was an impossibility.[20] Indeed, Gordon posits that it would be more appropriate to talk of American society as a number of "pots", rather than one pot.[21] Further, on a national level, hypothetically, a reduction of conflict between dominant and subordinate social groups could be possible only as long as contact and mobility were minimal. Yet, that was *not* the case, especially as the US entered the 1970s; nor is it true probably anywhere in the world almost one-half century later.

The above does not suggest that management education and educators in other fields were not being influenced by world and national events of the

1960s and 1970s. Broad concern with human rights throughout the world, the aftermath of conflicts between nations and peoples, economic interdependence due to advances in technology and the mobility of peoples, keen competition from industrialized and industrializing countries, and consequences of decision-making and their negative effects on the environment did impact education and practice.

One of the management approaches that grew out of the 1960s and 1970s is "systems theory," which generally refers to the interrelatedness of technologies, human resources, and environmental variables. Many other factors, such as Japanese management practices—influenced in the 1950s by American consultants such as W. E. Deming and J. M. Juran—impacted approaches to management. A primary concern was how to turn American business around in order to regain the competitive edge. An extensive body of literature addresses the issue of change in managerial thought and practice during these times. Although important, it is beyond the scope and specific focus of this book.[22]

Another field that grew out of the 1960s and 1970s which provided some insight into intercultural communication is the field of global education, and the work of R. Hanvey—discussed in Chapter 2. As global educators primarily ground their discussions around schooling in the US, this may explain why it still goes largely unnoticed in the business and related literature. Within the context of schooling, global educators generally advocate curriculums that engage students in study of domains of the human experience,—e.g., diverse and universal human values (cultural differences) and global and diverse historical, economic, technological, ecological and economic systems. (Hanvey advocated using "transspection" to develop "perspectives consciousness" in young people, rather than empathy.) There does not appear to be any published research specific to training and/or implementation of the transspection process within organizations. Nor does Hanvey offer advice as to how individuals are to transspect the perspectives of other cultures—i.e., what vehicles does one employ to access the puzzle of culture and experience? (See Figure 2.1.) What skills does one use to integrate diverse perspectives? If through verbal and written expression alone, then we are faced with the limitations of language addressed in Chapter 2.

Even in introductory management textbooks of the early 1980s and beyond, discussion of cultural differences among individuals and groups in the workplace was still relatively scant and (arguably) superficial. Diversity was generally addressed in the context of human resource management, conflict resolution and mediation of organizational behavior. Considerable attention was devoted, however, to the meaning and components of "corporate culture."

The new face of management

In US organizations in the 1970s and 1980s, management was arguably at a crossroad: What was to be the face of management—i.e., its role and functions? Aside from the challenges mentioned above, workforce mobility and decline in productivity were taking their toll on organizational productivity and longevity.[23] Additionally, opinions handed down in court cases specific to management of human resources added even more complexity to the aforementioned challenges. While discussion of HR law goes beyond the scope of this book, suffice it to say that a dynamic legal environment was evolving in the US specific to employee rights, occupational safety and health, management of discipline, and management–labor relations. As an example, in 1971 the Supreme Court handed down a landmark civil rights decision in *Griggs v. Duke Power* (401 US 424).[24] Regarding management of "diversity," difference could no longer be "melted away" through control. Managers would also be forced to comply with HR law and fair employment practices.

In the T&D literature, Noe and Ford mention the "need to *begin* [emphasis added] the process of identifying key managerial behaviors, work climates and aspects of verbal and nonverbal communications that are important for success in dealing with a highly diverse workforce."[25] The question was how?—and, how at a time when other individuals and groups were seeking protection based on age, disability and more?

In the quote that follows, Milton Gordon assesses the challenges facing American life as the US enters the 1970s. One could argue that it still prophesies the challenges facing the human resource management and development world for years to come, not only in the United States, but arguably—in light of the Chapter 3 discussion—throughout the world:

> The major problem, then, is to keep ethnic separation in communal life from being so pronounced in itself that it threatens ethnic harmony, good group relations, and the spirit of basic good will which a democratic pluralistic society requires, and to keep it from spilling over into the civic arena of secondary relations to impinge on housing, jobs, politics, education, and other areas of functional activity where universalistic criteria of judgment and assignment are necessary and where the operation of ethnic considerations can only be disruptive and even disastrous. . . . In sum, the basic long-range goal for Americans, with regard to ethnic communality, is fluidity and moderation within the context of equal civic rights for all. . . . Ethnic communality will not disappear in the foreseeable future and its legitimacy and rationale should be recognized and respected. By the same token, the bonds that bind human beings together along the lines of ethnicity and the pathways on which people of diverse ethnic origin meet and mingle should be cherished and strengthened.[26]

While Gordon's comments were sociologically derived and (admittedly) not intended for students of management, they point to two key management challenges of the future:

1   How can an organization of individuals work together as a group for a common goal?
2   How can an organization provide equal participation of different perspectives?

An organization cannot function as one unless there are shared values. Communication of thoughts and ideas cannot take place unless there are *shared symbols*. Alternatively stated, how could an organization or group achieve a pluralistic vision and still preserve and infuse identities and perspectives?[27] The answers to these questions were and continue to be complex, indeed, given the workforce characteristics and their implications to managers. Both have implications for communication skills and learning, and are explored in the chapters to follow. *Intermezzo is over. Allegro resumes.*

Key terms and concepts

assimilation, cross-cultural training, "scientific" approach to management, acculturation, diversity, training systems theory

Reflective exercises: These exercises require you to pause and reflect, and also provide the opportunity to evaluate how far countries have advanced, comparatively, specific to integration of diversity.

1   Some might argue that assimilation and acculturation is *less* salient today in the US than during the time of Milton Gordon. Consider what argument you could make either for or against this point of view. Is the US a "melting pot" after all?
     Ideas: Research groups that seek to revive their languages, heritage and ancestries. Research the impact of Alex Haley's *Roots* and the validity of the so-called "Roots Phenomenon."

2   a   Identify several laws that protect ethnic/racial/immigrant and/ or other "minorities" in the United States. Also consider legislation to protect diversities such as sexual orientation and disability.
     b   Pick another country and compare the relative legal protection afforded to the groups you chose for "a."

3   Search the Internet for web-sites of organizations which monitor "migratory" trends throughout the world, e.g., Migration Watch U.K. or others. What types of concerns do you see expressed regarding the influx of migrants from other countries?

6   Management's new face

This chapter revisits severalcal and contemporary theorists for their perspectives regarding the functions of management. The discussion has implications for communication, communication tool choices, situational applications across disciplines and organizational levels of planning, human resource development and management, training of trainers, and challenges of effecting change within and across profit and not-for profit organizations.

Introduction

The Administrative branch of the Classical School of management theory developed in the early twentieth century. The other branch was to be known as Scientific Management, and perhaps most recognizable in the work of Frederick Taylor. It is generally acknowledged that Scientific Management advocated application of scientific methods to analyze work and determine how to complete production tasks efficiently. The Administrative branch and Henri Fayol, as an example, focused on formulating principles for administering and structuring organizations. Much has been written about the Classical School as: (1) an important piece of management history; (2) a foundation for principles and methods that continue to have a huge impact on management practice throughout the world in contemporary times. Both approaches to management are mentioned briefly in Chapter 5 in the context of "The Changing Face of Management," a face challenged, in part, by a changing business environment. Chapter 3 profiles the US contemporary diverse workforce—a workforce that poses yet other challenges to the "new managerial work." While further discussion of management history is beyond the scope of this book, Fayol's contribution is important and useful to mention as a platform grounding traditional understanding of managerial roles. This chapter and the following sections address the need for reevaluation and expansion of traditional roles to include the role and functions of communication and the use of varied communication tools.

Managerial roles and functions

In 1916, Henri Fayol published his seminal work, *Administration Industrielle et Générale*, in which he outlined managers' routine functions as planning, organizing, commanding, coordinating and controlling. Numerous textbooks providing an introduction and overview of management continue to frame the functions of management around Fayol's early twentieth-century list of five. Some replace "command" with "leadership" to reflect contemporary concern with empowerment and/or shared visions; others omit "command" for "direct." Still others include "staffing" and/or "motivating." Frequently Fayol's functions seem to reappear dressed in new clothing. As an example, "management" is sometimes generally described as a process through which organizational goals are reached through people and resources. (Isn't this planning and organizing?) Communication is often a chapter in management-related textbooks, but seldom, if ever, discussed as a function or a role—where traditional functions are expanded to include that of communicating, and where roles portray the manager as a savvy communicator with a diversified communication toolbox.[1] Additionally, while communication is regarded among the important skills managers should have, generally nothing is mentioned regarding communication tendencies and choices in accordance with demographic realities. Given the challenges described in previous chapters, along with Chapter 2, "Limitations of Language," it appears that communication does indeed deserve a place of its own among the repertoire of roles and functions.[2]

Henry Mintzberg provides a complementary view regarding managerial roles, although he offers another rationale for the perspective:

> Over the years, I have grown increasingly dissatisfied with managerial roles as they are discussed in almost all the classic literature on management. In such literature, roles are always presented as a disconnected list rather than an integrated model.[3]

He further argues that managerial behavior is meaningful only if it influences people to take action. According to Mintzberg, managers' roles involve controlling and communicating, leading and linking, doing and dealing. He further states,

> Although almost all well-known writers on the topic of management have suggested that managers focus on one of these roles to the exclusion of others, I believe that all managers must apply all six roles to their work.[4]

While it could be argued that management theorists have not necessarily suggested a focus on one role to the exclusion of others, certainly an integrative model of managerial roles and functions is still somewhat elusive. If we could view the functions of management as the bricks of the manager's work, perhaps an expanded view of communication should be that of the mortar that integrates all managerial roles, however they are defined.

Defining communication

Communication has been defined as a process through which information— thoughts and ideas—are exchanged *through a common system of signs, symbols and behavior.*[5] As individuals generally do not share symbols for reasons that have already been addressed in previous chapters, a leadership perspective requires one to identify commonalties, and to employ as many or as few signs, symbols, etc. as may be required for communication to occur.

Figure 6.1 illustrates the elements of the communication process. Decisions about communication choices and elements of the process itself are as applicable to the virtual world as they are to the physical world. That dynamic process includes:

- Formulating the thought before it is "translated" through written messages, diagrams, symbols, pictures, and/or non-verbal cues. In this phase, the communica*tor* identifies what ideas he or she wants to transmit. Both detail and "big picture" relationships are considered. This phase is generally referred to as "ideation."
- In this stage the communicator decides on the "transmitters": Which words to choose? Why these symbols? Why diagrams or not? And so on. This phase, commonly referred to as "encoding," is a major challenge, indeed, as it requires both insight and knowledge of those receiving the message, an expanded view of communication choices, and time to make the choices and put them all together.

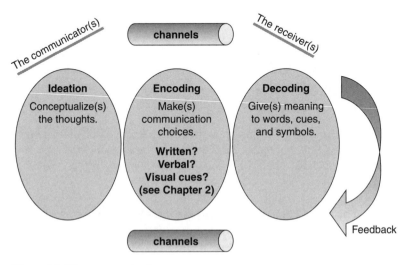

Figure 6.1 The communication process.

• Deciphering the message and the symbols chosen by the communicator(s) is the stage referred to as "decoding" by the receiver(s). Every communication involves a sender and a receiver.

Figure 6.2 illustrates that numerous factors may be constraints or cause interference to communication, the so-called "noise" that often precludes effective communication. Noise may occur for many reasons. Possible barriers to communication are identified in Chapters 2, 3 and 4. Workforce diversity: age, educational levels, working and learning styles, varied cultures and experience, inappropriate channels,[6] and time constraints, are all potential issues that may provide challenges to smooth communication flows. As organizations are pressured to manage their supply chains and balance the relationship between real time, quality, and customer satisfaction, communication choices become more and more challenging. Additionally, worker mobility, training for job rotation, and turnover can be costly to the organizational bottom line; therefore, training and orientation of a diverse workforce must be accomplished as expeditiously as possible. If expeditiously, then an ethnocentric perspective of communication, such as a Western predilection for words and low-context orientation, should be enriched to integrate high-context orientations as well. Recalling Chapter 4, production of change occurs in the

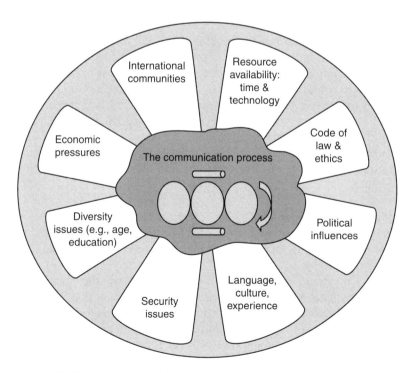

Figure 6.2 Communication interference and constraints.

process of communication. That process must be well designed—perhaps now more than ever.

Revisiting the classics

As effective management is a creative process, choosing effective tools of communication is as important to the effectiveness of the artisan as to the quality of the craft. However, for those who rely on "words," such tools may have to be gropingly discovered in much the same way Edward Sapir wrote of culture.[7] There is no need to invent many of these tools; most are there to be found. They simply need to be recognized as *communication* tools, and chosen in an effort to balance one's personal communication preferences with those of diverse cultures, experiences and cognitive preferences.

Revisiting Scientific Management uncovers many such tools, and perhaps points to other reasons why they may have been so readily accepted by the Japanese after World War II due to their HC preferences, rather than initially in the United States.

Tools to integrate planning, organizing, controlling, problem-solving

Scientific management and quality control processes

Tools of communication are at the heart of Scientific Management and of total quality control endeavors (TQ). Total quality management (TQM) focuses on job design, productivity improvement, and process improvement, or the most effective and efficient way of doing a job. Gantt charts such as the one shown in Figure 6.3, born during the era of Scientific Management and the work of Henry Gantt, still assist individuals in visualizing a sequence of events and the amount of time involved in which activities can (and should) be performed. The following are shipping industry examples. The maritime industry is one where mixed (diverse) crews are now the norm, rather than the exception:[8]

> In [Shipping Line Company Z] we follow something called the [LTV system] that is dedicated to process excellence. This is basically used to improve processes. It might be any process—be it Customer Service, Sales, or Operations. . . .
>
> Our [LTV system] team uses Gantt Charts, Visio, and they map processes done by Sales, Customer Service; and they found out that Sales and Customer Service were doing duplicating jobs, so they made up a detailed study, and with use of visual tools found out that an approx 30–45 percent of sales time was spent on Customer Service activities. They are right now implementing reforms based on this process to free up sales to do actual selling and not to do after-sales activities, which according to

our organization needs to be done by Customer Service. A clear demarcation of activities was mapped out, and we are following it diligently to ensure our customer is completely satisfied with us.[9]

. . .

Mitsubishi Heavy Industries' shipyard in Nagasaki, Japan, uses the Gantt Chart as a time line for vessels' overhaul and repair periods at their facility. The initial, temporary chart is delivered to the vessel approximately (1) month before the arrival at the shipyard. The chart's scheduling is discussed by shipyard representatives with key vessel personnel who will be remaining on the vessel during the repair period. If necessary, the chart is revised.

When the vessel arrives at the shipyard, the permanent chart is delivered to the necessary personnel and the overhaul and repair period commences. During the entire shipyard period the chart is revised weekly, as necessary, and new copies are distributed so that all departments, shore side and shipboard, are aware of revisions in the time frame.

The Chief Engineer who supplied the above quotation a decade ago, reconfirmed that these visuals would now also be sent electronically—but not necessarily. Both he and a captain, who worked for the same company, emphasized that such documents would also be delivered, since the Japanese prefer "face."[10] Cultural preferences toward communication choices are addressed further in Chapter 9.

The following quote illustrates that communication choices can cost time and confusion, particularly with diverse and changing crews.

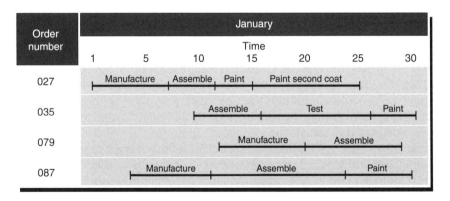

Figure 6.3 A Gantt chart.

Note: This Gantt chart shows the steps and timing of each step for each order.
Source: G. Dessler and J. Phillips (2008) *Managing Now!*: Boston: Houghton Mifflin., p.240.

The last vessel I brought in to the shipyard had been given no real information on what would be occurring during the yard period. The engineer had repeatedly sent emails and called in to the office when possible, but it wasn't until we were out of the water that any information could be obtained from the Port Engineer. I cannot think of any occasion where I have used a Gantt chart professionally, most often any work load we have will be sent in the form of a bulleted list.[11]

While Gantt charts are useful for relatively simple projects, more complicated activities—e.g., network planning and control projects, work flow analysis and numerous other interconnected events—can be communicated through program evaluation review technique (PERT) and critical path method (CPM). Both are illustrated in the PERT chart shown in Figure 6.4.[12] Note that events, such as the completion of a foundation, are pictured as circles. Activities that are time-consuming, such as the actual laying of the foundation, are illustrated as arrows. Through review of the PERT chart, individuals involved in a project can determine the critical path, or "the sequence of activities that form the longest chain in terms of their time to complete."[13] Equally importantly, the PERT tool gives individuals the opportunity to visualize what activities might be done simultaneously, and hypothesize risk factors involved in doing so. The stages of PERT chart development recall the considerations that are elements of the communication process. First, the communicator needs to identify all of the individual activities and stakeholders that are involved in the project, and formulate what needs to be communicated—i.e., the *ideation* portion. He or she must then choose the vehicles that will optimally transmit the ideas to be shared— i.e., *encoding* . . . and so on.

Networked activities are commonplace in today's virtual and physical workplaces. Therefore, the managerial role of controlling, which refers herein to include monitoring and network planning for quality and productivity, is imperative. Programs such as Microsoft Project and Visio facilitate visualization project timelines and networked activities, respectively. Numerous computer-aided drawing (CAD-like) software programs are widely available to track management projects. They facilitate tracking of strategy planning efforts, problem-solving, process improvement, balanced scorecard execution,[14] dashboard visualization,[15] benchmarking, business process reengineering, six sigma execution,[16] tracking progress and resources, and hypothesizing risk. Alternatively stated, these tools are important visual communication assistants in an era of mobile, virtual, and/or multicultural workforces. They should be considered an important element of the managerial (and leadership) toolbox to optimize organizational and intercultural communication.

Further communication aids can include charts such as the ones illustrated in Figure 6.5 which are generally referred to as *quality control tools* (total quality tools or TQT) and/or *improvement tools* used in problem-solving and continuous improvement. They are among *the* most important tools of the

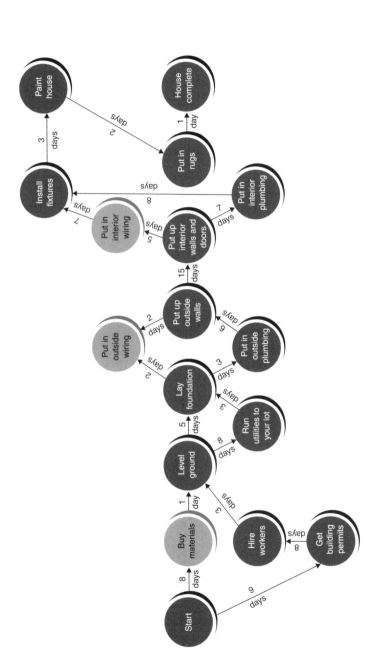

Figure 6.4 Chart for building a PERT house.

Note: In a PERT chart like this one, each event is shown in its proper relationship to the other events. The darker circles show the critical—or most time-consuming—path.

Source: G. Dessler and J. Phillips (2008) *Managing Now!*, p.241.

operational management (logistical, production/processing) trades, and prevail in theoretical and practitioner discussions in the production, operations, and management science and general management education and training literatures, in particular. The value of TQT is generally acknowledged as being a vehicle to help establish a common language of communication, a way

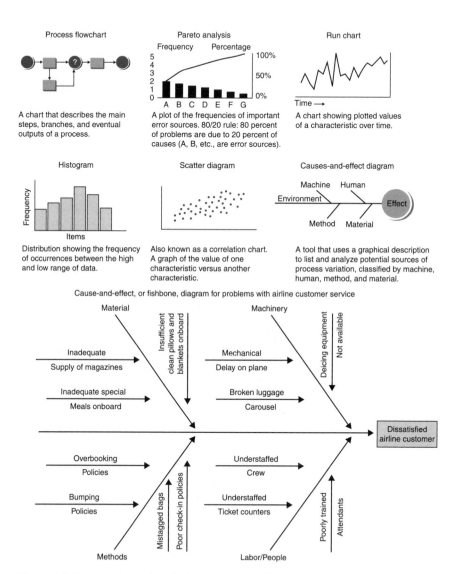

Figure 6.5 Commonly used tools for problem solving and continuous improvement.

Source: G. Dessler and J. Phillips (2008) *Managing Now!*, pp.248–249.

to guide TQC efforts, and as a map reinforcing organizational goals and direction, among others. Nevertheless, these literatures have not (as yet) mentioned another very important rationale for the use of these visual tools: namely, as a way to bridge communication preferences—the border zones, seen and unseen—between high- and low-context cultures and experiences.

Indeed, each stage of the communication process requires the manager, trainers and HR professionals to make choices: If "words," *why & which*? If graphs, *why and which? Why* a linear representation vs. a high-context illustration—OR, *Why not both?* as he/she journeys through the dynamics of the elements of the communication process. Undoubtedly, the new manager in the new economy workplace is well advised to integrate Eastern and Western communication tendencies. It is in this way that border zones are bridged.

Expanding the communication toolbox

The imperative to expand one's communication toolbox cannot be overstated. In this regard, people and organizational developers are challenged to create "learning landscapes"[17]: to map and present developmental inventories to optimize understanding of agendas as well as complex, culturally diverse and polychronic environments. A learning landscape may include visual representations of systems, processes, projects, and purposes—such as the company vision and mission—and be used for multiple applications. Those include, but are not limited to strategic planning, or a map of where the company is going, and succession planning. The applications are many: to training and development; to orientation of new employees and members of the organization's supply chain; to problem-solving; and so on.

High(er) context and non-linear communication tools

Tools for strategic planning, for charting complex developmental agendas and for orientation

As mentioned in Chapter 2, a number of quality control tools such as the fishbone diagram, or the cause-and-effect diagram, are linear by nature and somewhat limited for showing complex networked activities and possible courses of action. Brainstorming activities with organizational stakeholders often uncover relationships that are more effectively represented holistically. The manager makes his/her communication choices—hopefully—with a rationale.

Figure 6.6a provides a holistic view—a landscape of the caller's network in a glance. It is an excerpt of a former advertisement which aimed to show the advantages of a weekend, unlimited calling plan. The same information could have been communicated with a low context approach through text or written discourse. That is not the case here, however. This advertisement is very high-context. The primary encoding choice is highly visual as opposed to a LC-type language-based presentation.

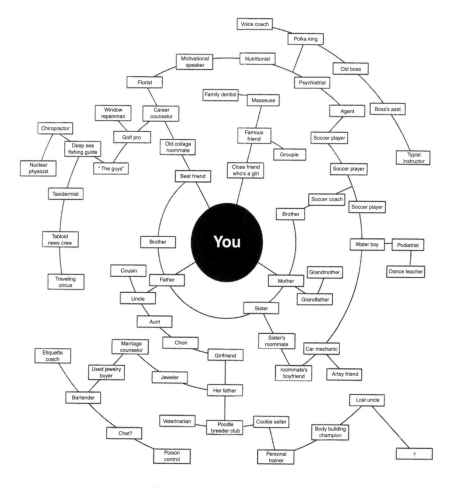

As if you need any more reasons to sign up for

Talk unlimited (TM)

Weekends are for catching up with the life you missed during the week. Introducing Talk unlimited(TM) weekends.

Now you can call anyone, anywhere in the U.S., all Saturday and Sunday for only $25 a month. And your calls during the week are just a dime a minute, anytime, anywhere. Plus, sign up now and get unlimited calling on the Thursday and Friday of the thanksgiving holiday.

Introducing unlimited weekend calling for only $25 per month.

Find us at

www.talkunlimited.com

Figure 6.6a Your communications network.

Figure 6.6b uses considerably more text, yet does offer a visual to illustrate how connectivity can be achieved through their Direct Connect network. The reader should recognize the rationale for both H/C and L/C approaches in light of the labor force demographic diversity discussion in Chapter 3. Most importantly, human resource professionals should appreciate the rationale for self-development and use of H/C and L/C modes even though they may not be a familiar or preferred mode of communication.

Figures 6.7a–d were inspired by a business conference regarding port development. How to get products to the right place at the right time places ports around the world in a very competitive logistical marketplace. Identifying and polling internal and external stakeholders becomes increasingly important in order to do a SWOT analysis—to assess organizational strengths, weaknesses, opportunities and threats. These visuals were generated through brainstorming. In essence, Figures 6.7(a–d) together form a teaching *and* learning landscape for marketing planning. Additionally they illustrate that ports are not just places where ships come and go to drop and pick up goods. Rather than talking about the future of ports, the visual cues helped to transspect the internal and external environments that influence them and vice versa. The figures also assisted the brainstormers themselves in crossing traditional operational and functional border zones through use of metaphor. As an example, the facilitator (myself) asked:

- Who might be among the potential stakeholders in (X) Port's supply chain if we were to view the port as an *entrepôt*, a place where goods are dropped? as a safehaven for ships and travelers, as an economic engine for trade and development?, etc."[18]
- How are we addressing those stakeholders now? Whom have we forgotten in planning efforts?

Figure 6.8 is effective due to its bare simplicity. Its applications are potentially many: as a marketing tool and as the organizational chart for employee orientation purposes, for example. Customer satisfaction is what matters at this organization. At a glance, this visual communicates who apparently leads the chain of command at Nordstrom.

Moving from talk to practice

For some individuals, "drawing on the right side of the brain" can be an arduous and (perhaps) distasteful task.[19] From personal experience, I have encountered managers who do not accept the implications of diverse contemporary workforce profiles for communication strategies. For others, a low-context orientation to communication is very ingrained and challenging to modify. As an example, during one workshop, attendees were asked to draw their network of suppliers, customers, and stakeholders—in essence, their supply chain. Some were unable to do so. They could discuss who they were, but could not put a pen to paper and sketch a network of connections. Another obstacle often is that of functional and linear thinking. It becomes

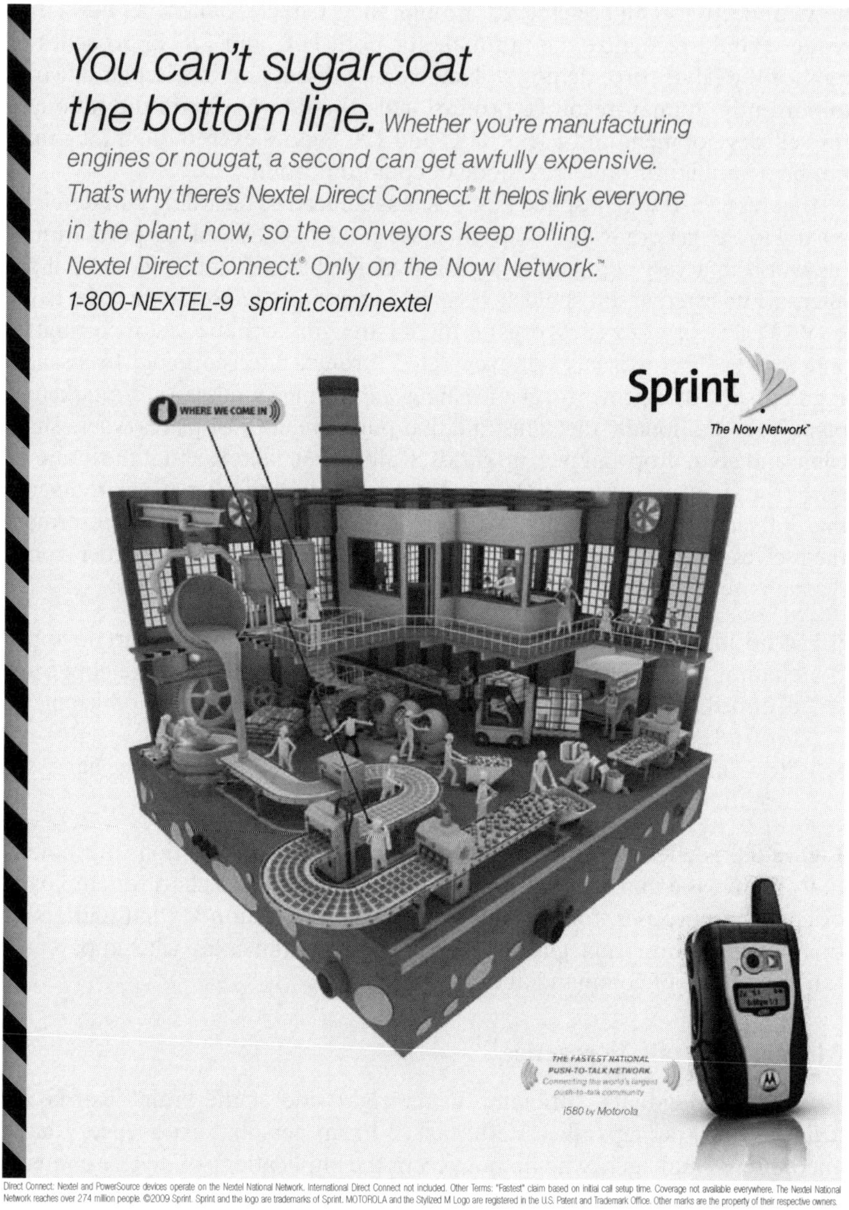

Figure 6.6b Sprint ad: Direct Connect.

Source: Sprint Direct Connect. Reprinted with permission.

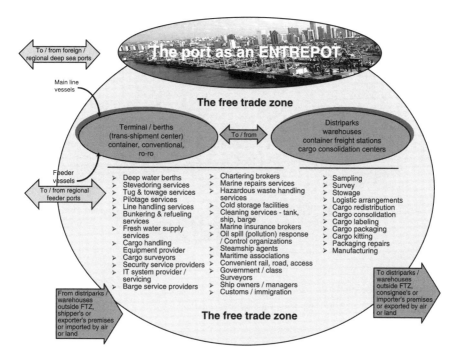

Figure 6.7a The port as an entrepot.

Source: Mohamad Salleh, 1998. Reprinted with permission.

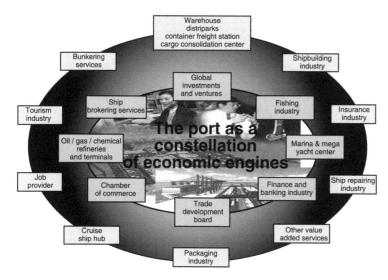

Figure 6.7b The port as a constellation of economic engines.

Source: Mohamad Salleh, 1998. Reprinted with permission.

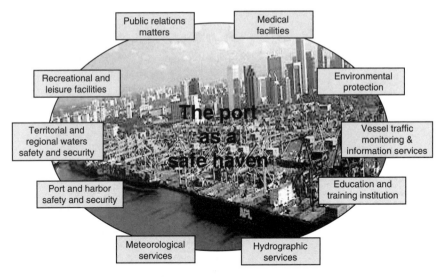

Figure 6.7c The port as a safe haven.
Source: Mohamad Salleh, 1998. Reprinted with permission.

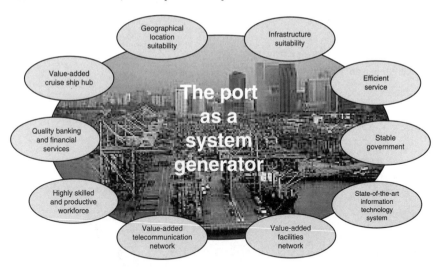

Figure 6.7d The port as a system generator.
Source: Mohamad Salleh, 1998. Reprinted with permission.

difficult for individuals to break out of operations and/or processes in order to see a bigger picture such as Figure 6.7 (a–d). The important first step, however, is for one to do an assessment of one's own communication preferences as was discussed in the Self-Assessment section of Chapter 2. We cannot know where we are going unless we know where we have been.

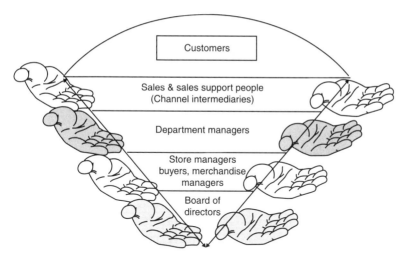

Figure 6.8 The organizational chart.

Source: Adapted from the "Organizational Chart" from Nordstrom, Inc. with permission.

An administrator/manager and educator reflects on an element of culture—formal education—based on his personal and professional experience in the maritime industry:

> Ship's officers in traditional settings are generally taught rational problem solving methods (left brain) to deal with operational issues. This method is most often reliable when sufficient information is available and the outcomes are predictable. There are those who suggest that during Operations Desert Shield and Storm it became apparent that many officers had developed an over-dependence on the step-by-step solution process. Reliance on empirical methods fostered conceptual blocks to creative problem-solving (right brain) required to resolve unpredictable situations. Situation awareness is a pivotal component to effective problem solving. The essence of defining any problem is "learning to look." In my opinion, course work (formal education) should stress the importance of viewing issues from different perspectives. The use of imagery and, in particular, conceptual drawing helps to define nebulous problems more clearly. Drawing images really impressed me. I will definitely incorporate conceptual drawing into my own teaching.

As Edward Tufte argues, "The world is complex, dynamic, multidimensional; the paper is static, flat." Consider: "How are we to represent the rich visual world of experience and measurement on mere flatland?"[20]

In summary, bridging border zones entails a diversified communication toolbox where all employees are trained to integrate effective LC and HC vehicles as necessary. Communication between bureaucratic levels is best considered as a *two*-way process, and it is never too late to learn new collaborative techniques. The following selectively presents defining hallmarks of leadership as they apply to this chapter's discussion.

Hallmarks of leadership

The leader—the cartographer

Organizational theorist, Richard Daft, equates change with innovation when discussing elements for successful change.[21] While some may disagree that they are synonymous, few would probably dispute that both innovation and change symbolize a "coming about" of something that was not there before. Additionally, to use an economic term, both have the potential to create positive and negative externalities in organizational life. While positive externalities or benefits may eventually be pooled expertise and improved market share, a merger in and of itself often is easier said than done in real organizational life. Employees often are fearful of the unknown and resist merging. Therefore, communicating the need for change (and innovation) requires the manager to be a master cartographer.

It is often argued that problem definition is one of the most difficult tasks to accomplish on the road to strategy formulation. Visualizing the issues and driving forces of change are brainstorming opportunities and challenges that are the first steps in strategy development.[22]

The leader—the storyteller

> Stories are central to human intelligence and memory. Cognitive scientist William Calvin describes how we gradually acquire the ability to formulate plans through the stories we hear in childhood. . . . Stories also play an important role in learning. . . . A good story (and a good strategic plan) defines relationships, a sequence of events, cause and effect, and a priority among items—*and those elements are likely to be remembered as a complex whole*.[23]

The above quote appeared in an article emphasizing the importance of stories at 3M Corporation. As organizational challenges are multi-relational and multidimensional, the 3M reverence for storytelling is based on their perceived need to explain themselves clearly and holistically to others. The authors also mention their importance in revealing who they are. In essence, they are an outgrowth of organizational transspection. Given the diversity profile of Chapter 3—particularly as it relates to adult learning and aging—and Chapter 4 discussion, it would appear that effective strategic storytelling and cartography should be placed in the arsenal for leadership competitive advantage.

Leadership toolbox 6: Management's new face

1   *Invite brainstorming activities through the use of diagramming, loops, and other tools presented in this chapter. View leadership as a process. "Process implies that a leader affects and is affected by followers. It emphasizes that leadership is not a linear, one-way event but rather an interactive event."*[24]
2   *Communicate the driving forces influencing the rationale for change, innovation and strategy.*
3   *Develop your mastery as a cartographer and story-teller.*
4   *Escape from flatlands. Enhance "the dimensionality and density of portrayals of information . . ."*[25]

In the following chapter, the Duromark case details how one organization works to improve organizational and intercultural communication in order to remain competitive and navigate through change. The case illustrates the importance of communication design, communication process considerations, managerial roles, and how all are employed for multiple purposes and to achieve competitive advantage: e.g., to track and monitor project procedures for team-based work design; to instill creativity; to develop individual, group and organizational synergies; and to problem-solve in situations when more complex interrelated activities are involved.[26]

Before proceeding further, however, the reader is reminded that the road to the leadership competitive advantage is more of a journey than a destination. This book aims to generate awareness: It encourages the reader to expand his/her communication repertoire, and addresses the rationale to do so. By no means does its author suggest that it provides a complete toolbox. Tools are *created*; they are created by *people*— the human capital of organizations—according to situational needs. With this in mind, please proceed to Chapter 7.

Key terms and concepts

Classical School of Management, communication, right brain orientation, TQM,
Scientific Approach, encoding, left brain orientation,
Administrative Approach, decoding six sigma,
PERT chart, Gantt chart, functions of management,
the control function of management

Exercises

1   Develop a strategic story for your organization or institution. Muster all the verbal and visual tools that are possible to integrate from this and previous chapters. Include no lists, or bullets. It must be a story with graphics to support.

2   Research "strategic storytelling" through a journal database. Find an article that illustrates the importance of storytelling through a business-related example. Hypothesize its importance to human resource development.

3   If you know of a story that is frequently told within your organization, critique it based on criteria from this chapter and others.

4   Visit the International Project Management Association (http://www.ipma.ch) and the Project Management Institute (http://www.pmi.org) for examples of the Chapter 6 discussion regarding process control, tracking or problem-solving tools. Report on one example.

Appendix 6A
Creating learning landscapes: selected practitioner examples

Ideation and coding of processes

Example 1: Drawing the organization's contextual environment

In Chapter 6, reference is made to Figures 6.7a–d. These were inspired by a business conference regarding port development. In this Appendix, the illustration is discussed in more detail. Reiterating, a large number of stakeholders representing diverse value-added industries assembled to discuss what might be the future of a port. The objective was to build consensus for a five-year action plan. Facilitators of this gathering, which involved over 200 participants, invited comments regarding the current Strengths, Weaknesses, Opportunities, and Threats. In other words, they invited a SWOT analysis of the port. Additionally, they solicited attendees' comments regarding environmental and industrial variables that might have bearing on the future of the port and its surrounds. The entire afternoon was an assembly of contemporary practice of the doing of marketing. The event also illustrated the power of relationship marketing as a brainstorming vehicle for marketing planning. Relationship marketing generally refers to the development of long-term relationships with internal customers and stakeholders—their "associates," external customers, and stakeholders along the physical supply chain.

At the close of the conference, one speaker offered suggestions regarding what the port city must consider doing for the future. He went through a list of items that addressed the experience(s) the port might provide. He also discussed services and infrastructural developments that might be considerations for future growth. On a flip chart, brainstorming ideas were listed pertaining to what might constitute a developmental agenda for the future.

Chapter 6 Figures 6.7(a–d), together, were developed as an outgrowth of that symposium. Rather than *talking* about the future of ports, the visual cues—developed with the assistance of graphic software—helped to transspect the internal and external environments that influence them and vice versa. The figures also assisted the brainstormers themselves in crossing traditional operational and functional border zones through use of metaphor. The brainstorming and drawing exercise began as follows with the facilitator (myself) asking,

"Who might be all the potential stakeholders in (X) Port's supply chain if we were to view the port as an *entrepôt*—a place where goods are dropped? As a safe haven for ships and travelers? As an economic engine for trade and development?" and so on.

Figures 6.7a–d comprise the teaching and learning landscape for marketing planning; additionally they illustrate that ports are not just places where ships come and go to drop and pick up goods. Therefore, the visuals served to illustrate in a broad sense what is and what could and should be an agenda for development of planning partnerships.

The need to get products to the right place at the right time requires businesses around the world to operate in a very competitive logistics marketplace. Identifying and polling internal and external stakeholders is increasingly important. The drawings, while initially difficult for some participants, were beneficial to visualize the gestalt of a developmental agenda for planning relationship marketing. One individual described the experience as follows:

> The metaphor of the port as an economic engine could go on and on as a constellation, all of which are interconnected. The constellation is really the support structure for the port's hinterland and beyond. The key to the interconnection is stakeholder involvement; it is important to *see* that.

Example 2: Drawing the contextual environment

An illustration for a not-for-profit[27]

In the Chapter 7 case of Duromark, we will see that developing an orientation to work, environment, and organizational goals is challenging, especially as workforces move and change. Orienting new associates to organizational life is also especially challenging in not-for-profit organizations that rely on volunteers from diverse socio-economic and cultural groups. As the following example illustrates, identifying what matters within the organization, important stakeholders, ongoing issues, and other ongoing planning concerns must be communication choices aimed to optimize transfer of training across diverse and mobile groups.

The visuals included herein were prepared by a former District Executive of a not-for-profit service organization that relies upon volunteers. Figures 6A.1 and 6A.2 were selected from many that could be used as an orientation piece. Rather than talking about recruitment, Figure 6A.1 illustrates that the organization and district operate in a very open environment. Volunteers would need to be recruited from each town in the district, as the future of the organization would depend upon successful recruiting. As stated by the former District Manager,

> The . . . District is quite open to its environment. It is partially composed of its charter organizations—churches, schools, fraternal orders, and

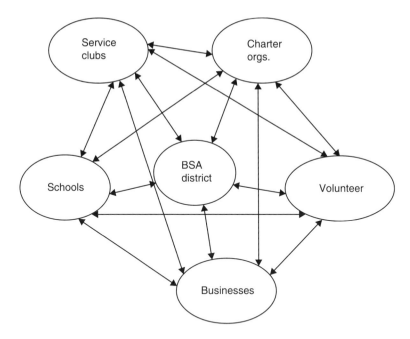

Figure 6A.1 Organization and district operating in an open environment.

businesses. The executives are generally members of service clubs. Local business people conduct the annual community fundraising campaign. Local schools provide market data and recruiting opportunities. District volunteers come from all corners of the district, and many of its major and minor employers. All these elements, as members of the same communities, interact with each other independent of the district, as well. This organization is quite closely bound and open to its external environment.

As illustrated in Figure 6A.2, the relative success of the organization depends upon the balance between environment, organizational mission, technology (to accommodate networking), resources, and organizational structure. The balance of all these factors is the developmental issue—the *yin* and *yang* of the future, and a notebook reminder (enhanced through computer graphics) for the future (Figure 6A.2).

Example 2 revisited through diagramming

Loops and lines

As illustrated in Chapter 2, Figure 2.4, Appendix 2, Figure 2A.2, and Chapter 6, the Fishbone Diagram is linear by nature, and generally considered effective

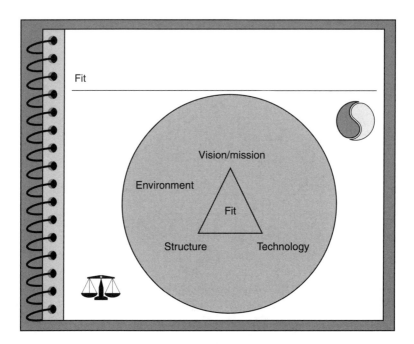

Figure 6A.2 Balancing factors for organizational success.

for analysis of simple "a"-causes-"b"-type operations. However, it is not so useful for analyzing complex and multiple relationships between individuals, stakeholders and/or processes. Therefore, other encoding tools are necessary to optimize decoding and understanding.

Management consultant, organizational scientist, and educator, Gareth Morgan, cautions against "falling into the trap" of linear thinking. Rather, he advocates "an alternative way of thinking about [a] problem by revealing [a] pattern of relations" that may be involved, or "multiple causalities," such as power, authority, influence and relationships. Morgan also uses loops (not lines) for visualizing (projected) change processes. In his view, loops "encourage us to understand how change unfolds through circular patterns of interaction. . . ."[28] The result is a rich visual that provides insight into the system under consideration. As an example, in his *Images of Organization*, he points to the sequence of circular relationships that caused Great Britain's "mad cow" disease to mushroom into uncontrollable proportions.

Referring to Figure 6A.3, after diseased sheep brains were used in cattle feed, the "mad cow" phenomenon was identified, or an encephalitis disorder that was exhibited when cows stumbled in British fields. A series of events sent other events into motion—*not* one cause that caused one effect, but

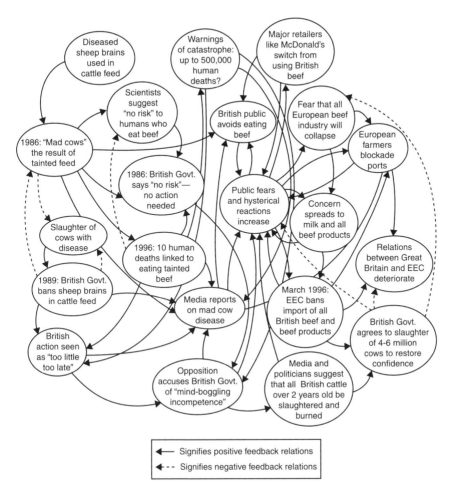

Figure 6A.3 The "mad cow" phenomenon.

Source: G. Morgan (2006), p. 269.

rather multiple causes. In short, loop analysis is a very powerful tool, particularly because it facilitates system thinking, management of systems, and identification of optimal points of intervention before problems escalate out of control.

There is significant theoretical grounding for application of Morgan's discussion of "loops, not lines" and mutual causalities to the discussion herein from the literatures of systems thinking and systems dynamics.[29] Other literatures that ground the application are those addressed in Chapter 4 specific to adult learning, intercultural communication, and art education regarding culture's influences on cognitive processing.

Relational diagramming

Imagine that a hypothetical not-for-profit wishes to explore why volunteer turnover has increased. For this example, another celebrated quality control tool, the Relations Diagram—also called the Interrelationship Diagraph—is useful, especially when a team is having difficulty identifying what is causing a problem. Frequently, there is not just one driver that is causing a situation. The Relations Diagram pictures the multiple cause-and-effect relationships of a particular incident or problem. It facilitates identification of possible root causes or drivers, and helps team-members project potential change measures to remedy the situation. It is a useful way to bridge border zone preferences between high-context and low-context orientations.

There, potential applications for relational diagramming are unlimited. A <www.google.com> search points to virtually millions of examples: e.g., public school settings to encourage critical thinking, health care and more.[30]

Figure 6A.4 is an example of a Relations Diagram format that represents the problematic volunteer retention issue. To draw this diagram:

1 Agree on the problem. At first glance, "Volunteer Turnover" appears to be the foremost problem this organization is facing. The complaint: "What are we going to do about volunteer turnover? We're losing 80 percent of our volunteers annually!"
2 Draw a box or circle to show all the elements involved. Brainstorming for causal factors reveals that the situation is much more complex than it seems. A decrease in major donor giving apparently influenced the organization to close offices and reduce the number of paid employees. As a result, the current organizational structure is strained as there are not enough

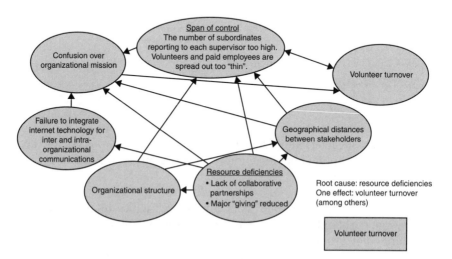

Figure 6A.4 Relational diagramming: anonymous not-for-profit.

resources—human and financial—to train and orient volunteers. Paid employees and volunteers are complaining of "burn out." As positions were eliminated, the span of control, or the ratio of number of supervisors to subordinates continues to be much too low. Volunteers express that they do not feel a sense of satisfaction from doing a job effectively, and so on.

3   Draw arrows to show what is influencing what. Sometimes there are mutual influences. As an example, the current organizational structure is the reason for large distances between stakeholders (volunteers, community). Relocating the home office could help with that. In turn, the geographical distances between stakeholders are also straining the current organizational structure. Nevertheless, the arrow should be drawn to show which one is the stronger influencer. For example, "Resource Deficiencies" explain why the organization has not invested in updating computer technology for internal and external communications through the Internet. Having that would help with training and orienting volunteer membership. Geographical distances between volunteers in the physical world appear even larger without integrative communications.

4   Analyze the diagram. Once all the connections have been drawn, the team counts all the in and out arrows and decides which one appears to be the major driver.

5   The team projects and prioritizes countermeasures to address the problem. The team recognizes that they have few cooperative partnering agreements that could extend their resources and reduce financial outlays. They also need to attract dynamic board members who are networked and experienced in fundraising.

Volunteer turnover turns out to be only a *symptom* of the real issues the not-for-profit is facing. The diagram illustrates that the root cause of many problems is "resource deficits." "Resources" include the lack of collaborative partnering agreements with other profit and not-for-profit organizations, major donor giving, and technology integration that would facilitate communications across distances.

Example 3: Ideation—the concept of **doing** *marketing*

Over my professional career, I have done many workshops for executive and middle management. I am often overwhelmed by the number of people I see who continue to view marketing as sales and/or advertising. Contemporary marketing management and marketing activities still involve the conceptualization of needs, and the transformation of those into utility creation in the form of pricing, promotion, and distribution of ideas, goods, and services: aka the American Marketing Association (AMA) definition proliferated in the mid 1980s. This "marketing mix" is known as the famous 4 Ps, or those elements of *p*roduct/service, *p*rice, *p*romotion, and *p*lace (which includes the added value and cost-saving considerations of time, location of distribution intermediaries or channels, and other supply-chain management considerations) that satisfy customer needs in accordance with organizational resources. Development of the famous Ps also must be a fit with organizational capabilities—after all, the customer can't have *everything*, right?

Fast forwarding to 2007:[31] In that year, the AMA advanced the concept of marketing's activities to capture the importance of the extensive relationship development that effective *doing of* marketing activities entails in an era of globalization. The following is that most recent definition:

> Marketing is the activity, set of institutions, and processes for creating, communicating, delivering, and exchanging offerings that have value for customers, clients, partners, and society at large.[32]

Yet, despite the espoused academic sea change, where production and sales era mentalities have apparently evolved to the globalization and relationship marketing era, the perceptual screen of "sales and advertising mentalities" continues to prevail based on baselines taken by the author at the onset of professional workshops and in academic settings.

As culture and experience are often reasons why individuals do not see marketing in the same way, I decided to attempt to effect a change in the everyday discourse and understanding of marketing as a discipline—away from linking of *marketing* solely to activities of promotion and selling of goods and services.[33] How could I initiate some modest changes? That was my challenge, and still is; the following illustrates how that challenge can be addressed.

I decided I needed a "learning landscape" to illustrate marketing as an ongoing *process*, as words alone were not beneficial as a developmental agenda. For starters, I began to speak of the "*doing of*" marketing activities, rather than discussion of where firms might plan to market goods and services, as I felt that the latter, or the verb, "market," inaccurately conveys that its practice is largely promotional in scope. Example 1 illustrates the *doing* of the *many* activities of marketing. My challenge was to try to conceptualize magnitude of the *process* by design.

Concurrently, I moved to drawing and metaphor to encode the concepts I wished to ingrain in my multicultural and national audiences. As the audiences change, so do the metaphors. The following details the process in more specific terms.

The idea. . . .

If we were truly in the global, relationship marketing era, then we would notice, perhaps remarkably, that the everyday discourse of marketing would involve discussion of its many activities. Alternatively stated, let's imagine it as a process of inputs and outputs. What might be the daily "production and operations schedule"? If marketing is being practiced as it is being preached, the *process* would probably involve gathering of marketing intelligence outside of the business itself—buyer behavior, internal and external environmental variables, competitive analysis and others that point to new products/services and positioning.[34] In essence, this is the process that evolved in Example 1.

Marketers (and/or marketing management) often perceive an information need that is not being satisfied. Therefore, marketing intelligence is gathered and funneled *constantly*. This process is illustrated in Figure 6A.5. Information shapes an organization's purpose and the evolving definition of the business, or the organization's (unique) mission. In the information-gathering part of the market research process, businesses are advised not to view their scope too narrowly, for that would be practicing "marketing myopia."[35] Indeed, many industries and environmental variables influence industries and other variables. These factors often become reasons why management may decide to close, divest, acquire, reengineer and/or all of the aforementioned strategies.

Turning data into information is what marketers are supposed to do throughout the dynamic funneling process. The marketing manager in all of us then tweaks what (we think) we have learned to fit with the capabilities and

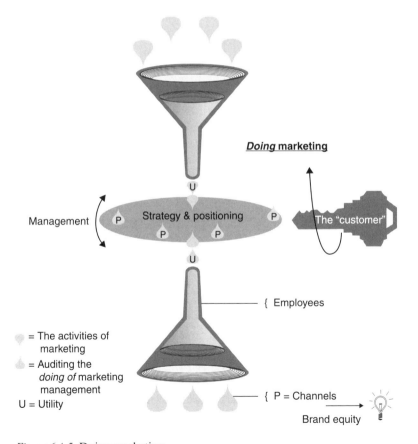

Figure 6A.5 Doing marketing.

culture of the organization. An analysis of Strengths, Weaknesses, Opportunities and Threats (SWOT) is often employed at this introspection stage. Tweaking involves positioning the business to be different from rivals. In Figure 6A.5, that tweaking is illustrated as a key that is turned and adjusted by customers, channel members, managers, and employees, in other words, all those stakeholders/relationships which should be viewed as "customers." The customer always wants more—meaning that the customer is always turning the key and has rising expectations. Management, however, weighs what the customer wants or demands against organizational resources. Therefore, management may adjust the key in accordance with organizational capabilities. In positioning, management sets the organization apart from its rivals, and identifies a strategy that embodies its unique mission and lofty vision. That distinction may be brand, technology, cost, supply-chain savvy, and/or a combination of these and other factors.

Strategy considers how to differentiate the organization from others over the long term. As Michael Porter argues, "operational effectiveness is necessary, but not sufficient."[36] Quality and process improvements in contemporary times are an expectation. In reviewing the above, it is understandable why Peter Drucker argued that "management is a creative action."[37] The visual supports the discourse.

In the gathering-of-intelligence process, students are frequently introduced to methods and rationale for doing exploratory research. This initial research, depending upon time and cost factors, may evolve into a formal research design involving qualitative and/or quantitative research. I often discuss the ongoing imperative and importance of doing research in a variety of academic and corporate settings. Frequently, it is necessary to emphasize that research is not to be regarded as something organizations do only when they encounter a problem, but rather as a necessary marketing activity to feed the desire for growth. (Problems *and* opportunities are viewed as normal dynamics of growth and the growing process. The food for all phases of growth is marketing intelligence.) In Chapter 6, Figure 6.8, "The Organizational Chart," illustrates who matters in the marketing process—who is serving whom, so to speak.

In countries that are in varied stages of marketing evolution, i.e., from a sales era mentality to the globalization and relationship marketing era mentality, the visual illustrations have elicited interesting reactions throughout the years. Among former command economy workshop attendees, the words sound nice, but the idea of *doing marketing* can potentially be quite foreign to culture and experience. Therefore, the figures also help to optimize understanding of the challenges that individuals and organizations may encounter when attempting to do business in former command economies. Actually, nothing of the funnel may work—and, of course, that is the whole point.

In former command economies, needs were decided, demand controlled, distribution channels established by governments and by "connections," and flows of goods and services were decided by others. The constant doing of marketing as a process was not a dimension of culture and experience. The following essay illustrates the challenges that marketing posed in former command economies. It is included here, as it points to the importance of education and training in nurturing experiences that are not commonly shared.[38]

> The official year of birth of the Russian market [economy] is 1990. Thus, it may look as if we (the Russian people) have had a market for seven years in a row. However, this short period of revolutionary transformation toward a free market was preceded by seventy years of a centralized planned economy. The history of this economy has not experienced the idea [concepts] of contemporary marketing. Under this [the former Russian] condition, a 'market-[driven orientation'] simply did not exist. All branches of the economy, at least in theory, were synchronized and planned on the basis of a five-year plan. All the demands were calculated and predicted 5–15 years ahead, so there was no need for the individual organization making its own studies. All data was directed from Moscow and results were sent back. [Market research as we know it in the Western world was non-existent]. Governments were responsible for distribution, movement and collecting the goods and providing services. Any entrepreneurial activities were considered unethical and illegal. Marketing was proclaimed a "capitalist's science" and replaced with "political economy." As such, marketing became illegal too.
>   Sensationally and starting from *perestroyka*, marketing became the most popular and the most fashionable field of economic study. Suddenly, all levels of management started to experience strong craving for knowledge in this area. Unfortunately, the art of marketing still remains for Russian business a great mystery of the free market. . . .
>   . . . Currently, Russian entrepreneurs are struggling with low operational effectiveness and shortage of financing. There is, also, a lack of business culture and ethics. As a result, management thinks in terms of pure, fast profit, not positioning and long-term strategy. (Dmitriy V. Koniaev, July, 1997, unpublished, reproduced with personal permission of author)

The essence of what is described above is why the funneling process was so challenged in the homeland of the above author. Funneling of intelligence requires diverse inputs as part of the *doing of* marketing. The marketing managers of the future must seek ongoing input from associates as part of the marketing intelligence, continuous decision-making and controlling process. Additionally, if management is practicing the marketing concept, customer satisfaction audits should include employees and others along physical and virtual value supply chains. If the entire organization is practicing the marketing concept, the organizational diagram probably resembles something close to Chapter 6, Figure 6.8, which illustrates who drives the process of marketing. Indeed, marketing and the marketing concept are "bottom-up" activities, as Figure 6.8 also illustrates. They work to defy the gravity (of death, denial, and/or extinction). Grass-roots polling of stakeholders becomes key to the process.

Ongoing research probes buyer behavior and environmental variables that marketing professionals translate into ongoing utilities—the **U** of Figure 6A.5—or the creation of customer want-satisfaction. From research and analysis of need a dynamic marketing mix evolves—the **P**'s (probably not just in contemporary times)—that are churned out from the funnel. Along the way, organizations should be channeling information into brand equity and brand extension decisions. The brand identity, extended, is at the core of product strategy and organizational identity.[39]

The promotional strategy—evolving from the conceptualization of *utility*—is likened to the execution of a touchdown after skillful strategizing, controlled risk-taking, and gaming. Advertising, public relations and promotional give-aways, as examples, deliver the message that evolved from *doing of* marketing. If marketing has done its work, then brand identity: what the organization thinks of its brand, will equal brand equity: what the customer in its broadest sense thinks of the brand.

One limitation of Figure 6A.5 is the fact that it is a two-dimensional landscape that needs enrichment. Computer technology might enhance communication of the process tremendously by placing "the everything" in motion. Virtual visits to those who practice the *doing* would also help us tremendously to "escape from flatlands," as Edward Tufte (1990) would encourage us to do (Chapter 6).

Example 4: Web-site design

The following is an exercise based on readings of the previous chapters. Ask several colleagues to choose five web-sites that they enjoy. Choose five of your own. Do an item-by-item analysis of their choices and yours in accordance with the following:

*   How many are high-context in nature? Explain.
*   How many are low-context in nature? Explain.
*   Which sites mix both low- and high-context orientations?
*   Which sites do you find difficult to follow? Easy to follow?

Try to analyze why

*   What are the communication preferences represented by the group? By individuals?

We will return to web-site design in Chapter 9, "Communication Design Issues of the Future."

***

Key terms and concepts

marketing, marketing concept,
relationship marketing, SWOT

7   Building learning organizations through learning landscapes

> Most successful change efforts begin when some individuals or some groups start to look hard at a company's competitive situation, market position, technological trends, and financial performance. . . . Two factors are particularly important in institutionalizing change in corporate culture. The first is a conscious attempt to show people how the new approaches, behaviors, and attitudes have helped improve performance. When people are left on their own to make the connections, they sometimes create very inaccurate links. Helping people see the right connections requires communication.
>
> ("Leading Change: Why Transformation Efforts Fail")[1]

Chapters 4 and 6, in part, point to the extensive literature addressing the role and importance of effective and diverse communication modes in navigating through the process of change. In this chapter, the reader is encouraged to create "learning landscapes"—to map and present developmental agendas to optimize understanding of complex, culturally diverse, and polychronic environments.[2] Indeed, as John Kotter argues in this initial chapter quote, transformation efforts often depend upon clear understanding of where the company has been and where it needs to go.

In the following case study, the reader is reminded that culture is, after all, *learned*. The reader is engaged in a fieldwork experience whose objective is to convey how shared meanings are created. The rationale for the engagement is inspired by the work of anthropologists, Rosalie Wax, Magoroh Maruyama, and Melville Herskovits:

* Recalling the transspection discussion of Chapter 1, it was Magoroh Maruyama who argued the importance of the emic or culture-laden, rather than culture-free approach, whereby one walks in the shoes of those being researched to gain understanding of their world.
* Rosalie Wax concurs with the view that the process of understanding comes about when one has the opportunity to witness others struggling with their reality. She mentions that "initially, [the fieldworker] finds that he does not understand the meanings and actions of a strange

people, and then gradually he comes to be able to categorize peoples (or relationships) and events. . . ." She further states, "some readers may feel that I am giving too much weight to socialization, since it can, after all, be considered simply a form of 'learning.' One of the reasons for my procedure is that learning, as conceived by most psychologists, is a culturally static procedure (as the learning of nonsense syllables or mazes), whereas socialization implies a participation in the cultural dynamic and a corresponding development or enlargement of the self."[3]

• Melville Herskovits used the term "enculturation" to refer to the socialization process that societies pursue to integrate new members into their ranks.[4]

And so goes the rationale for this chapter's field-walk. Welcome to Duromark Incorporated, where the reader witnesses that culture *is* learned. Not only is it learned, but apparently it can be learned at any age, in whole or in part, and—while perhaps alien to one's own—without loss of personal or group identity. The whole or part involves shared modes of cognition and communication, language, values, and more. Witness how one organization makes communication choices, in particular, that are integral to the topography of their learning landscape.

Duromark Incorporated: case study

> **learning landscapes:** a holistic visual representation of planning, processes, developmental agendas and other organizational activities that contemporary and future managers are challenged to create in order to maximize organizational and intercultural communication.

While the organization as described herein is fictitious, the interviews and examples are based on empirical research at a large manufacturing facility over a period of two years. It is noted that considerable effort was taken through peer review to assure that the identity of the company and its employees are not revealed. Therefore, enough information is provided specific to the firm's organizational history and demographics only to enable application of the material presented heretofore. As a general overview to the site: It is Japanese-owned; the parent company has had a sales presence in the United States for over four decades. Presently there are manufacturing operations worldwide to include its US locations. Duromark excels in integration of both Eastern and Western communication strategies that aim to maximize organizational and intercultural communication as described in Chapters 1–6. This profile explains why it was chosen among other case possibilities for this field-walk. It is a rich case, suitable for use in many settings for many reasons. However, given this era of mergers and acquisitions, it appears particularly impelling as an exemplar to those who are charged with building organizational culture and/or implementing a culture change, and seek insight into the process and what it entails to do it effectively.

Organizational dynamics: "culture and experience"

The following key organizational variables characterize the firm's locations: (a) job rotation and Japanese and American interaction; (b) the significant role of training; (c) American–Japanese exchanges; and, (d) team-building and self-managed work groups.

Job rotation/Japanese and American interaction

Job rotation and interaction between Japanese and US associates are significant to organizational history and developmental efforts. While Japanese associates represent only 3–4 percent of the workforce of the location described in this case, their role is important in the following way: Their presence is related to technology transfer, and their average length of stay is from two to five years. When there is expansion and/or new research and development (R&D), Japanese individuals trained in a particular technology visit to train American workers.[5]

Role of training

The firm hires from a 15-county radius. A common denominator of many individuals interviewed is that none had similar job responsibilities in their previous employment. Therefore, the role of training and orientation is a huge component of organizational life, as is the need for effective communication due to workforce mobility and diversity. The significance of training, however, cannot be understood without discussion of corporate culture and how training design functions as a resource to meet organizational objectives. That issue is addressed later in this section.

American–Japanese exchanges

Added to the dynamics already mentioned above is another piece of "topography" (Figure 2.1) evolving from the history of the organization. The following dialogue illustrates that associates at different managerial levels are also sent to Japan for training.[6]

AM: Our very first program was called [p], and it was for first-line supervisors; and to make a long story short, what we were looking at in [year] was a full series of multiple challenges for the year [x].

The manufacturing challenges that are described by AM include: meeting customer satisfaction, increasing the domestic content of product(s), and improving quality. Her comments not only illustrate the role training played as a resource to meeting the firm's objectives, but also the rigor that training involved. "Training rigor" generally refers to the degree of cognitive involvement of the trainee, and the duration and intensity of the program.

> All these things were driven by our company philosophy. When we looked at the situation we said, 'wow, that's a lot that we're trying to do. So we were looking at how can we be successful at all of those, and, of course, the answer to that is associates. They were the ones that were going to implement all of this. So we wanted to grow their capabilities— to strengthen their capabilities. But in a year and one-half time, we couldn't train 8,000 associates. So we picked first-line supervisors because they had close, connected, day-to-day contact. And what we did with those first-line supervisors was that we took them away from their jobs— and it was a business decision too because we were going to be transferring 71 team leaders to [plant x] sometime between [the years x–y]. So we could add this excess 71 members to manpower to accommodate getting people off to work for training. . . . What we did is we put them in the classroom.

Further to training rigor:

> We put them in the classroom for two weeks; we sent them to Japan for four weeks; brought them back to the classroom for two weeks. We basically burnt them out, but they learned a great deal. And at that time they had not taken very many courses; we had some offered, but we did not have a strong customer base at that time.

AM's comments further illustrate that training rigor, job rotation, and HC communication practices such as *minarai*, discussed in Chapter 2, were and continue to be factors of training design ingrained in organizational history:

> And the time in Japan was to let them work side-by-side with their Japanese counterparts; people who had been doing the team leader's job for ten, fifteen years. And it was amazing what happened—that they could look at that and say, 'Oh—that's what my job responsibility is.' They had only been team leaders for six months; most of them were high school grads; most of them were from rural areas around here; they didn't have a clue as to how to be a supervisor. And we needed them to learn that real quickly, and that helped. That did that. That accomplished it for us. And I've really oversimplified the program because there are a lot of details that go into making something like that work. But evidently it was successful because we met all the challenges, and the team leaders that were in the first 10 groups are now teaching new team leaders. So we've passed that along, and they stay here in the States and go to all the

[number] plants, and we still do some Japan sites; so that program is still running; and it's in its 4th stage—we keep changing it. . . . One of the neat things that happened, and why we keep changing it—is when the customers came out here through the [p] to experience some of the classes, they would go back and talk about that, and we started having people take our general classes more; so we have had to shrink the amount of time in the classroom because the people have already had the classes—which is fantastic. So those are the types of things that we do.

Other associates spoke of returning to Japan for training; these associates train others. In other words, they function as mentors themselves when they return to the US Job rotation is also a factor here. Individuals might rotate to Japan but also travel to other locations in the US. A senior vice-president (SVP), who is Japanese and who had been with the company for 25 years, indicates how these individuals represent a challenge to the future of the company, and points to implications of AM's comments:

EP: Could you comment on some of those things that challenge—that you feel are [company's] greatest challenges?
SVP: [The SVP mentions several challenges].
. . . Another challenge is that we hired many college graduates; now we have many engineers managers—and particularly engineers; how can we encourage them, their education background; how can we expect their growth in the corporation?—those kinds of things.

Workforce demographics/team-building/self-managed work-groups

Aside from the percentage of Japanese mentioned earlier, one associate describes the degree of cultural diversity at this location:

EP: What other kind of cultural make-up would you say is in place here?
C: About twelve percent of our associates here are from minority groups. That would include Asian and African-American. I don't know what the breakdown is within that twelve percent. I would assume the majority would be African-American. [He mentions the 15-country hiring radius.]
EP: Any Spanish-speaking?
C: Not that I know of; not that I've heard of. Females make up about a third of our workforce. And they do any and all jobs.

Could it be argued that the above figures (i.e., 3–4 percent Japanese, and a 12-percent minority comprising Asians and African-Americans) portray a highly culturally diverse workforce? In fact, based on the above figures, could it be argued that this company's workforce is relatively homogeneous? In fact, neither can be argued. The data show that cultural diversity is a highly significant factor in this particular organization, and therefore, a key consideration to training design. But the reason has little to do with the actual numbers reflecting "diversity." Rather, it has everything to do with the corporate philosophy (discussed later on) and the importance of team-building and group work in meeting organizational objectives. Let us visualize a hypothetical quality control (QC) team: Assuming it is composed of eight to ten individuals, one of those individuals may be Japanese, one or two may be African-American and/or Asian, one-third to one-half could potentially be female. Teams do not necessarily reflect homogeneity. Therefore, cultural differences at Duromark are highly significant since problem-solving involves teams of individuals.

During a recent workshop devoted to problem-solving techniques, several concurrent classes were in session regarding the subject of "Cultural Diversity Training." One administrator of the workshop indicated that all associates are required to attend a cultural diversity training program. She also mentioned to me that she has noticed an increase in Hispanics and "people from the Caribbean." On the bulletin board in a hallway near an eating and beverage area, or "break area," is a diagram of a company product. Its parts are labeled in Spanish. Nearby, a newspaper article is posted. It reports that by the year 2010 Hispanics will pass blacks as the largest minority group in the US. Also posted is a schedule of English-language, Japanese-language and Spanish-language classes available to all associates.

An American firm? A Japanese firm? A Japanese-influenced firm? Andlor, a Japanese and American-influenced firm?

Respondents acknowledge their firm's Japanese ownership. Additionally, each can recount, *almost verbatim*, milestones in organizational history and important contributions Japanese founders have played in organizational growth and development and corporate philosophy. This recalls the Chapter 6 discussion of strategic stories. Company history and philosophy are addressed in company training programs. Nevertheless, associates view their company as an American firm. Their comments are based on actual numbers of American workers versus the dwindling number of Japanese, and the multiple country hiring radius from which they draw their workforce. Analysis of company literature also shows that the firm is committed to purchasing where they produce. Their commitment to local suppliers is reflected in not only purchasing policies, but also in supplier involvement in training at the company locations. The SVP comments on the dwindling role of the Japanese:

SVP: . . . at the beginning, of course, Japanese [were the most]; gradually we added American associates. Now less than five percent . . . four percent are Japanese population. In the office area maybe same thing—maybe we have three . . . five percent Japanese. But so at the beginning almost all the decision making and so forth was done by Japanese; now the decision making is done by American managers and so forth. That's quite a difference. So for Japanese, at the beginning, Japanese have to be teacher sometimes. And now the Japanese could not be the teacher; so the *function* of the Japanese changed for us. That's one difference if you compared the beginning and now.

Another employee's comments are similar:

C: They [the Japanese] rotate. And that [x number] is an approximately dwindling number. So we're involved in a great deal of technology transfer. And technology transfer—since [the company] has been around since [year], and we [i.e., at this plant] have only been around since [year]—there's obviously a lot more that they know, especially in the R&D process and development process than we do; and there are a lot of technology centers that have developed in Japan that simply don't exist here in America.

EP: When you say the number is dwindling, is that because there is more—or as a result of training, there is less of a need? Do these people come over in a training and development capacity and then return?

C: They come over for various periods of time. Probably the shortest would be two to three years. So they may be here from two to five years—I think that's the standard period. And they come over to do a job—to do a specific job. We have been expanding rapidly since our inception in [year]. What that means is that every year—almost every year there's a new plant, there's a new process, there's a new expansion; and most of that is something that has been done in Japan first. So what you have are people that are trained in that technology to come over here and train Americans in that technology.

The following exchange points to the reversal of roles whereby Americans are now mentors to other Americans:

C: But what we've been doing over the past few years is trying to reverse that. So we're sending more and more Americans over to Japan to learn in Japan, and then bring that knowledge back with them and then teach their fellow Americans. We have a couple of programs set up to do that. AM will tell you more about the [p] in which we send over a large number of American associates to do just that—to be over in the Japanese factories; to learn production methods. And we've actually been able to take what we've learned here and the different ways we do things here, and transfer some of that knowledge back over to Japan. So Japan has actually learned things from our production here. So now the flow is going both ways. The idea is that eventually we will be a self-reliant organization. That is we'll be able to design, develop, produce, sell and export [products] here without any significant help from Japan—a self reliant organization within a world-wide network of self-reliant organizations.

Data display the efforts of associates to portray the firm as *American* (as opposed to a *Japanese* firm). An illustrative example involves an off-site conference presentation by an administrator from Division C.[7] He began his talk by asking the audience if he looked Japanese. The answer, of course was "no" as he is an American. When he began his presentation, he immediately grabbed the audience's attention with his question. They looked up immediately. While these comments were incidental to the focus of the presentation, the American portrayal was a theme throughout. Portrayal standardization is achieved through training and storytelling.

In interviewing, it was obvious that both the Americans and the Japanese had been influenced greatly by one another. However, I often wondered if they recognized it? Of the Americans interviewed, some obviously did. For others, Japanese influence in their daily activities appeared so imbedded and practiced so unconsciously, that it was barely recognizable to them. Recalling Sapir (1927), the influences apparently surfaced as unconscious patterns of thought. One such influence is related to the company's corporate philosophy.[8] Another influence is related to the use of nonverbal communication (NVC). Both influences are discussed in the sections that follow, where the intention is to make visible what may be argued as the "invisibility of everyday life" specific to use of varied communication strategies within this organization.

Communication strategies

The concept of "learning landscapes" was inspired while doing fieldwork at Duromark. Additionally, data showed that the organization devotes considerable attention to the use of space to optimize learning.

Visual cues

Recalling Chapter 2, "visual cues" refer to actions or symbols that are representative of a concept and/or something to be said or done. Forms of visual cueing are addressed in the following subsections. They include, but are not limited to, visual aids such as use of diagrams, and cartoons, as well as the use of space.

Visual aids

At the site I visited, use of visual aids is noticeable virtually everywhere—on bulletin boards and classrooms, on the shop floor for tracking production, in company literature, in problem-solving efforts, in public relations, hiring, and in R&D. One might ask, "How is this different from other US firms?" My perspective is based on my own business experience. Prior to visiting this firm, I had never seen visual aids used to the extent they are at this site.

The following are examples.

Example 1: A Division C workshop, visual aids for problem-solving and QC, emphasized the importance of the Fishbone Diagram, the use of histograms, pareto diagrams, graphs, etc. One associate's comments during a two-day workshop for company suppliers are illustrative in this regard:

SL: Presentations must be accompanied by diagrams, etc. Once you put the charts and graphs up there it helps tremendously. We have Hispanics; we have Japanese; we have people from the Middle East.
   Everybody speaks the same language—that includes diagrams. . . . Presentations should be done without a lot of words. Everyone should understand what you're trying to say.

SL also mentioned on several occasions that visuals create a common language that assists with problem-solving and analysis. In informal conversation during a break, she discussed teamwork, and mentioned how important these tools were for socialization of the culturally and nationally diverse mix on teams. Referring to the Japanese, "Culturally, they don't talk. Hence, the importance of the visual aids."[9] Pointing to a fishbone diagram, SL adds:

   You look at this; it's not just numbers and words. That's why we want to show things on charts and graphs.

QC literature includes numerous fishbone exercises and cartoons. As an example, a drawing of two cartoon-like feet is used to introduce each chapter of the manual. They represent the steps a group should follow in forming and executing a QC team effort. Explanations in manuals are frequently illustrated with line drawings of the product. In the classroom a procedural picture hangs on a wall by the door. It illustrates, without the use of words, the instruction that paper cups, etc. (garbage) should be thrown in the pail, rather than left in the classroom.

Example 2: When AM was describing the different programs of Division B, she automatically grabbed for paper and drew a chart to illustrate her points. Yet, when queried for other examples of use of diagrams, etc., initially she did not think of many examples. Nevertheless, as the interview progressed, she recognized how ingrained they were in her daily practice.[10]

EP: You used a diagram to show me how you're set up. Do you use many diagrams or even stick figures to show cultural or other types of situations?
AM: No, the closest thing that can come to [mind] is part of what we do in orientating in the Japanese language. We have a hand-out that we have that has little cartoon figures on it.
EP: Do you have a copy of that?

AM: Yes, but I am not able to give you that. [laughter]

EP: Would you be able to show it to me? [She makes a phone call and obtains a copy from someone on second shift who delivers it to our conference room.]

AM: It's real possible they're still using it as part of our orientation. It was one of the favorites 'cause we [had] this stack of things. Everybody and their brother wanted to give us things, and we just weeded out what worked and what didn't. Typically text doesn't work with our people. Our people are action oriented. So pictures were worth 1,000 words. And that's why we use a lot of videos and slides.

EP: So you use this . . . in training? . . . the cartoons?

AM: And we also use it in orientation. The cartoons got the message across so quickly that we use it—you know—it is not at all uncommon if somebody is going to go to Japan for a new model trip for example. . . . and that's always the first thing I reach for—because it is so good in demonstrating.

. . . The fishbone is the basis of our inner circle activities.

. . .

EP: So . . . you talked indirectly about some visual mapping you do.

AM: That falls in line with what we were talking about before. One of the biggest struggles is getting, making sure that what we trained is implemented, taken to the plant floor. And we use a lot of visuals for that, and our team leaders when they went to Japan picked up *a lot* of visuals—*very simple* situations of tracking attendance, tracking quality, tracking rejection.

Later AM mentions how US associates have also influenced training. Her comments concerning how the process sparks creativity are also interesting.

AM: But what happens is—you know what I'm beginning to recognize as we go through our questions is that—what will typically happen is— rather than somebody use that *same* situation, it will trigger for them: this would work good in this class if I modified it in this way— so that somebody else might use another strategy. What it does is it sparks creativity. So we don't necessarily copy—but we copy the concept. The more I think about it the more I think we do—we just take it for granted, so it's hard for me to tell you all these visual things that we do.

AM adds that visual aids are used to show management how they have used training. As an example, associates will do a video to show results.

Face-to-face interaction

Taking someone to the spot (i.e., the on-site location) is regarded as much more valuable than "talking" about it in a classroom, as in the following two examples.

Example 1: For hiring a prospective employee is likely to be taken to the "spot" along with his family, to view the nature of the work he/she will be expected to perform. In the mid 1990s, "going to the spot" was not being done virtually—through computer-based technologies at Duromark. It is being utilized as the technology becomes more advanced, and is an "architectural piece" utilized when personal visits cannot be accomplished due to time constraints and/or other reasons. Face-to-face, however, is still the preferred social interaction regime due to organizational history, culture and experience.

Example 2: Solving a manufacturing problem involves observation at the site of the problem with associates representing cross-functional areas of expertise such as assembly and engineering. Face-to-face, and "taking someone to the spot" is also known as "walking the talk." Rather than talk about it, they just go there. The following supports this view:

C: First of all, I'd like to say that the use of visual images here for my department is very, very important because basically instead of having words or features—or something like that—what we try to do is just take people out to the spot. . . . If you go out to the plant, you'll see that the offices are right beside where the line is. So you walk through the doors and you're right out there where it is happening. The plant manager is right there. . . . People are constantly out and about going to the actual spot—wherever, whatever the problem is; where things are going on. And so in that way, we use visual images all of the time to convey what the message is to whomever needs to get that.

EP: Is that at shop level?

C: That's at shop level all the way up.

C adds that going to the spot is very important in teaching on the subject of problem-solving.

C: How do we solve a problem? Instead of taking a textbook, and having a hypothetical problem written down there, they [in AM's Division] would ask someone, 'what's the problem in your area? Let's take a look at it—let's analyze it.'

Going to the spot also sends an important visual cue to the associate working on the line. By going to see that person, the associate's value to the company is acknowledged. The action could also be viewed as a form of back-channeling, or *aizuchi*, mentioned in Chapter 2, as it provides immediate feedback to participants. C expresses further support of this view:

C: Another thing that we say here is that the person doing the job is the expert. So if there is a problem out on the line with a certain process [(C) explains a manufacturing problem]—obviously you can pinpoint that to a certain team in a certain area—whether it is an [x] problem or a [y] problem or whatever; and then you can go to the [z] people who go directly to that group, and say, 'we notice this problem; how can we attack this? What is happening here? Let's analyze the situation.' And they go directly to the associate that's doing that process, because that associate knows more about that process than anything else; and it could be at that time that the associate says, 'Yes, I'm having a problem doing this.' At that time the engineers, people from whatever department that is the [z] people, and the associate himself will get together and see how they can eliminate that problem by going to the spot—not by having an engineer sit in his office two miles away, and say, 'you know it should work right because we designed the process to work this way.'

Therefore, a typical problem-solving scene on the plant floor might include an assembly-line worker, engineer/designer, a customer, and a supplier all at the same spot solving a problem. Here again is another example where computer-based technologies and virtual chats may be utilized along with traditional, physical space, team problem-solving.

Toolboxes of integrated communication strategies

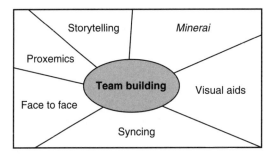

Placing individuals together from different managerial levels also character-izes many classroom activities. This is a striking contrast to firms where inter-actions are based on managerial levels. At this site hierarchy is de-emphasized. An illustrative example is a Division C workshop on QC tools that took place over a two-day period. Attendees were from various firms that supply parts to the company. Twenty-one people attended—a combination of middle managers, lathe operators, and QC team leaders. Each firm's associates had never met prior to this workshop. Participants, to include this author, were divided into four groups by counting off from one to four.

The number of men and women were about equal. Experience levels with their firm ranged from 11 months to 25 years. Several were dressed in work jeans; others in slacks; others were dressed in their company uniform; a few men had long hair; their hands showed signs of manual labor—grease/oil-stained and/or nails not carefully groomed. Language use in group-discussion also indicated that individuals did not share socio-economic backgrounds. There was no "top down" or "management-centric" approach to learning and interaction apparent. Rather, all these people had an equal say in group problem-solving activities. In group work there was diagramming, brain-storming and multidirectional, versus one-way communications.

In group discussion a young man—a lathe operator with 11 months' experience at his firm—[incidentally] articulates the concept of "walking the talk": "[you have to] talk to the people that run the machines; *the human being* with the problem; the engineer [only] may be interested in the design [and in] improving the design."

Other visual cues confirm the equal value of all associates. As an example, all company employees, regardless of managerial level, wear a white pant-suit uniform. Additionally, space is not used in ways that symbolize hierarchy or status. As an example, there are no fancy offices for executives. Additionally, space is employed in such a way as to minimize hierarchical boundaries, facilitate communication, and show that all associates matter. Data provide many interesting examples of the above: One associate mentions during the presentation described earlier, which occurred off-site, that all associates are treated with equal respect at this company. "There are no private offices; there is no reserved parking for any one of our [number] employees, except for the nurse."

Another associate compares his firm with another for which he worked. Note how visual cues at another firm were used to emphasize status:

NN: . . . Then I came to the [company]. Now the interesting thing was still working part-time . . . when I worked part-time and I was going to school, I worked for a manufacturing company that was truly what I would call Americanized in the old tradition of American management. I am glad I had the experience to do that because I was able to see two totally opposite environments. Going from that kind of environment to this environment was almost like a culture shock.
EP: Tell me how that was. How was this a shock . . . a culture shock to you?
NN: Taking, for example, the supervisors. They were signified different; they wore blue hats. That's how you could tell they were supervisors.
EP: So *there*—while here you dress alike—*there* you accentuated the fact that they were at a different managerial level.
NN: They were at a different level. You were asked to come in and do your job for eight hours—and basically that is it. It was interesting too because it was a union environment, and the interesting thing that I saw was that,

for example, if I had a problem, the supervisor could not do—he could stand there, and talk to me, but he wasn't allowed to touch anything. And I found that very unique, because here it's almost like everyone rushes in to deal with that.

The SVP comments are similar:

EP: How would I know your [company] culture if I saw it? What makes [the company culture] different from other cultures?

SVP: I think if you study the corporate culture or philosophy whatever of the leading two companies, you'll find quite a similarity. Everybody talk about their respective people; many people talk about customer satisfaction; the way of the description is a little bit different, but the essence is very similar. So I don't know what differentiates [our company] from other companies. One thing I can say is that maybe we are—sometimes the way of implementation makes a difference. You can say that we expect everybody—we think that the people are the most important asset of the company.[11] We believe that training—everybody has to be respected; everybody has to be treated as a human being— people talking about status symbols. Now so many companies are talking about—I often times [am] invited to the companies who are now trying to change their culture; and last week I was invited by one of the big part suppliers for us—a big company. And they are trying to change their culture. But, for instance, you say that, ok, 'let's make a culture which denies the different treatment, the different—way to treat the people in the same company.' So not about how we make all kinds of status symbols. In our company there is no problem here; everybody has the same uniform. This is one of the most gorgeous conference rooms for visitors, but not for the company executive [laughter]. . . . I think that one of the differences between other companies and our company is that how we are trying to do in accordance with what we are saying. We are not successful, sometimes we have problems too. A good example is that now many companies say that 'we believe in teamwork. We are one single team . . . an [x company] team or a [y company] team.' But at the same time there are many different treatments for the executives, managers vs. the people walking around. So what the many people are now saying is that, 'ok we believe that everybody should be treated as equal; everybody is a member of a team; but . . . I do not want to give up my comfortable, deluxe office. I believe that the size of my desk is appropriate in conjunction with my ranking in the company. I never want to go to the cafeteria where all these maybe production people [are] eating; but I would rather prefer to have dinner or lunch with the corporate executive in the corporate executive dining room.' We don't do that. So to make an analogy people can say that, 'generally speaking I agree, but when it comes to me, I don't.' That's the difference.

C, NN, DH and SL all mentioned the open door policy of the firm. Aside from a "wall-less" environment—a workplace where there are no executive offices—workspaces are one huge room with no internal walls or partitions. One can go right to the President if you can show that something can be done in a more efficient way. All three respondents provided examples of situations where this has happened. Several had done so themselves.

The SVP pointed to team-building as one of three key areas emphasized in training; problem-solving and understanding corporate philosophy are others. The SVP comments, "It is important that they work together as a team—not as an individual person." How—in addition to the above—is this objective facilitated? Recalling the Chapter 2 discussion of "syncing" and proxemics, one strong physical visual cue for syncing is, of course, the uniform. Additionally, role-playing is used extensively to confirm and clarify information learned in a classroom setting. For an example, one strong visual is the "ball of yarn" technique—a role-play and follow-up activity. To summarize, the group starts with a ball of yarn and traces the progression of a particular process or procedure. If associate X needed to follow up with Y, then X holds the yarn, and the ball is passed to associate Y. The process continues until a web of connections is created that is realized both visually and kinetically:

AM: And they make a web; and they have to put a pop can on top of it to hold it up—so that's a repetition of what we use there, but instead of doing the pop can exercise, what we do is we have these flip charts that go around the room—'O.K.—you said you're going to do this—tell us about it. How did you do it? O.K.—who was going to do it with you?' It says it on the flip chart: 'so-and-so was going to follow-up.' O.K., 'did you follow-up with him?' And then they take the string and pass it to the person that was going to follow-up—if they followed-up. If they didn't the string gets dropped in the middle of the floor—so it makes this visual image of what happens when somebody doesn't follow through with their responsibilities.

In essence, the above simulation incorporates many dimensions of previous chapters. The final effect is a web of relationships illustrating how the process was supposed to work and where, procedurally, it may have gone wrong. Recalling AM's earlier words, "text does not work with our people," this particular activity is obviously very high-context, as it places less emphasis on the use of words for communication. It is also a powerful visual cue confirming associate value. According to AM, "it's a demonstration of teamwork, and how important it is that *every single member* of the team is important—whether you like that member or not. Specific to Division B's programs, she mentions, "We don't just do things in classes; we do programs, because we believe there is some value to having a group experience, and then we create what we call significant emotional experiences that carry the learning from the classroom to the floor." The "emotional experience" described by AM is a factor of creative brainstorming across managerial levels and functions and involvement of team members.

Data show that teams "spark creativity," and are [therefore] "significant emotional experiences. Teams nurture human potential; teams nurture feelings of company and group ID, or membership. Team-building is fostered through group experiences, a wall-less environment, and proxemics. Each is a factor of how space is utilized, and how a common language is created—through a combination of visual cueing, storytelling of corporate philosophy, and *minarai*—discussed further in the following section.

Minarai

Learning by observation continues to be important to organizational history and training and development efforts. The Japanese were teachers; they continue to be, albeit dwindling in numbers. Americans teach other American associates. Americans, many without any international experience prior to employment with the firm, had their first experience overseas in Japan. Americans in increasing numbers go to Japan for training. They, in turn, return to the US and teach other Americans within and across sites. Learning by doing, *tenarai*, is also part of the *minarai* experience. Role-play, observation, returning to apply concepts at site, back to role-play, back to classroom, observation, etc. are evidenced throughout the training programs.

Indeed, it is argued that *minarai* enhances team-building efforts. A team, much like an organization, is a group of people working together. Yet, within that team, and/or across teams, there are also *sempai–kohai*-type, teacher–student relationships as were described in Chapter 2. Recalling the earlier comments of the SVP, originally, the Japanese were teachers. Teacher–student relationships continue; mentoring continues. The following comments reflect both team-building and the role of *minarai*.

AM discusses some training she has attended:

AM: . . . and then we teach each other. It's very common to have a mix of all levels of the organization in a classroom. So there are some managers that are learning it from me when I teach.

In describing associates the point is elaborated further:

AM: In the case of [p], our customers are our team leaders, and team leaders are associates. And we're all associates.

    . . .

AM discusses the various programs created to train individuals at different levels of management by creating an in-house network, or teaching pool. Again, strategic stories are key.

AM: . . .

Our [x-p] is like a behavior science college. You've probably begun
to see that there is a lot of . . . 50 percent, for example of the [y-p]
is philosophy. We're teaching the [company philosophy]. We have senior
managers, vice-presidents for teaching these classes on the [company
philosophy]. Not from the standpoint of trying to get people to buy it,
but what they do—in fact, I call it facilitating, rather than teaching—
because what they're doing is sharing how they learned what our
philosophies are, and how they used that in making decisions; and then
our people take it or leave it. And nine times out of ten, of course, they
take it because they've been living with it. It's not really anything they
don't know, but now there is a formal way of sharing it, and they hear
the stories of the managers and the senior executives, and how they use
it every day. So it is a sharing type of experience.

Note the use of the term "sharing" in the above. "Sharing" at this company
is a process of planned acculturation.

It is generally agreed that organizational culture is revealed through
three common artifacts: Its myths and sagas, its communication systems and
metaphors, and its behavioral norms and attitudes. Sharing of information
and sharing of experiences can be likened to a socialization process where
cultural artifacts and legends are reproduced. This is accomplished through
Training and Development (T&D). Mentoring is a primary vehicle for
reproduction of cultural artifacts, and explains why respondents' comments
often were identical in discussions of corporate philosophy, organizational
history, etc.

NN talks about the role of the facilitator in a fishbone exercise session.
Notice the words he chooses to describe his role. Admittedly, his choice of
words may have been coincidental; or they could have been a factor of his
experience with the firm.

EP: What function then does the supervisor perform?

NN: I think the supervisor provides more of a . . . I use the term . . . father
figure. Everybody has input, but you need somebody there who can
control . . . You don't want people who are making decisions or
implementing ideas that are going to mess up your entire area. You *still*
have to have somebody there who is a father figure, who is more of a
trainer. Not only do you have to instill in the environment or in the dept.
or whatever area, but you still have to be able to create the experience of
illustrating, 'here's why you can't do what you're doing . . . here's
guidance—here's where you need to do more instead of less.' You also
need to be the type of person—a—you used the term, *facilitator*—not
that you have to do this or you have to do that. So I see it as not being a
dictator, but more as a father figure.

NN could have chosen to describe the role of the facilitator as a "group leader," a "manager," or a supervisor. Yet he said, "father figure." This is an interesting choice of words if viewed in the context of the history and training and development efforts at this organization. Choosing discourse carefully, a Chapter 1 Guideline, is definitely obvious at Duromark. All these strategies foster a sense of company identification among "associates."

Learning landscapes

The above findings show that learning at this site is an outgrowth of numerous communication strategies and other factors working interactively for a common goal. Indeed, this firm qualifies as a "learning organization" (LO) in the spirit of Senge (1990); but, obviously, they work at it. Data display that associates participate in goal setting. Shared visions permeate the data. Additionally, data show plausible explanations of why the company has evolved as an LO: This was not only an organization in which teaching and learning occur, but also one in which landscapes of learning are systematically and sequentially *constructed*.

The expression "learning landscapes" reflects many dimensions of the learning experience at Duromark. As examples, those include the architectural use of space to facilitate learning and the proxemics and creative activity of teamwork they generate. It is dynamic, indeed. Said alternatively, to come to know this firm, one would have to discover its landscape. The following visual images of that 'scape were represented in the data:

Stepping stones: AM refers to programs that build on other programs as "stepping stones." Learning activities are not independent or unrelated classes; rather, learning activities are understood within the context of programs. Teams are emotional experiences sparking creativity beyond the program to the shop floor and back into the next program level.

Building blocks: Layering of learning within a program and between programs is referred to as "building blocks." The programs are in sync with organizational goals and objectives. Training classes may begin with teaching concepts in the classroom and follow with an interval involving practice or application at the work site. Alternatively stated, learning is broken up into intervals to give associates time to implement what they are learning, digest it, and then return to the instructional setting to "get the next piece." Associates then return to the classroom to share experiences, and then progress to the next stepping stone in learning. Note AM's comments specific to the construction of learning experiences:

AM: . . . We use that type of strategy—that stepping-stone strategy—in every single class we do.

EP: So not only is it ordering of a particular learning experience—where you're starting out with something, but then you give them an opportunity to work it out and practice it; and then you go on and you add the next level on.

AM: Exactly, exactly. . . .

Later she adds,

> . . . We confirm and clarify what they learned, and that they're using it; and then the next part of the follow-up purpose though is always to give them a new piece. There is always something new to learn. And by doing this on an annual basis and making it just like coming in for a physical, we're hoping to develop after a five-ten year period a culture where they are looking for it—that constant learning environment.

Developmental road maps: Additionally, learning landscapes are also visual representations of a comprehensive training and development agenda. They are utilized as agendas/guidelines for training. For example, AM discusses a "developmental road map" one department was creating to help associates put together the skills, or the pieces they need to grow. Simplified versions of tracking production on the shop floor were mentioned in an earlier section.

AM: The more complex [tracking systems] is that there are some departments— there is a program called [z-p] that's going on at our [x] plant, and is slowly being spread throughout the organization. What they're doing is putting together human skills, business skills, and technical skills; and what they're looking at is almost like a road map of, 'what pieces do you need to grow?' And it starts at the basic associate level and what classes that we have to offer in [Division B], some department-specific situations, on the job, classes together—basically everything—it's like a road map for development—a developmental road map.[12]

EP: And is it a chart?

AM: There is one department that has gotten so sophisticated with it, that it is a huge chart. They haven't figured out how they're going to implement it yet, but at least they have the road map. It's a very new creative thing at this point.

So here we have a landscape of learning that could be utilized by an associate or associates for tracking their own development. Rather than talking about developmental objectives for departments, groups, and individuals, the visual representation lends assistance to understanding and planning. If it were a fishbone diagram, each bone might represent particular knowledge, skills or abilities (KSAs) that need attention—the "what's to be learned" inspired by Gagné (1962), and mentioned in Chapter 4.[13]

Visual cueing: Asking how the company understood the term "globalization," also suggests another possible use of learning landscapes: to facilitate sharing of organizational goals not only through verbal discourse, but also through visual cueing. Data showed that Duromark's globalization philosophy was described as a standard that does not change. In other words, regardless of the context—whether it be US locations or overseas locations—the company philosophy remains the same: standards of quality, respect for the individual are basic tenets throughout the world. In a meeting with SL and DH, I drew how I viewed the company philosophy. The meeting also turned out to be an opportunity for me "to confirm and clarify" if my understanding was correct. In my thinking I recalled AM's words:

AM: In our globalization philosophy, there is a *core* [emphasis added] in every single organization we are working for synergy among [companies] worldwide.

In a meeting with SL and DH I drew that concept as a circle.

(Reader: imagine a circle about here)

AM: [continuing]
... But then understanding that even within each plant there is a different culture. We are different from [x and y plant . . .], and certainly different from one country to another. We are different from Japan, obviously; we can learn from one another, and we share the knowledge. We have a fundamental knowledge that is the same, but we have differences from one plant—just like a family; you have a fundamental core value system, but the brother and the sister, and the second brother are different from one another. We have differences as well.

EP: So you have your core—if I could re-articulate that—so you have your core philosophy that involves globalization.

AM: Right.

EP: ... and you have your principal statements there, but then you recognize as you go from context to context here, and as you go overseas that there are modifications.

AM: [acknowledges]

EP: The *core* doesn't change.

AM: But some of the methodology of carrying it out may be different because of the different cultural implications. So those are the three pieces—the globalization pieces that the [program] points to, and then we have a module for interpersonal skills, and we have a module for diversity. And in the diversity segment we want to get into, of course, cultural diversity; but we've done a lot with—we have Japanese language classes; we have English language classes, and the Japanese language classes are open to all of our associates.

The globalization landscape, therefore, evolves from a standard core and includes pieces, or modules addressing diversity and interpersonal skills.

EP: How in your training with these different concepts you've talked about, have you utilized other forms—not necessarily verbal, but nonverbal approaches?

AM: Good question. [the p], obviously, we had to prepare these people to go to Japan.

This is the program mentioned earlier where many team leaders had to be trained in a relatively short amount of time.

> It was a real culture shock. Many of our team leaders had never even been on a plane before, let alone an international flight, you know. So we had eight hours plus another four hours of what we called orientation— getting them prepared. We would bring in maps, and each group would come back and we'd have pictures—we put together picture albums. [AM explains that within "p," they performed skits to demonstrate cultural differences, invited family members and other activities to illustrate the overseas experience.]

I questioned the SVP of his understanding of the term, "globalization."[14] His comments were similar to AM's. He mentioned that he didn't see any deviation from the company philosophy wherever they went—i.e., regardless of location. Duromark, as an outgrowth of its environment and corporate philosophy, trains for the core. Through face-to-faces, mentoring and virtual and other visual assistance it trains for "glocalization" strategies. Communication becomes shared experiences.

The following excerpt illustrates this point:

EP: Does the term, "globalization" have any special meaning for you? How would you explain it?

SVP: [The SVP indicated that he did not have a good understanding of "globalization"—he offered that perhaps "glocalization" is better— thinking globally but recognizing local differences. As an example, being globalized is integral to the company philosophy specific to quality, but then recognizing local differences.]

The visual that began with the circle mentioned earlier might be elaborated as follows to represent the words of both AM and the SVP: A center circle— i.e., the "core"—is the company philosophy. Within that circle are training modules—i.e., subcircles that represent such elements as *kaizen* and interpersonal skills, or "people skills". They are the behavioral science foundations mentioned earlier by AM. That circle travels to all company locations in the

US and throughout the world. Drawn from the circle, in the form of fishbone diagrams, are the developmental guidelines for training specific to the contextual differences—the "what's" to be learned at each location. *I purposely have not drawn this visual, to illustrate how much more effective it would be if we had it.*[15]

The visual representation could also be drawn as an "eye of the tiger" where globalization is the "eye" and "glocalization" strategies are the spokes. The drawing, in essence, cues an organizational developmental learning agenda. Additionally, its application, as one example, is a developmental map for the international assignee (IA—Japanese, American, etc.) to track his or her own developmental milestones, or to inventory potential differences in other locations or, alternatively stated, the visual cues areas of development for the trainee and others.

Summary

The interviewees all described the use of visual tools for problem-solving, and acknowledged their other potential applications as a heuristic tool of analysis. As mentioned in Chapter 2, the fishbone is already proven for TQC—for tracking production and for systems analysis, as examples. Data derived from the interview with NN show that it is also used in office environments for problem-solving. As examples, he mentioned two departments: In one, its use resulted in an improvement in workflow; in another it was used to improve a computer program. He also saw it utilized for setting goals and objectives. Comments by the SVP also suggest the feasibility of further applications:

EP: The Ishikawa Diagram (I notice)—the fishbone is used in tracking processes in production at [company] and in [other divisions]. Can you explain what your experience has been with this tool and/or how you have seen it used when you were in Japan?

SVP: I am familiar with the fishbone as an analysis tool that could be applicable to many areas. It helps to identify the problem itself and the root cause of problem. . . .

[I asked if he knew how use of the fishbone was regarded in Japan when Ishikawa introduced it for TQC. I mentioned that, after all, its use was predicated on the fact that people would sit down at the table and discuss problems and identify causes. Weren't there skeptics that questioned its feasibility?—i.e., could individuals do this if they feared it might mean their job, embarrassment, etc.? His perspective triangulates earlier comments by NN specific to why the process works. I asked this question especially because of the tendency of the Japanese to be concerned with saving "face."]

SVP: Americans often want to emphasize the fact that someone is wrong.

The SVP related a personal story that involved analysis of the cause of a problem at an account. The SVP accused someone of being wrong in the analysis. The person became defensive, and they proceeded no further. Then the SVP said, "let's forget this" and a meeting was called. At the meeting the fishbone was used. [Note: In the process of using the fishbone, no person's ideas are criticized; this is a ground rule.] They analyzed the problem. During the meeting, the person accused was quiet [but this was probably so because he had been accused earlier]; yet, no fingers were pointed at anyone. According to the SVP, the advantage of using the fishbone is that there are many more opportunities to analyze causes; and invariably, the process uncovers that often what is believed originally to be the cause is either more complex or not the cause at all.

SVP: Maybe only one element is the real cause of a problem, yet the process allows everyone to see much more than just one potential cause of a problem; and this becomes insight into other 'by-products' for the future. It is time-consuming; it may seem easier to say someone is wrong.

   [In other words, the process is time-consuming. A "quick fix" might be to blame someone for a problem or to enforce punitive measures.]

Recalling the Quality Circles Tools, Division C workshop, the Fishbone Diagram was used as a visual cue to "root out" causes of several manufacturing and production problems. As mentioned earlier, the second day the class was divided into groups; each group was given a problem to analyze. Obviously, this was an opportunity to apply what we had learned (i.e., an example of *tenarai*). SL maintained that the fishbone, for example, could be used in problem-solving for just about anything—even situations that are not job-related. To prove her point our group tackled "why someone might be overeating?"[16]

   The group selected a team leader to do the drawing. Referring to Figure 2A.2, the effect, or the problem, was written as "overeating." The group analyzed possible reasons for the problem under each category. Through group brainstorming various possible causes were identified such as stress and/or a nervous condition, body chemistry and metabolism rates, idle time in that person's schedule, and/or a schedule that was not conducive to eating regularly. In the "methods" category, they posited that perhaps a rate of eating was too fast, schedule of eating and/or shopping were prohibitive to eating properly, and method of cooking. The group combined "material and machines" as a category, and identified the accessibility of vending machines and convenience or "fast-food" as other possible causes. The group diagram pointed to the fact that the problem was not overeating after all. Rather, overeating appeared as a possible symptom of another problem or problems. The real problem might be related to lifestyle and schedule, or a health disorder. After potential root causes were identified, they briefly discussed the countermeasures that could be pursued to identify and remedy the real problem.

The limitations of this tool mentioned in Chapter 2 were supported in interview with Duromark's associates. Additionally, other variables that were key to the effectiveness of the method involved the need for someone to facilitate the process.

EP: . . . What do you think really drives the use of that technique? What's going to decide if it's going to be successful?

NN: I think you need somebody to direct it. I think you need someone who is a leader of a group or a secretary of a group to stand up and say, 'all right, what other ideas do you have?' They *have* to be led through the process versus everybody just sitting and trying to throw out ideas without somebody leading the process.

EP: So that the *trainer*, if you will, is a very important person.

NN: Very important.

Data show that Duromark is as much a factor of culture and experience as are the Ojibwa of Manitoba or the Quiché people of Guatemala mentioned in Chapter 2. If one were to attempt a graphic illustration of this organization, a learning landscape to enable others to discover it, Duromark's communication strategies would definitely be a major piece of this organization's cultural puzzle. Yet, it was Duromark's SVP that cautioned against overemphasis on "techniques," pointing to the overriding importance of a nurturing culture to achieve organizational effectiveness. He argued that given all the rationales for this or that technique, nothing was necessarily fail-safe if people were not motivated. Given the positive atmosphere, however, the chance of success was optimized in his view.

Every interview pointed to organizational and individual commitment to learning. One associate also emphasized that when suppliers are having problems, management sends its own employees to be of assistance. Another mentioned that out of all the training he received, the most eye-opening was the training that focused on development of an anticipatory taxonomy to guide identification of training needs. That effort is optimized with an expanded communication toolbox, a nurturing organizational culture, and a supporting technological fit. Duromark apparently escapes from flatland in many training and development scenarios.[17] Indeed, it could be their operative motto.

Consideration of the market forces affecting Duromark and many other contemporary profit and not-for-profit businesses are reasons why enriched communication skills continue to be vital to organizational effectiveness. Indeed, these skills are as important an investment in "training the trainer" and "teaching the teacher" as they are for the individuals whom managers, trainers and developers hope to serve.

Diverse orientations to work and space are subtle and perhaps unrecognized challenges in an era touting teaming and cross-functional work. As teams may include potential individuals who delight in gestalts, so should the communication strategy include encoding choices that depict the "big picture." Chapter 9 explores this further in the context of communications technologies.

Communicating the need for change

John Kotter writes extensively on the subject of leadership and change management. He argues that organizational change efforts typically fail for a number of reasons, and lists eight common errors that managers often make. If managers wish to lead change, Kotter's list suggests the following recommendations:

1 Establish a sense of urgency. This means managers should "[examine] market and competitive realities, identify and discuss crises, potential crises, or major opportunities, or major opportunities".
2 Form a powerful guiding coalition.
3 Create a vision.
4 Communicate the vision.
5 Empower others to act on the vision.
6 Plan for and create short-term wins.
7 Consolidate improvements and produce still more change.
8 Institutionalize new approaches.[18]

Hallmarks of leadership

Successors and followers

It is often said that there are no leaders without followers. In the Chapter 6 Hallmarks, leadership was described as an interactive *process* of leaders and followers. Robert Kelley argued the importance of "followership" development, and researched the qualities of effective followers. Aside from being committed to organizational goals and effective group membership, other principal characteristics included: (a) self-management—demonstrating independent, critical thinking, not requiring close supervision; (b) commitment—to something other than self; (c) focus and competence; and, (d) credibility, courageousness, and honesty.[19]

The socialization process observed at Duromark did not just happen coincidentally. Mentoring, planned-for stepping stones, shared visions, and commitment to leadership, followership, and a nurturing organizational culture for each were evident. Indeed, it may also be argued that without leaders and followers there will be no successors. Development of successors appears extremely important, perhaps particularly in times of economic and other uncertainties.

Context creators

Gareth Morgan argues that "effective leaders and managers are skilled in the art of managing context." This hallmark is complementary to the role of the master cartographer mentioned in Chapter 6, and to that of chief honcho of organizational learning, described in Chapter 4. As master cartographer, the leader sets organizational strategy and vision. However, the context creator, as described by Morgan, appreciates and addresses "the importance of the *internal* context and how it shapes almost everything they do."[20] And so it is at Duromark. Contexts were created by every manager interviewed through brainstorming activities, reward systems, and more.

 Leadership toolbox 7: Building learning organizations

1   *Do not take learning, strategy, or context for granted. Provide the developmental landscape for leadership and followership to take place.*
2   *Be cognizant of the effects of downsizing and early retirements. Take care to monitor that succession management is being addressed in planning efforts.*
3   *Beware of a management-centric approach to communication. Develop structures and practices at all levels that nurture two-way communication.*
4   *Collaborate with other departments or divisions to evaluate existing and future organizational, team, and individual capabilities for building of learning landscapes.*
5   *Build learning landscapes whenever possible and appropriate! Be a context creator!*

Key terms and concepts

training rigor,
visual cues

Exercises

1   List how qualities of followership are fostered at Duromark.
2   How was context created at Duromark? Identify and discuss the stepping-stones that were put in place to build organizational culture.
3   Do a self-evaluation of your followership capabilities in the four areas described in this chapter.

4 Explain how your organization fosters both leadership and follow-ership qualities within groups and as individuals, or identify one that you feel does both.

5 Think of an organization for which you have worked or one you studied that went through change. How was the need for change planned, organized, controlled; and how were all these managerial functions communicated throughout the organization?

6 If *you* were leading that organization, how might you have maximized organizational and intercultural communication. Provide your own managerial perspective and learning landscape. Hypothesize what high-context oriented visual tools might have been created to communicate any or all of the above. In other words, construct a *learning landscape* that might augment efforts to navigate your firm through the change process.

7 In a team or individually, identify a merger or acquisition that was either successful or not. Investigate through secondary and primary resources (as may be available to you) why it was. Explore which cultural elements were challenged and possibly redesigned during and subsequent to the merger.

8 Best practices in IHRD

Previous chapters point to the many factors that may influence the practice of human resource development in foreign and domestic settings. Chapters 1 and 2, in particular, largely convey a culturally laden or *emic* perspective, focusing primarily on "differences" in working styles, communication preferences, protocols and other issues involving work and perceptions of work. In other words, the reader is prepped to be cognizant of those work-related, cultural factors that may be different from his/her own, to include the demographic profile of the workers themselves (Chapter 3). Theoretical and real foundations for the existence of those differences are provided, along with implications and suggestions for training and development.

This chapter evolved from consideration of the following question: *Should a book addressing human resource development from a leadership perspective focus solely on difference?* Clearly, the answer was *"no."* While it is true that "webs of rules," national dimensions of culture,[1] nepotism, communication preferences, and much more influence organizational design and management practice, certainly there remains the imperative to share some best practices that can be taught and applied (to varied extents) wherever one goes, and so the focus of Chapter 8. An *etic*, culture-free perspective is provided herein to selected roles that are generally accepted as functions of human resource trainers, managers, and other HR workplace-related professionals.

The following discussion focuses on best practices—identifying and consistently executing the optimum way of doing a particular activity or process(es)—specific to the topic, "How to Recruit the Right People for A/Your Business." It addresses what should have been done *prior* to the recruitment and selection process. *Why is an entire chapter devoted to this process (vs. other HR functions and roles)?* Answer: Because human capital is a critical, indispensable factor of production to all organizations of all sizes. Plus, as Chapter 3 indicates, selecting the right people continues to be particularly challenging, given the mobility of the global workforce. Once employees walk through the portal of the organization, many other functions of HR must be aligned to desired organizational outcomes. Frequently the organization does an internal, regional, national, or international search for an employee or employees through a "want ad," but does not devote sufficient attention to the generation of the ad through careful prior analysis. Therefore, the following addresses the organizational audit and job analysis, and best practices related to those activities. Subsequently, discussion turns to the implications of these practices to fair performance appraisals.

How to recruit the right people for a business

Wait! Don't be so quick to post those ads for job positions!

This seminar points to ongoing due diligence processes and considerations that optimize your selection and allocation of the right people for the right places *before* the recruitment begins.

Discover the value of:

* an organizational audit
* proven job analysis techniques
* the ABCs of effective job ads, and more.

Whether you are a new business or a business that is in the process of reinventing itself, this seminar is not one to miss.

Who should attend? Those who are decision-makers and accountable for organizational development and productivity.

The advertisement for the above seminar is one that travels well internationally. It appears that no organization is immune from hiring the wrong people. The seminar begins by asking attendees, "*What is meant by the 'wrong' people?*" That question generally attracts many responses, often to include laughter. The "wrong" people profile generally includes, but is not limited to, those who are not qualified to do the job, those who apparently do not understand their job or their role within the organization, and those who are not motivated to perform the functions of the job (and do not stay). All these reasons often lead to costly turnover. *And why?* Often the problems begin with the job ad itself. Therefore, we begin there, and return there later on.

The job I want ad

The following three advertisements are fictionalized samples of real-world postings that circulated on the Internet. Discussion then follows that points to the importance of the organizational audit and the job analysis. These activities are key elements of what is viewed herein as the *process* of recruitment and selection. It is a systems view. Once institutionalized, effective follow-through optimizes hiring of the right people.

Exhibit A: True Sweet Beverage Group

Job Description:

- Merchandise chain store accounts
- Supply back stock at assigned accounts
- Build displays
- Fill racks and coolers
- Maintain designated sections of displays

Exhibit B: True Sweet Beverage Group

Job Description: Supervisor of Delivery Service Personnel

- Make sure deliveries are on time
- Paperwork and administrative duties
- Run routes as necessary
- Hire and train qualified drivers
- Dispatching schedules

Job Requirements/Minimum Job Qualifications

- Must have a valid commercial driver's license
- Must be 21 years of age
- Prior supervisory experience
- High school degree or equivalent

Exhibit C: Director, National Sales/Marketing and Logistics

Company: Safety Transport Corporation
Job Location: Erie, Pennsylvania
Career Level: Experienced (3–5 years as a manager).
Overview: Can you MOVE mountains. Are you DRIVEN to succeed? Safety Transport Corporation is a growing transportation company that offers logistics services. We need a seasoned, skilled professional with strong capabilities in sales and marketing. This person reports directly to the company president, and plays a key role in strategic planning.

About Safety Transport Corporation: [Ad shows three pictures here: the corporate office, the job site, and an activity of the job itself] Safety Transport was recognized in "Trucking News" as one of the 100 best companies to work for in North America. Founded in 1950, our customer base encompasses numerous industries where transportation safety and on-time delivery are of paramount importance.

Job Description:

- Build a sales force to develop our account base and growth strategy
- Implement and exceed sales goals
- Identify and develop new accounts
- Improve and monitor sales cycle process, including but not limited to prospect lists and leads, prospect qualification, analysis, pricing, proposals, presentations, and planning
- Provide our value proposition to our customers
- Engage in continuous learning of product and industry knowledge
- Create, seek, and manage effective information to support strategic sales efforts
- Liaison with corporate office in Ipswich, Suffolk, UK.

Job Requirements/Minimum Job Qualifications

B.A. degree in business, marketing, or logistics
3–5 years of experience in sales, marketing, and logistics in union and non-union environments
PC proficient
Able and willing to travel
Strong communication and presentation skills.

Discussion

If viewed from the perspective of Chapter 3's discussion of high-context (HC) versus low-context orientation, the above job ads fall along a continuum of low-context (Exhibit A) to higher-context orientation (Exhibit C). From a best practices perspective specific to recruitment, what are the strengths and weaknesses of these advertisements?

1   Ads A and B obviously provide no context whatsoever to the positions— e.g., location, important relationships. Recalling Chapter 1, only "the job itself" tasks are marginally addressed, but nothing more. Job tasks refer to the activities that the employee needs to perform to fulfill expectations of the job. These ads have the potential to make the recruitment process a nightmare since many individuals may apply, or none at all, due to the low-context approach.
2   The job tasks themselves are not entirely clear. Best practices discussion in the field of training and development clearly supports that performance statements should include action verbs. Without those, it is difficult to identify clear performance expectations and measure whether and when they were accomplished.[2] As an example, under Exhibit B, "Paperwork and administrative duties" lacks a verb; as a statement it is quite

vague. What exactly is the employee expected to do? If the employee is expected to "prepare certain reports" and "monitor work activities of subordinates specific to X," then those tasks should be delineated. "Dispatching schedules" represents another error of omission. Changing "Dispatching schedules" to "Prepares route runs; schedules drivers" provides action statements that are clear, and most importantly, measurable; they establish milestones for further development. Action statements also have implications regarding the necessary cognitive abilities of the worker that are important to the job—addressed in a subsequent section of this chapter.

3   Exhibit C provides a sense of what matters to the organization. Job tasks are viewed in the context of organizational safety and on-time performance. The others do not.

Best practices: Job ads, in fact, should be viewed in the context of the demographics of today's mobile workforce, and consider both high- and low-context orientations of the readers. Yet, starting the recruitment process with job ads is not advisable without reflection regarding what should be driving the ad placement in the first place. That issue is the subject of the next sections of both the seminar and this chapter.

The organizational audit

If we want to know what a business is, we have to start with its *purpose*. And its purpose must lie outside of the business itself. In fact, it must lie in society since a business enterprise is an organ of society. . . . It is the customer who determines what a business is.[3]

The organizational audit (OA) refers herein to a periodic review of alignment or fit between the organization's strategic direction—or its mission and vision, with its environment, human resources, mid- and short-term activities, and its organizational architecture or design. Design also influences workflow. Research regarding business successes and failures illustrates that if any one or a combination of these elements is out of alignment, the organization is generally unable to deliver its value proposition or functional benefit to those whom it wishes to serve. Each, i.e., mission, vision, design, etc., works in tandem with the other, or nothing works at all over the long term.

Therefore, specific to human resources, an institutionalized OA is essential to the recruitment process to identify those knowledge, skills, abilities (KSAs) and attitudes/values that are necessary to progress the organization's strategic direction. Discussion regarding the job ad pitfalls addressed earlier is usually an eye-opener and a useful entrée to consideration of recruitment in a much larger context—that of the organizational vision and mission. HR is, after all, the operational arm of strategy. To make the connection between strategy and operations, attendees are encouraged to reflect on the Peter Drucker quote (above): *What is your purpose?*; additionally, the work of David Aaker is integrated: *What value proposition do you provide to your customers?*[4] If it takes more than one minute to answer these questions, it becomes quite clear that management has a great deal to think about before posting job positions for new recruits. The work of Jim Collins (2001; 2005) is also useful to reinforce the importance of these considerations, and particularly his discussion of the Hedgehog Concept.

The Hedgehog Concept[5]

The protagonists that inspire the Hedgehog Concept are a hedgehog and a fox, based on the essay by Isaiah Berlin.[6] The fox rushes from one idea to the next while the hedgehog moves along deliberately, with commitment, goals and direction. While the foxy leader is looking for short-term gains (and hires accordingly), the hedgehog is committed to producing the best long-term results. When asking those tasked with recruitment, i.e., managers, HR and related professionals, and others: *"What is your Hedgehog Concept?"* they answer the following questions as they relate to their organization. Specifically,

*   *What is your organization passionate about?*
*   *What drives your economic/resource engine?* This question is concerned with more than profits. It also considers that other resources must be sustained and developed to support the organization's vision and mission.
*   *What are you the best in the world at?* This consideration goes beyond the organization's core competencies. An organization may have core competencies such as managerial and engineering expertise, but that does not mean it is the best in the world.

If organizations hope to recruit the right people, these are very important questions to answer. The answers are essential to identify the individual and group KSAs that will support the organizational mission and vision.[7]

Workflow analysis

Workflow analysis refers to the review of how work moves from the customer through the organization. Every job in the organization may be viewed as an input that should create or add value. Sometimes these jobs work in tandem, sequentially, or reciprocally—where work is handed off to others to be returned for more value-adding work. Workflow analysis examines how the order of these activities may be improved, combined, or deleted. It is very important to evaluate workflow prior to the recruitment process as part of the organizational audit.

An effective way to illustrate the importance of the workflow analysis to recruitment and selection processes is through sports analogy.

Management professor, Robert Keidel, encourages managers to follow sports to gain insight into the types of relationships that drive an organization. Each sport represents a different business model and a set of worker interdependencies that are required. Following Keidel's inspiration, let's compare organizational workflow and the inputs of individuals and groups to that of four different sports: baseball, US football, and soccer or basketball to gain insight into important considerations for recruitment and hiring.

- **Baseball:** Individuals are "loosely coupled."[8] This low degree of interaction is generally referred to as pooled interdependence by numerous writers in the field of management and organizational science.[9] In other words, while the goal of the entire team is to win and play effectively, each player's position is largely independent of others compared to the other sports. Work does not flow between the units except at the start when the catcher throws the ball to the pitcher. On the field, players are spread out—field density is low; players engage relatively little, interactively. Coaches carry out tactical goals: As tacticians, one coach focuses on the first baseman; the manager may focus on the pitcher. It is hoped that each will play effectively in order to contribute to overall team performance. Recruiters focus on the technical (hard) skills of individuals. They don't necessarily care about how each player interacts with others (i.e., soft skills). Understandably, many times a high-performing soloist can become a baseball prima donna.

- **US football:** Most players are tied to units of work. They largely play having a role as part of a group. That group might be defense, offense, and/or special teams. As Figure 8.1 shows, players are more tightly coupled. Obviously, there is more interaction among the players and more concentrations of players upon the field than in baseball. The manager of a football team is comparable to a strategic planner. Managers are strategists; they create the game plan. Players must be skilled in following the game plan. While it is true that players may act independently, e.g. quarterbacks may call their own plays, there is generally centralization of authority. Interdependencies are mainly sequential as each unit plays after certain activities take place (or do not). In hiring for a football team, the most effective players will primarily be group performers of a highly orchestrated team.

- **Basketball or soccer:** Comparatively, basketball and soccer require the highest level of interdependence. Outputs and inputs take place interactively. Players are tightly coupled on the court or field. The game plan and strategic manager of US football would not be ideal for these sports. Rather, his or her role is that of a flexible and responsive integrator whose role is to improve the flow and transitions of the game. Would football's John Madden, former head coach of the Oakland Raiders, be an effective substitute for basketball's Phil Jackson of Laker's and vice versa?—probably unlikely.

Characteristics	Baseball	Football	Basketball or soccer
Basic unit*	Individual [loosely coupled]	Group [tightly coupled to roles]	Team [tightly coupled to all]
Management	Tactical	Strategic [game plan]; coaching hierarchy	Integrative
Density	Low	Moderate	High
Interdependence	Pooled	Sequential	Reciprocal
Hiring	High performing soloists	Group performers of orchestrated (predictable) activities	Flexibility

Figure 8.1 Sports analogies.

Source: Gleaned and adapted from the collective works of Dr. Robert Keidel. Permission obtained in an email exchange of Dec. 7, 2009.

Note: * "Basic unit" refers to how significant individuals or groups are to outcomes.

What does this all mean to recruitment considerations? Technical skills and expertise in a particular discipline, task, etc. or hard core skills are not always prime determinants of job success. Interdependency considerations also matter; following directions and other factors of cognition and memory also matter in varying degrees. In short, workflow analysis is an important part of an organizational audit. In a workshop setting, attendees are asked if the "game" their organization plays is the right game, given its purpose, stakeholders, and external environment.

Job analysis and critical incident technique (CIT)

Most academic textbooks devoted to international human resource management generally include discussion of job analysis, or the process of capturing work-related information important to job decision-making and job design. This is often done through observation, interviews, and/or through diaries kept by the employee/employees. Some textbooks recommend a workflow analysis as part of the job analysis process; others suggest that job analysis follows job design, whereby work is organized around those job tasks, responsibilities and duties of job position; subsequently, these expectations are communicated to new and existing employees. It is argued herein that job analysis is an essential part of the recruitment process, and should be done prior to recruitment efforts for new, replacement, or realigned employees. Additionally, this section will define the term "responsibility" in accordance with the demographic realities discussed in Chapter 3.

An article by J. Flanagan in the *Psychological Bulletin* (1954) is an early reference to attention to "The Critical Incident Technique." He defines it as a "set of procedures for collecting observations of human behavior in such a way as to facilitate their potential usefulness in solving practical problems. . . . [It] outlines procedures for collecting observed incidents having special significance and meeting systematically defined criteria."[10] According to Flanagan, the "critical incident" or activity itself is one that is important to drawing inferences about the person performing the activity. Flanagan acknowledges that the process of observing humans is nothing new; indeed, it is centuries old. His discussion of early use of the CIT during World War II is particularly insightful to understand why the CIT is considered to be a very powerful tool, or handmaiden to job analysis. In the early 1940s, the US Army Air Forces' Aviation Psychology program used the method to determine why pilots were eliminated from flight training school. In other words, why were they the wrong pilots? After reviewing vague statements in reports such as "lack of inherent ability," "poor judgment," "unsuitable temperament," the board moved to establish clear procedures and criteria for selection.[11]

In the context of this chapter, the critical incident technique (CIT) refers to a particular methodology of collecting significant information about the job itself, and the worker behaviors that are associated with incidents themselves. This view of critical incident technique may vary or be applied differently within the field of IHRM or other disciplines/fields/professions, but it is the one which will be used herein. Incidents are divided into major dimensions or categories of job performance. For example, the following positive behavior for a nurse specific to the dimension, "dispense medication to patients," might be to assure that the medication was correct:

> When picking up meds for the patient in Room 107, the nurse thought that the quantity seemed high; she returned to the nurse's station to check the patient's chart.

Unacceptable (negative) performance behavior might be to dispense the medication without verifying it was correct.

Based on interview, etc., those analyzing the job identify what worker characteristics, cognitive and physical: e.g., memory, aural comprehension, written and oral communication skills, problem-solving, ambulation, and more, are required to perform them. There are numerous resources that are useful to the process of job analysis. For example,

- The US Department of Labor provides an extensive *Dictionary of Occupational Titles (DOT)* on-line, and it is available through many sources. The DOT lists job categories, descriptions and respective tasks that are commonly associated with the job. Figure 8.2 is a sample extracted from that resource. Note that while it is useful as a reference guide—particularly for those starting a new business, for businesses that are downsizing or realigning employees, or for use simply as a benchmark—there is no

Code: 582.685-122buy the DOT:

Title(s): Scrubbing-machine operator (textile products)

Tends machine that washes and dries twine: Turns valve to admit soap solution to starch pots (tanks) of machine and to admit steam to drying cylinder. Creels machine with bobbins of twine and threads twine through starch pots and drying cylinder. Attaches ends of twine to takeup bobbins. Starts machine and observes movement of twine through machine and onto takeup bobbins to detect malfunctions, such as tangles and breaks. Doffs bobbins of cleaned twine. Scrapes accumulations of dried soap from machine.

Figure 8.2 Dictionary of occupational titles, sample.
Source: http://www.occupationalinfo.org/58/582685122.html

information provided regarding those worker characteristics such as cognitive abilities that are essential to effectively perform the job.
- There are also "competency and position analysis" questionnaires (PAQ) and respective software packages that can be utilized to gather information about work as it is performed in a particular organization. Although these resources may not help managers, HR professionals and others to "break the code" entirely (Chapter 1), they are helpful guidelines for gathering some of the Items 1–10 discussed in that chapter. PAQ guidelines also consider the worker's cognitive abilities, or mental processes, as well as the tools necessary for the job.[12]

Preparing the CIT Matrix

All of the above analysis, research, and discussion lead to preparation of a matrix that identifies the job tasks, job duty or title, worker characteristics, and minimum qualifications of a particular job position. Figure 8.3 is a sample of a job and worker characteristics matrix that should be generated prior to all recruitment efforts. For ease of discussion, it will also be referred to as the CIT Matrix.[13] In a classroom, workshop, or seminar setting, individuals are asked to pick a job they know and a partner or two who may not know the job at all or as well; subsequently, they generate the matrix together. This kind of activity illustrates how the process is not only a recruitment tool, but also a basis for writing job descriptions, developing an interview team or search committee, and for generating job advertisements, to be explained later on. Regarding Figure 8.3,

- **Responsibility**. This term focuses on the contribution that the employee makes to the organization. In this case, a physical trainer's overarching role is to *ensure customer satisfaction and safety*. For Westerners, the term "responsibility" often causes confusion, as frequently there is a tendency

Job duty: physical trainer Responsibility: ensures customer satisfaction and safety	Mathematical reasoning	Analytical ability	Ability to follow directions	Memory	Comprehension–aural	Comprehension–written	Expression–oral	Expression–written	Problem-solving ability	Clerical accuracy	Physical dexterity
1. Creates friendly atmosphere for customers. [Greets customers; provides assistance with use of machines; compliments achievement.]	0	3	3	3	5	2	5	2	4	2	2
2. Provides maintenance and custodial cleaning of the gym.	0	2	4	4	2	1	1	3	3	3	5
3. Maintains machinery.	0	3	4	2	0	2	0	0	2	2	4
4. Answers telephones.	2	2	3	3	5	3	5	2	4	2	2
5. Demonstrates proper usage of machines to customers.	0	3	4	5	1	1	4	1	4	2	5
6. Stocks cooler.	0	3	4	3	2	1	1	1	1	2	5
7. Assists in preparing memberships/contracts.	4	3	4	5	5	5	5	5	3	4	2
8. Organizes and files all paper work.	0	3	4	2	3	3	1	2	2	2	2
9. Mixes and serves dietary supplement drinks.	2	2	4	4	2	3	2	2	0	3	3
10. Spots for lifters.	0	3	3	1	1	2	4	1	1	2	5

Rating scale

1	2	3	4	5
Very low	Low	Medium	High	Very high

Worker's characteristics

Minimum requirements

Must be 18 years of age
Must have reliable transportation
Must be able to lift a minimum of 50 lbs.
Available to work early mornings, nights, and weekends

Figure 8.3 The CIT matrix.

to think in low-context terms, or of job responsibiliti*es* that are to be performed. This chapter encourages a high-context view of the term "responsibility." For example, a captain's responsibility is to ensure safety of passengers and others at sea. A nurse's responsibility is patient care, and so on. This is not simply a semantic exercise. Understanding what matters first is critical to doing the "right" thing in challenging or stressful times.

- **Job title/job duty**. Consider these terms interchangeable. The job title illustrated in Figure 8.3 is that of a "physical trainer" who generally works in a fitness center.
- **Job tasks**. These are the activities to be performed on the job. Figure 8.3 is greatly simplified. However, many of these tasks generally may involve extensive descriptions of activities related to the primary task itself. For example, "spots for lifters" might also require the physical trainer to assure that the area is clear of debris or weights that could cause someone to trip and fall. In other words, safety or other performance issues should always be considered and integrated with performance expectations, as applicable.

1. Cleans chip plugs in the top conveyer.
2. Prepares inventory report summary for weekly analysis.
3. Minor maintenance.
4. Has a general appreciation for the principles of navigation.
5. Shows initiative.
6. Removes wood scraps from the #4 motor area.
7. Knows Excel.

Figure 8.4a Writing action statements.

They must be <u>measurable</u> and written with <u>action verbs</u>.

1. *Prepares* inventory report summary for weekly analysis.
2. *Performs* daily maintenance on #4 conveyer belt.
3. *Demonstrates* the principles of navigation.
4. *Performs* safety checks by doing...
5. *Develops* one new product/service per fiscal year.
6. *Removes* wood scraps from the #4 motor area.
7. *Uses* Excel to prepare financial statements.

Figure 8.4b Writing action statements.

As stated earlier, all tasks should be stated using action verbs to assure expectations are clearly understood and are measurable. "Measurable" means that one can assess whether the performance statement was accomplished (or not). Figure 8.4a lists seven performance statements. Items 3, 5, and 7 are unacceptable performance statements. Number 3 lacks a verb: What is the employee to do? And, what is he or she supposed to maintain? Numbers 4 and 7 are vague: What are the performance expectations? Reminder, "Understand" and "knows" are not performance statements, and should never be used when itemizing job tasks. Number 5, "shows initiative," is also vague and may be interpreted quite differently across cultures. Figure 8.4b offers suggestions for improvement in accordance with discussion heretofore.

- **Worker characteristics**. Figure 8.4c details a limited number of potential worker characteristics that are important to the job responsibility described. It is advisable to consider cognitive and gross and fine motor abilities.
- **Minimum qualifications**. These are not to be confused with worker characteristics. These statements refer to certifications, degrees, experience and other non-cognitive factors that are important to the job position. Recruitment can be a time-consuming process, particularly if this section has not been well thought out.

All of the above considerations are incorporated into the CIT Matrix, or Figure 8.3, in this case. Subsequently, each job task is rated against the worker characteristic on a scale of 1–5 to assess relative importance to job

---

Cognitive abilities, physical dexterity, communicative abilities

- Memory?
- Ability to follow directions?
- Ambulation, and physical dexterity?
- Analytical abilities?
- Oral communication skills?
- Comprehension skills?
- Written communication skills

Figure 8.4c Worker characteristics.

success. For example, the success of number 1, "creates a friendly atmosphere for customers," requires no "mathematical reasoning ability." Therefore, the rating is zero (0). Yet, number 7, "assists in preparing memberships and contracts," does require a significant amount of mathematical reasoning, following directions, oral expression and other abilities that are rated from 4 to 5 on the matrix. The matrix also addresses the relative importance of ambulation—important to ascertain if a wheelchair-bound candidate, for example, might be able to successfully perform the job functions.

When the matrix is completed and reviewed by job incumbents, managers and others, it becomes a tool to be used for screening applicants, for interviewing, and for rating applicants who are best suited for the job.

The job/want ads: revisited

By now the reader should appreciate why one should not be too hasty in posting advertisements for job positions. After all of the above considerations have been addressed, the optimum advertisement captures the 4s and 5s of Figure 8.3. It provides context to the job itself, and states the overarching responsibility of the worker in a motivational way. It considers the relative degree of physical dexterity that will be required to perform the job successfully.

Legal implications

Recruiting the right people obviously requires careful analysis of organizational goals, the worker characteristics, minimum qualifications, and the job to be performed. Let's assume 100 people apply for the job of "physical trainer." In the United States, as an example, the American with Disability Act (1990) and Age Discrimination in Employment Act (1967, 1986) are only two of many reasons why great care should be taken to identify the critical worker characteristics for the job without bias. The job matrix optimizes fair selection practice; plus, it helps those who recruit to document the rationale that was used for selection. For example, if a candidate is not able to lift a minimum of 50 pounds, cannot bend and stoop to maintain machinery, does not have strong oral communication skills, then he/she is likely not to be the best candidate for the position—i.e., not qualified.

Performance appraisal implications

The CIT Matrix sets the stage for expectations of job performance once the candidate is hired. Let's assume that Cindra S. is hired for the position of physical trainer. Let's also assume that a standard instrument is used to measure Cindra's performance. One item listed on the evaluation instrument is, "advises customer regarding nutrition and dietary choices." Cindra receives a low rating under this dimension, and questions why this statement is there in the first place—and rightly so. She was never hired to give nutritional advice; nor was an academic background in nutrition stated as a minimum qualification for the job. In short, the matrix used for recruitment purposes becomes the foundation for the performance appraisal instrument used to evaluate the employee.

Hallmarks of leadership

A culture of best practice

Leaders are advised to develop a culture of *best practice*.

According to L. Carter and P. Carmichael, *"best practice* is a program, intervention, or system that achieves sustainable positive results, as measured within a six-step framework—diagnosis, assessment, design, implementation, continuous support, and evaluation."[14] Implementing a vision depends upon recruiting the right people. In order to do that, developing and supporting a best-practice focused culture is essential to all organizations.

Have [CIT], will travel . . .

In the late 1950s, early 1960s, "Have Gun—Will Travel" was a well-known US TV series starring Richard Boone as Paladin, a Western gentleman gunfighter. The title became an expression that was used to convey a sense of readiness for anything. A review of the literature specific to Critical Incident Technique supports that the CIT has many applications in many disciplines. The CIT apparently "travels" well internationally—to include application to leadership training.[15] Consider "packing" it to identify worker characteristics and job performance skills that are essential to leadership.

 Leadership toolbox 8: Best practices in IHRD

1   *Management author, Jim Collins (2005) argues that getting the wrong people off the bus and the right people on differentiates the good to great companies.*[16] *Identifying the right people involves careful analysis of many factors. View recruitment and selection as an ongoing process. Institutionalize the organizational audit, workflow analysis, and job analysis to optimize hiring of the right people.*

2   *At a strategic level, transformational leadership requires a clearly stated vision. At an operational level, be sure performance expectations are clearly stated and aligned with your vision for the future. Recall the limitations of language (Chapter 2).*

3   *From a workflow perspective, is your organization playing the right "game"? Use the sports analogy to assess the nimbleness and responsiveness to your customers and stakeholders, and play the game that aligns well with your organizational purpose and passions.*

Key terms and concepts

emic, organizational audit, job task, workflow analysis,
etic, job analysis, responsibility, Hedgehog Concept,
recruitment, job design, critical incident technique

Exercises

1   What is your personal and/or organizational Hedgehog Concept?
2   Focus on an organization for which you have worked or are working. Review the discussion of sports analogies. Are you collectively playing the right game?
3   On February 9, 2001, the US Navy nuclear submarine *Greenville*, captained by Scott Waddle, sank a Japanese fishing school boat, the *Ehime Maru*. Review the inquiries regarding Capt. Waddle's conduct on that day and subsequent. What do you feel was Captain Waddle's *responsibility*? What is your reaction to the results of the administrative hearings regarding this incident?
4   Prepare a CIT-generated matrix for a job you know well. Use your matrix to coach another individual regarding the dimensions of the job and the worker characteristics that are required. Subsequently, arrange a role-play whereby several individuals interviewed for the job claim varied qualifications. Rate these individuals in accordance with the matrix you created.
5   Based on Figure 8.3, and an interview with a physical trainer (if possible), write a want ad for that job position that incorporates the best practices addressed in this chapter.

9   Communication design issues of the future

The leader's task, as Chester Bernard recognized long ago, is to develop a network of cooperative relationships among all the people, groups, and organizations that have something to contribute to an economic enterprise.[1]

Previous chapters relate the role of leadership to organizational learning, knowledge, followership development, communication choices, and more. This chapter focuses on culture's effects and the context of work on electronic communication choices that require careful consideration of issues that are more complex than they may seem. Indeed, being an effective communicator is no longer just a factor of one's speaking, reading, writing, and listening skills. Not only the "new manager," but also trainers and associates at all levels need to demonstrate skill in choosing an appropriate communication medium to fit the intended purpose and audience. This explains why communication design choices are addressed in a book devoted to international human resource development. Recalling R. Moss Kanter's call to action two decades ago, building effective "collaborative forum(s)," where managers develop peer networks and work across boundaries with peers and partners,[2] may be easier said than done. The following sections place these imperatives in a larger context, where they need to be, beginning first with a broader discussion of knowledge management, and knowledge sharing.

Managing capital in the digital age

It is generally agreed that no organization or economic system can survive without effective management of essential inputs known as factors of production. These factors include natural resources, capital, human resources, and entrepreneurship. While a century ago, the term "capital" might have meant only financial resources, tools, production-line machinery and equipment, and basic inventions, today the term involves much more. Having *digital* capital among one's competitive arsenal, or the ability to store information such as sound, graphics, text, and video by computer, is a critical component of contemporary "capital." Some might argue that this is the currency of the future. Having management information systems (MIS) and processes in place to store or "warehouse" information, and retrieve, or "mine" information is essential, and frequently referred to as the data warehousing and data mining or consumption processes. Having it, however, although important and vital, is not enough. Knowing how, when and where to use it, effectively . . . now that's another matter.

Knowledge management (KM), enculturation, or the socialization process that societies (and organizations) pursue to integrate new members into their ranks, organizational learning, and electronic communications should be viewed as very interrelated in contemporary times. There is a growing and extensive literature on the subject of knowledge management, referring to how an organization develops its capacity to warehouse, mine, share and utilize information with its stakeholders. Stakeholders include employees, suppliers, investors, customers and other constituencies. Recalling the Chapter 6 Duromark case, the enculturation process potentially begins the minute a stakeholder member enters a physical or virtual door or portal. What information should be stored and how, and how and which information should be shared makes the twenty-first-century workforce developer somewhat of a "media artist", "critic", and culture builder. Therefore, choosing wisely is an important skill to develop.[3]

This chapter does not address the "what information should be stored," or the knowledge acquisition, knowledge-building side of knowledge management decisions. That is the subject of a book by itself. This being said, it is still important to mention, however, that utilization of this knowledge is no longer a linear, one-at-a-time activity. Recalling earlier Edward Hall references, rather, they tend to be quite polychronic by nature. There is the hyper-textual quality of knowledge usage today: Machine-readable text, pictures, video, sound and graphics are frequently organized so that related items of information are connected. Every field has been impacted by usage of the Internet, intranets—computer networks that enable data sharing and communication within an organization and its various workstations, and extranets—generally referred to as computer networks that allow the flow of information via the Internet between the organization and elements of its external environment.

Marketing research such as gathering of customer information, new product-service development, information retrieval, and stakeholder feedback takes place simultaneously. The linear, siloed approach—waiting for research to be compiled, followed by production, and without input from stakeholders—is a phenomenon of the past. The same is true for HRM. Human resource information systems (IHRS) and retrieval of stakeholder information are essential to organizational development. In short, knowledge accumulation has become much more relational—requiring input from those who need to use it, and time-sensitivity. Both these factors have implications to the "which information should be shared and how" side of knowledge management, to be discussed later in the chapter. Before that, several more contextual understandings are addressed.

Knowledge management: explicit and tacit

While *information* is derived from raw data—facts and figures—that have been organized to explain some phenomenon, *knowledge* herein refers to information that has been learned and applied to use.[4] No evolving business activity can do without either and expect to be successful or long-lived. As mentioned earlier, this chapter does not delve into "what and how information should be stored"—or the knowledge acquisition, knowledge-building side of knowledge management decisions. These are explicit or content knowledge management issues that are vital to building organizational memory and learning through activities and infrastructures involving data warehousing and data mining of documents and text. Considering web-sites as an example, explicit knowledge might include repositories of policies, competitive information, electronic libraries, investor information, and more. An "About Us" section, if included, establishes the organization's view of their market and their world, emphasizing to stakeholders "what matters here" in an acculturating way. In short, explicit knowledge is information that can be codified rather easily. This, perhaps, explains why it has received more attention in the literature than tacit knowledge.

Tacit knowledge, unlike explicit knowledge, is not as easy to codify. It is acquired through discovery and via vehicles that facilitate collaboration, and discussion. Video conferencing, chat groups, discussion boards, list servers, and other interactive media get conversations going.

For example, in construction projects, compiling and passing on captured knowledge can be quite challenging. In a study of eight leading Turkish contractors working in the international construction sector, researchers set out to ascertain how knowledge was warehoused, mined, and applied to projects going forward. Research shows that most of these project-based firms did not have a knowledge management strategy for storing and retrieving information that could be shared to advantage. The study shows how this could be accomplished systematically through a web-based system called Knowledge Platform for Contractors (KPfC).[5]

As another example, Eastman Kodak Co. pursued a pilot project involving Tacit Knowledge Systems Inc.'s KnowledgeMail. Company management utilizes digital technologies to facilitate improved information sharing. The pilot project manager, Brendan Regan, also manager of engineering design for the company's imaging group, explains that they chose software that "is more focused on people than on documents." He claims, "Engineers will talk your ear off, but the majority of them aren't interested in documenting anything."[6] Rather they prefer to seek out other engineers to collaborate on issues they are facing in person. The engineering example recalls the Chapter 1 discussion "Breaking the Code." This emphasized why it is so important to analyze the nature and complexity of work as both have implications for working styles. Taking that discussion further, contemporary managers, trainers and/or developers also need to decide which information should be shared and how.

This evaluation process is complex, indeed, as culture and experience greatly influence what should or should not be shared, how, and why.

Effective tacit knowledge management also has implications for the building of organizational culture. Organizational culture refers to the rubric of values, social norms, and beliefs that are shared by the members of an enterprise. It is the mortar that holds together diverse individuals of the workplace. Organizational culture is what transforms *e pluribus* into *unum*. Returning to the Eastman Kodak story as an example of enculturation at work, one could hypothesize that over time, stories will evolve from dialogues between the engineers. From stories and social norms or best practices, knowledge evolves that guides what to do and not do, given certain circumstances. Hence, the tacit knowledge manager is also somewhat of an ethnographer, having the potential to record and represent the social realities of others. Oral histories become learning histories and fact sheets that become stored in organizational memory.

Anthropologist John Van Mannen, in *Tales of the Field*, explains that "ethnographers occupy a literary borderland somewhere between writers who reach for very general audiences and those who reach for a specialized few".[7] The same is true of those who manage knowledge in contemporary organizations. Which borders to cross and which to bridge? Those are difficult decisions, regardless of one's functional role. Blurred boundaries should be understood as issues of power and resources; personal preferences may be underlying reasons for conflict, stress, resistance to change, or general confusion. The following section provides some general guidelines regarding media decisions, and then moves on to culture's effects on selected choices.

The media richness continuum

In Chapter 6, communication is defined as a process through which thoughts and ideas are exchanged through shared symbols and patterns of behavior. Effective encoding is part of that process, whereby the media critic chooses which channels will most effectively convey the intended meanings. As personal preferences could easily influence choices, research on the subject of media richness is useful to sharpen effectiveness and objectivity. The following metaphor of a pipeline effectively illustrates why understanding of media richness matters: "Media differ markedly in their capacity to convey information. Just as the physical characteristics of a pipeline limit the kind and amount of liquid that can be pumped through, the physical characteristics of a medium limit the kind and amount of information that can be conveyed."[8] What criteria determine media richness? Over three decades ago—obviously well before the advent of the digital age—Lengel and Daft pointed to these criteria:

1   Does the channel choice have the capacity to provide prompt feedback?
2   Can it transport more than one cue at the same time?
3   Does it give the receiver the feeling that it is directed to him/her personally?

These criteria continue to be important considerations for making suitable communication choices internationally. While the array of communication channel choices continues to grow due to the diversification and proliferation of computer-based technologies, media richness may still be viewed as a continuum of low to high, if viewed from a culture-free, or etic perspective. Alternatively stated, concepts underlying media richness are important considerations to those who develop human capital and to self-development.

The Figure 9.1 Media richness (MR) Flowput Meter provides an etic perspective to the relative MR capacity of channel choices. Face-to-face communications, to include video conferencing, rate relatively high on Lengel and Daft's criteria. Face-to-face is very rich as individuals are physically present, interacting, and available for eye-contact, aural, verbal and nonverbal communication messages such as those conveyed through posture and gestures. A study by Massachusetts Institute of Technology (MIT) showed 30 percent more employee productivity in an organization having "the most cohesive face-to-face networks."[9] If other individuals are present, group dynamics influence cues as well. Access to as wide a range of cues is not possible during video conferencing. One might see only a frame of several individuals represented on a TV monitor or screen.

Computer-mediated communications (CMC) refers to those communications that are transmitted electronically from one computer to that of another in the form of text, and may be viewed in real time on a monitor or screen. As

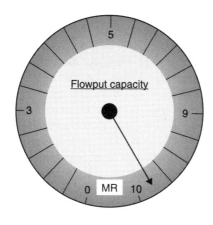

Low		High
1–4: general information, not personalized	5–6: written communications that are personalized (letters, memos)	9–10: Personal presence (face), and video conferencing
		7–8: phone, text messaging e-mail, CMC, social networking

Figure 9.1 Media richness (MR) Flowput Meter.

an example, in virtual chat rooms physical or aural cues are neither possible nor available. Therefore is it not as media rich as a communication that involves personal presence. Impersonal junk mail and spam mail or virtual junk mail register at the low end of the media richness spectrum. In other words, the higher the degree of personal or social presence, the higher the degree of richness of the media—from an etic perspective. The MIT study mentioned earlier supports that employees having "the most extensive personal digital networks" demonstrated 7 percent more productivity than their associates. It concludes that Web 2.0 and Wikis—sites that allow simultaneous content development by multiple authors—may advance employee productivity.[10] Indeed, reports show that participation in social media, referring to computer-based networking activities through tools such as YouTube, Facebook, Twitter, MySpace, and others, will grow considerably in coming years. These forums are media-rich forums providing feedback, reinforcement and engagement opportunities.[11] Research on team productivity and team dynamics supports that face-to-face settings are preferred for quality of interaction and team productivity.[12] Other research argues that video conferencing can be just as effective as, or more effective than face-to-face interaction.[13]

Research regarding negotiation outcomes suggests that great deal of care be taken when choosing communication media. Choices often influence the amount of time spent to achieve negotiation outcomes. Studies in this field show the more rich the media, the more satisfaction with the process; the more satisfaction with the process, the more the tendency to collaborate versus compete. The clarity of the communications perceived in the minds of the participants also contributes to satisfaction with the negotiation process, and may be an incentive to participate in future negotiations.[14] CMC also appear to foster group identity and learning within teams that are spread out over countries and time zones.[15] This chapter does not delve into research in effectiveness of one media choice over another. Many variables such as culture, experience, and nature of the work and the industry influence media selection. Nevertheless, universal flowput capacity principles are a useful place to begin for an introductory guide to media choices. Consider these principles as the *etic* perspective to media selection. However, the etic perspective, while necessary, is not sufficient. The emic perspective, which records the viewpoints of the participants, is also vital. Therefore, we turn again to transspection, culture, experience, and recall themes from earlier chapters.

Culture, experience, and the nature of work, revisited

Given a critical global organizational objective, what is the influence of culture on . . . the technology used to deliver learning solutions in an efficient and effective manner?[16]

What influences individuals to choose one communication channel over another? This is a complex topic, indeed, and an area of ongoing research in many fields, including, but not limited to, negotiation, retailing and marketing, education, and information technology. Chapter 1, "Breaking the Code," emphasizes the importance of discovering the "web of rules" that guide each society's work, and argues that "human work cannot be understood merely in terms of efficiency of exchanges in the market."[17] This perspective is as applicable to the virtual world as it is to the physical world. It may seem expedient to encourage use of CMC to facilitate exchanges due to distance. Nevertheless, there may be other variables worth considering. The following are illustrative examples:

Media perceptions: culture and experience

While email registers as being relatively lean in terms of media richness compared to other options on the Figure 9.1 Media Richness Flowput Meter, it is generally acknowledged as a popular option for virtual workplaces, particularly in Western countries such as the US. Yet, in workplaces that are steeped in centuries of Confucian tradition, such as in Korea and Japan, media selectors are well advised to investigate cultural protocols. As an example, one study investigated the use of email among marketers in several textile goods divisions of a South Korean conglomerate that were separated geographically. It was discovered that email was readily exchanged among team-members who were peers. However, team members avoided emails when communicating with their team leader. As one interviewee explained, "Whenever I feel like to report something and try to send the document via email, I often hesitate and somehow give up on using email and decide to go to see him in person, or make a telephone call, or send him a fax, or an express surface mail."[18] In South Korean culture, showing respect for seniors is paramount as a social expectation that applies to the virtual world as well as the physical world. Sending a fax or a letter suggested that more effort was being made while email might be construed as rudeness to a boss.

National cultural tendencies such as preference for working individually versus collectively, uncertainty avoidance,[19] and high-context versus low-context communications[20] may be significant considerations for individuals working globally in virtual teams. Cultural variables, or the emic perspective, do matter and will influence technology choices. More research is necessary to uncover how global virtual teams "can work and exchange knowledge effectively across space, time, *and* culture."[21] There is no one template that can be used everywhere. IHRDers pay heed!

Media perceptions: educational delivery modes

While the etic perspective views CMC in the moderate to high range of media richness, there may be other subtle reasons why potential users might view it as relatively low or lean in richness compared to other channels. Consider, as an example, the field of education or training and development and the potential array of course delivery modes that are available. Students can attend class through synchronous courses, asynchronous delivery modes, or a combination of both. Synchronous courses are those that take place in real time with live instructor–student and/or student–student participation and interaction. As an example, it might be a course that is offered three times per week, with attendance required. Live chat rooms, audio/video conferencing, and real-time presence of teachers and students are examples of synchronous deliveries. Asynchronous courses allow students to attend class on their own schedule. The student logs in to lectures for a certain amount of time per week to view text, presentations, exercises, audio/video clips, and/or leave messages on discussion boards. Frequently, courses may involve combinations of asynchronous and synchronous deliveries.

Preferences for course delivery modes are probably as varied as are working styles. Individualist vs. collectivist orientation can potentially influence preferences for synchronous and asynchronous technologies—with the former generally favoring individualist orientation and the latter often favoring collectivist orientation, but not always.[22] For example, in one on-line humanities undergraduate course, one student explained that choosing an asynchronous course seemed very attractive at first. On-line delivery would give Rebecca the opportunity to be more flexible. Her peak learning time was morning, and morning was not an option in the traditional in-class synchronous mode. Yet, after completing several weeks of the course at a time that was apparently convenient for her, she withdrew. Her reasons for disenrolling involved the "Discussion Board" requirement. Forty percent of the course required that she post her views, and respond to the comments of others according to certain criteria. Rebecca explained, "I just froze in those discussion board situations . . . to think everyone was viewing how I felt about a certain subject. It just wasn't comfortable for me. I realized I prefer the in-class experience . . . I like the one-to-one with the instructor." Let's take Rebecca's example further: What if we are in a country where trainers and educators are highly regarded? What might the reaction be if they were replaced by a computer?[23]

Another example of how these tendencies can be culturally influenced involves a cross-cultural training session where individuals were asked to fill in the missing words to the following proverb: *God helps those who help_____.* Apparently Westerners, primarily those of White, Anglo-Saxon origins, usually complete the sentence with *themselves*—a reflection of their individualist tendencies. Yet, when Asians are tasked with the same exercise, they generally complete the sentence with the word *others*.[24] Each group solves the problem in his/her culturally appropriate manner.

Recalling the discussion of "Generational Differences" in Chapter 4, hypertext and Internet-based training might work for some, but not necessarily; group-based activities and "techno-centric focus" may or may not be well-suited for Generation Ners,[25] along with media-rich methods (Figure 9.1) in order to provide frequent feedback. In short, demographic and cultural effects on learning are very important to the design of learning systems and the training and development of others. The reader is well advised to transspect his/her training and learning environment.

Media perceptions: spam and privacy

There is an extensive amount of research regarding consumer perceptions of on-line and phone privacy. Global marketers, for example, are eager to communicate messages to potential buyers, yet must be careful about the impact of spam on consumer perceptions of privacy and trust—not only within one country, but also when targeting other countries and consumer groups.[26] As databases continue to be warehoused and mined through increasingly sophisticated technologies, consumers are becoming increasingly vocal about arbitrary inclusion on shared lists that evolve into annoying spam and voice mail.

One US survey by Hanrick Associates found that "control over personal data remains central for consumers."[27] Yet, the study cautions companies against a one-size-fits-all policy regarding consumer-directed privacy messages. Even perceptions of what is meant by the terms "privacy" and "spam" are not generally shared. Legal definitions of spam refer to phony offers that are sent via email. However, general definitions point to the popular notion of spam as that unsolicited junk mail that one receives on-line and through the post office. In one study, apparently 51 percent of respondents over the age of 45 years were very concerned about spam; yet only 23 percent of the age range of 16–24 shared the same view![28] Organizational employees are also internal consumers. How consumers use the Web is apparently greatly influenced by culture, experience and perceptions of privacy and trust within those frameworks. Again, IHRD and related professionals need to carefully consider how to disseminate information.

Media perceptions: socialization and experience

Perceptions of CMC's richness are also apparently influenced by numerous knowledge factors such as the degree to which the communicators know their partners. Once that is ascertained, there is more ability to select communications to suit the needs and working styles of the recipients. There is a learning and socialization process that may be necessary to expand the users' communication experiences. Recalling the earlier Eastman Kodak engineering example, a new engineering employee might feel the same degree of discomfort with collaborative KnowledgeMail as Rebecca experienced in an asynchronous discussion group.

The number of variables that could potentially have an effect on usage of computer-based technologies is well beyond the reach and focus of this book. Additionally no attempt is made to engage in advocacy or review of technologies, hardware and/or software of the Information Age. It seems likely that whatever technologies we know and use today may not resemble their current likeness in the future, given the exponential growth of technological development. Nevertheless, while the technologies may change, the imperative for effective communications and networking will not. Therefore, the communications designer will need to view his/her role as a creative manager with access to many artisan tools: voice, graphics, images, text, space, interactivity, hypertext and more. Communications networks may indeed be superhighways, but cannot necessarily be linear ones, low- or high-context ones, Western or Eastern ones. One must know the audience for whom the message is intended, and uncover existing communities of practice to determine if technology integration is effectively aligned with strategic objectives. How that might be done is the subject of the next section.

The organizational audit

> Although the formal chart of an organisation is intended to prescribe how employees interact, ties between individuals arise for personal, political, and cultural reasons. The understanding of the formation and structure of such informal networks are key elements for successful management.[29]

While no two organizations may be alike, they all share several defining characteristics that are worth identifying in the context of this chapter:

1   They are *and should be* "goal directed";
2   They are *and should be* "designed and *deliberately* structured and coordinated activities";
3   They are and *should view themselves* as "linked to their external environment."[30]

Numerous disciplines argue the importance of performing an organizational audit to assess the fit between business functions and the organization's mission, or its *raison d'être*. As an example, a Human Resource (HR) Audit generally refers to the periodic evaluation of how effectively the organization engages its employees based on turnover, return on investment, compliance, and accomplishment of organizational objectives. The context of the workplace and the industry are factored into this assessment, particularly as these factors are bound to change. Similarly, a Marketing Audit encourages utilization of qualitative and quantitative research methodologies. It determines whether the organization is meeting customer needs through effective product, service, pricing, distribution, promotional and other strategies. Qualitative research might include focus groups, observation, and interviews with customers, management, and other extended stakeholders involved in the organizational supply chain. Quantitative research might involve a review of sales reports, and buying and usage patterns. In other words, the organizational mission—what it says it does and why it exists—is measured against what it does.

Therefore, because communications practices and technology integration are vital elements of an organization's infrastructure, they too must be carefully scrutinized as part of an organizational audit. Specific to technology integration and communications, the operational question is: *Are technology and communications practices a fit with organizational culture and strategic objectives? How is that determined?*

Numerous companies employ consultants to perform organizational audits for a wide variety of reasons. Often anthropologists count among those consultants, as they have studied the relationships between individuals, society, and the environment for decades. Anthropologist Marietta Baba has researched the relationship between technology integration and culture, and argues that individual biases can be quite problematic, causing interference with strategic direction.[31] An important methodology in the research process is "ethnographic inquiry", an effort to describe the various aspects of culture—those puzzle pieces of Figure 2.1, in Chapter 2. Generally a long-term process, ethnographic inquiry could include interview, participant observation, observation, and data collection. As Baba points out, the researcher(s) do "direct field observation of habitual practices at the operations level; participant observation and ethnographic interviewing to gain insider perspective, informal interactions to build rapport and access insider knowledge . . ."[32] The idea here is to discover communities of practice, or how employees really *do* work and group themselves through collaborative networks. Findings regarding practice frequently differ markedly from representations on the formal organizational chart. As with the Confucian protocol example, the more individuals are encouraged to enter into collaborative relationships, the more important it is to ascertain the nature of those relationships. To not do so might cause distrust among workers and work groups, which in turn might directly influence organizational effectiveness.[33] Because ineffective or effective knowledge management influences perceptions of trust or distrust, KM and risk management are quite interrelated.

While traditional ethnographic inquiry through interviews and surveys can be effective for auditing purposes, they can also be time-consuming and costly. An example of an alternative method involved researchers at Hewlett-Packard who used email exchange logs to map existing communication networks. As illustrated in Figure 9.2, aside from identifying communities and sub-communities, data also revealed power flows as they really existed as opposed to how they were formally assigned. Other means of communication such as instant messaging, telephony, and mobile communication usage are among the possibilities for data sources.[34]

Restructuring and cost-cutting frequently dominate the headlines of contemporary business news in many areas of the world. Companies are well advised to consider doing a cultural audit to assess the fit between media choices, technology and users—to include an audit of the available

Figure 9.2 Email log of community structure.

Source: Tyler, Joshua, Dennis Wilkinson, and Bernardo Huberman. (2003). *Email as spectroscopy: Automated discovery of community structure within organizations.* Retrieved April 17, 2003 from http://lanl.arXiv.org/abs/cond-mat/0303264.

technologies at varied locations. Then if changes need to be made to fit with new strategic direction and available factors of production, managers, trainers and HR professionals will have an important baseline, and be aware of what border zones may have to be bridged and/or redesigned.

Cross-cultural effects on human–computer interaction

> Our newest generation of learners: If we build it, they will come; if we build it well, they—in the broadest sense of the word—will learn.[35]

While discussion of hardware, software and technologies are excluded from the scope of this chapter, it would be remiss to fail to mention the importance of context when designing computer-based technology systems. The field of human–computer interaction (HCI) addresses the relationship between people and computers, by asking how computer systems should be designed to meet the needs of the people who use them. Designers of computer systems will need to know a great many things beyond wires, bytes, bits, glitz, and boards. Even in this domain, and when configuring on-line systems, it is important to guard against ethnocentrism.[36] A researcher from Siemens AG Corporate Technology Information and Communication User Interface Design cautions,

> . . . assumptions about the future user groups and the future situations in which the products are to be used should be part of the planning and design process. These assumptions are heavily influenced by the culture in which the design engineers were raised. Design engineers pay less heed to or have no real understanding of product requirements that have little significance in their own cultural context.[37]

A multinational company such as Siemens has reason to be concerned with issues such as these, as new product development and design success relies upon accurate interpretation of customers' wants and needs. Computers are, after all, tools, and, as tools, the socio-cultural context, to include history and the environment, influences their usage.

The following are a few examples of how cross-cultural effects may be detrimental or influential to HCI designs—depending upon who the user(s) may be.

- Interactive experiences such as turn-taking are not the same wherever one goes; indeed, this dimension of social interaction varies a great deal across cultures.[38]
- Whether to prepare displays and web-sites for electronic commerce—as contexted syntheses, having high-context orientation, versus compartmentalized facts, or having low-context orientation—is an important consideration. The entire Chapter 2 discussion of high-context (HC) and low-context (LC) cultures and "The Limitations of Language" is pertinent here. Development of effective web-site displays is important to all organizational functional areas.
- Determining the impact of culture on depth perception and the ability to perceive patterns of lines is essential because not all cultures see the same things in the same way. Recognizing parts of a whole picture might be influenced by colors, backgrounds, density gradients, and height perceptions. Clearly, art education and cultural psychology research, among others, support that different cultural groups do not process pictorial information in the same way.[39]
- Identifying how the organization of work activities and the context in which computer-based technologies will be used influences the design of the structure and its systems. Many computer and microprocessor manufacturers study the environments of consumer and business users through anthropological and other research. Research findings are then translated into new product development.

The following is a Japanese perspective regarding the subtle impact of cultural effects on HCI:

> . . . I have had chances to work in western academic societies . . .; those experiences helped me become aware of the importance of 'culture' in the design of computer-supported communication tools. These experiences can be compared to the sudden awakening from a deep sleep.
>
> The same 'code' can be interpreted in a variety of ways, depending on the undersea part of the iceberg—the framework for interpreting words, gestures, and expressions that is part of membership in a culture. Japanese and Americans and others have fundamentally different decoders at the cultural level, and communication difficulties result when that isn't taken into account.[40]
>
> When I became aware of the differences between American and Japanese social protocols, I began to understand more deeply my own cultural background.[41]

With the advent of the 1990s there were those who warned against ethnocentricity when developing computer-based technologies:

> Sadly, many American and UK developers still think they are at the centre of the Universe. Most computer operating systems and online searching and retrieval systems owe their origin to the major North American and European software houses and centres. Such systems are then sold to an international market in spite of being conceived originally for local needs. The conversion to an international version often only involves adjustments to support diacritical and other special language characters. However, feedback from users and sales representatives of online systems tells us that a user interface which is appropriate and effective in a particular organisation setting, a particular country or a market segment (linguistic barriers notwithstanding) is not directly transferable across widely different cultures to produce efficient cognitive coupling and thereby sales![42]

Language is a defining element of culture. Yet, until the 1990s, the ASCII system for encoding language characters and symbols was grossly inadequate to support multiple languages, as only 96 characters were within its repertoire. Furthermore, the Latin alphabet is not the foundation of many languages. Other languages have special syntactical and other requirements. Consider, for example, Chinese that is read in columns, or Arabic that is read from right to left. Therefore, it was necessary to address how to format text according to the needs of each respective language. Although "the granddaddy of Western encodings" was replaced by Unicode, "a universal character encoding system . . . that can accommodate more than 1,000,000 [characters, with] . . . room for every symbol and sign from every language that ever existed,"[43] there are still many technical challenges awaiting knowledge managers who develop organizational learning globally.

Character encoding is definitely a concern for software developers. Consider India, as an example. This is a country that is rich in cultural diversity due to its many languages, religions, and customs. To move into the Internet era, libraries are faced with the challenge of digitizing extensive resources that have been stored in diverse print media in the form of monographs, pamphlets, manuscripts, palm leaves, and tamra-patras or copper plates. The need to know how to do this points to the importance of Unicode and issues that relate to the challenges involved in multi-script database development.[44]

One IT administrator from Nanjing of Jiangsu Province of the People's Republic of China describes such technical challenges specific to the problems of Chinese transcription as follows:

> There are two different Chinese languages used in computer systems. One is simplified Chinese, which is used mostly by mainland Chinese people. The other is traditional Chinese, which prevails in Hong Kong, Taiwan and GuangDong province (the closest province to Hong Kong). The same Chinese character looks a little bit different in these two different systems. As for me, I can make out some words in traditional style, but some I can't. That is the reason why Microsoft company offers two Chinese version operation systems every time. So in the computer system, a Chinese character has two different unicodes for its traditional glyph and [the] simplified one. And if you use [the] simplified Chinese operation system, you need to install [the] traditional Chinese language package in order to display the content of some websites which use traditional Chinese characters. I think that it adds the extra burden to transcription to Chinese.[45]

Therefore, knowing how text should be presented in the global marketplace is probably as important as knowing which encoding medium to choose. Buying software from different vendors and piecing them together will not be effective to create single search engines that will work effectively anyplace in the world. There is obviously still much work to be done in this realm. However, as Woolliams and Gee point out in an earlier quote, although adjustments to support diacritical and other special language characters may be necessary, they will not be sufficient. Understanding of the socio-cultural context that influences technology usage is also critical.

International and multidisciplinary collaboration is also key to effective design. As argued by A.Dix *et al.*,

> HCI is undoubtedly a multi-disciplinary subject. The ideal designer of an interactive system would have expertise in a range of topics: psychology and cognitive science to give her knowledge of the user's perceptual, cognitive and problem-solving skills; ergonomics for the user's physical capabilities; sociology to help her understand the wider context of the

interaction; computer science and engineering to be able to build the necessary technology; business to be able to market it; graphic design to produce an effective interface presentation; technical writing to produce the manuals, and so it goes on. There is obviously too much expertise here to be held by one person (or indeed four!), perhaps even too much for the average design team.[46]

Art educator, Renee Spitz, presents a similar perspective to the above in the following, but also turns to the artistic community for collaborative advice:

Since culture does affect human perception and cognition, one would expect cultural variations to be reflected in computer graphics images developed by artists from widely differing cultural backgrounds.[47]

For, as Spitz points out, just as cognition is influenced by culture, aesthetics is "a system of conventions established within the artist's cultural group."[48] The conventions that are embedded in one culture may be rich; but as *one* system they are limited. The reality or realities the conventions represent are *a* lens, but not *all* lenses of reality. Therefore, the hypertext and/or linear choices imbedded in one culture may be limiting in and of themselves. Obviously, HCI enterprises of the future will need to utilize teams of designers representing diverse cultural and multidisciplinary backgrounds. In addition to those disciplines mentioned above, others that ground this book are also valuable to optimize HCI.

   "*Why*," the reader may ask, "*are these literatures important to inform the Computer Integration Technology manager and/or the HCI designer? Isn't the business of technology enough?*" Isn't it enough to know about psychology, marketing, engineering, programming, technologies, cognitive science? Or, alternatively stated, what insight might other disciplines provide?

   Recalling the "Introduction" to this book, adult learning theory, as one example, considers the role of cognition, or how individuals perceive and mentally process information, in the learning process. If cognitive processes are not generally shared among adults, then the manager must know where similarities and differences may be bridged. The literature of intercultural communication helps here. Intercultural communication is grounded in theory derived from empirical study of verbal and nonverbal exchanges between individuals and groups of individuals. Bridging border zones between peoples of different cultures involves conscious choices of *which symbols to choose?* If we know or can learn about that, (hopefully) the designer may be further informed by the research and practice of training and development (T&D). T&D professionals can plan and implement learning experiences, approaches, and/or training and design procedures that help the organization, groups and individuals to achieve a common purpose.

   As cognitive processing is largely determined by the way individuals perceive and respond to the world around them through culture and experience, the literature of anthropology, sociology, art education, and adult learning theory enrich insight into how and why adults learn they way they do. Together they provide guidance to managers attempting to discover their *own* (perhaps) unconsciously preferred communication modes. They also provide insight into how one might go about learning and employing other, perhaps unfamiliar, modes. Indeed, as Chapters 2 and 3 illustrate, people are *not* the same wherever one goes as regards preferred modes of communication. Therefore, research in these fields *also* has much to offer to designers of computer-based technologies in the global Information Age.

A subfield within the field of HCI is computer-supported cooperative work (CSCW). CSCW explores how people work together, and is generally considered to be strongly interdisciplinary, to include sociolinguistics from a variety of perspectives. Although the subfield and social context are important to the communication process, both are beyond the scope of this chapter.

In short, the managers and training and development professionals need insight from all these disciplines. As with the popular song about love and marriage, this book posits that *"we can't* [apparently] *have one without the other* [any longer]." Without a doubt, there are many things in the users' environments that may potentially influence preferred communication modes; these, in turn, may affect choices, which in turn may affect usage. Managers and designers obviously need to research their users and design systems to meet their needs. It is not intuitive, but wouldn't an HCI designer's life be easier if it were? . . . which brings us to the rhetorical question of this last section.

Could there ever be a theory of a person?

Anthropologist, Richard Shweder, points to the failure of the "cognitive revolution" of the 1960s to develop an adequate theory of the "person."[49] Shweder emphasizes his point when he summarizes the respective positions of proponents of general psychology vs. cultural psychology. Although he was not writing with the focus of this chapter in mind, his words are applicable and insightful as they point to the imperative for research and integration of cross-cultural and multidisciplinary perspectives when training those who will manage HCI design:

> "People are the same wherever you go" is a line from the song "Ebony and Ivory" by Paul McCartney and Stevie Wonder; that line describes pretty well a basic assumption of general psychology. . . . The aim of general psychology is to describe that central inherent processing mechanism of mental life. . . .[50]
>
> Ontologically speaking, knowledge in general psychology is the attempt to imagine and characterize the form or shape of an inherent central processing mechanism for psychological functions (discrimination, categorization, memory, learning, motivation, inference, etc.) Epistemologically speaking, knowledge seeking in general psychology is

the attempt to get a look at the central processing mechanism untainted by content and context.[51]

   The main intellectually motivating force in general psychology is the idea of that central processing device. The processor, it is imagined, stands over and above, or transcends, all the stuff upon which it operates. . . . Given that image, the central processor itself must be context-and content-independent. . . .[52]

Shweder describes the contribution of cultural psychology as follows,

   The basic idea of cultural psychology is that no sociocultural environment exists or has identity independent of the way human beings seize meanings and resources from it. . . .[53]

Interestingly, HCI educator discussion regarding the design of cognitive architecture frequently portrays humans as Shweder does above, or from a general psychology perspective. References to the effects of culture and experience are often limited to adjustments to support diacritical and other special language characters and symbols. Frequently, caution is advised with use of metaphor and icons. There can be no doubt that research within the field of general psychology has contributed greatly to the understanding of biological processes shared by humans. As the following states,

   All communication systems involve the detection and encoding of patterns of information. Surely designers of artificial communication networks can learn something from biological communication systems, which have stood the test of two thousand million years of evolution.[54]

Nevertheless, as with all single, perhaps functional approaches, one vantage point is never enough to inform contemporary human interactions. Therefore, Shweder's essay is useful to emphasize the importance of both the emic and etic perspectives to communications designers. Both fields of study provide further grounding for multidisciplinary collaboration regarding HCI education and design. In a transnational, consumer-focused, dynamic and interconnected era, exploring the *intentional* worlds of users will continue to be vitally important.[55] As computers are used to "mediate" actions between users, designers need to formulate a mental model that responds to system events which relate to users.[56]

   In summary, developing a network of cooperative relationships among individuals, groups, and organizations requires organizational associates to discover a great many things: the socio-cultural context that surrounds usage of tools, the nature of work, how culture and experience influence cognition and learning, communities of practice, and much more.

   The following selectively presents defining hallmarks of leadership as they apply to this chapter's discussion.

Hallmarks of leadership

The leader as transformer

In the context of this chapter, the transformer refers to the leader as a converter of energy. Just as the person who throws the switch to enable or disable a train that may be unseen, the leader enables unseen individuals and groups through knowledge management, auditing, and ethnographic inquiry. Doing these activities helps to bridge the border zones of diverse working styles. This is not to be confused with popular discussion of the "transformational leader"—one who looks beyond self-interests and transactions and creates followership, provides and implements an impelling vision, invests in stakeholders, and develops an environment in which change can take place. There can be no doubt that the twenty-first century requires global leaders that are comfortable and confident with technology.[57] However, leadership of "digital capital" involves many other complex challenges to leadership. As stated by the authors of "Digital Capital: Harnessing the Power of Business Webs," "The information age is bringing forth a new business form: fluid congregations of business—sometimes highly structured, sometimes amorphous. . . ."[58] Therefore, those who create fluidity, value, and connectivity in physical and virtual worlds will have the competitive advantage.

The leader as logistician

It is impossible for one individual to be all-knowing, particularly in an era of mobility, virtual space, and exponential change. Therefore, now more than ever, transformational leadership requires careful recruitment, selection, and training and development of individuals who can add value and be enablers themselves with regard to knowledge management objectives. In this sense, the leader is a logistician, assuring that the right people are in the right place at the right time.

In the parable of "The Wheel and the Light," authors W. Chan Kim and Renée Mauborgne tell the story of third-century BC Chinese Emperor, Lui Bang of the Han Dynasty. At a banquet celebrating the unification of China, many were puzzled why Lui Bang was emperor, since he was not of nobility; nor were his credentials as a warrior, logistician, and diplomat as impressive as those of his heads of staff. When questioned by his disciples regarding this enigma, Lui Bang replied through the analogy of the wheel of a chariot. "Sturdy spokes poorly placed make a weak wheel. Whether their full potential is realized depends on the harmony between them. The essence of wheel-making lies in the craftsman's ability to conceive and create the space that holds and balances the spokes within the wheel. Think now, who is the craftsman here?"[59] And so with the leader. He or she must develop harmony through selection and development of human capital and construction of supportive KM systems.

The leader as artisan and craftsperson

Recalling the introductory statements to this chapter, effective communication is no longer just a factor of one's reading, writing, and listening skills. Leadership requires careful honing of tools to meet the needs of their users, and careful media choices to provide organizational glue of geographically and virtually dispersed entities. One size does not fit all. Therefore, one should appreciate that there is a great deal of artistry involved in making the choices that will yield optimum results.

 Leadership toolbox 9: Communications design issues of the future

1   *Assure effective knowledge management is integrated with organizational culture-building, socialization, and learning to bridge the border zones between diverse working styles.*
2   *Employ ethnographic inquiry and other methodologies to assess if communities of practice are aligned with organizational goals. If they are not, then analyze what transformational processes may need to be employed to create urgency for change.*
3   *Assure that the organizational audits are implemented at all levels in physical and virtual worlds, and in accordance with cultural protocols. Verify that what the organization says is the same as what it does.*
4   *Recognize that digital and human capital count among the most important weapons of a competitive arsenal in the information age.*
5   *Guard against enthocentricity when choosing and developing computer-based technologies. Integrate multiple perspectives, artisanship, and craftsmanship for team and product development.*
6   *Recognize that the etic and emic perspectives are not mutually exclusive in organizational life. Strike a balance between the two.*

Key terms and concepts

knowledge management, explicit knowledge, tacit knowledge, information, organizational culture, media richness, computer-mediated communications, etic vs. emic, synchronous vs. asynchronous technologies, organizational audit, HCI, social media

Exercises

1   Evaluate your personal comfort with the media choices that are popularly employed within your organization. What choices are most rich and least rich, in your view?

2   Ask the same question (1) of a co-worker, or a personal friend. Compare and contrast your views with the views of the person you questioned.

3   What contextual circumstances were similar to yours regarding the organizational characteristics of your co-worker or friend? Which were different?

4   Relate the discussion regarding "communities of practice" to your own organization.

5   From a professional and personal perspective, how would you rate your degree of technocentricity on a continuum of 1–10? Rate "professional" and "personal" separately. Consider technology-based social networks you count on (e.g., Facebook, Linked-in, MySpace blogs, wikis, YouTube.) Also consider the portable communication devices you depend upon and their respective features. Why are they indispensable to you? What implications does this profile have for those tasked with building training and development infrastructures?

10 The future of IHRD

Readers of this book might wonder why the author has not yet defined the meaning of "international human resource development (IHRD)." Isn't this generally done straight away in Chapter 1? Why this brazen unorthodoxy? The rationale for this decision is threefold: (1) It seemed important to *first* guide the book's target audience—i.e., "all those who are committed to workforce development, through subtleties that affect learning and communication choices in physical and virtual spaces; (2) to *first* introduce the demographics and mobile nature of the global workforce itself and the implications of all of that to training and more, and *then* turn to a definition that might encompass all of these factors; (3) to present compelling reasons to the reader to *first* evaluate personal preferences, assumptions, and possible biases regarding how individuals learn or should learn, choose to work, choose and use technology, make communication choices, and so on. After addressing the above, it appeared logical to identify a definition that might be useful and appreciated going forward. Therefore, Chapter 10 first discusses several fields that are related to the broad field of IHRD. Subsequently, it addresses developments that may (or should) impact theory and practice of IHRD in the future, particularly the evolution and integration of organizational science and organizational development (OD) with the field of HR. The information is based on ongoing fieldwork and interviews by the author with practitioners in both fields.[1]

Toward a definition of IHRD

> One of the very first requirements for a man who is fit to handle pig iron as a regular occupation is that he shall be so stupid and so phlegmatic that he more nearly resembles in his mental make up the ox than any other type.[2]

Human resource management (HRM)

Chapter 5 provides an overview to the evolution of management in the twentieth century and beyond. The *management* perspective is one that largely dominates the academic literature specific to the field of human resources. This field has obviously evolved from the days of Scientific Management and Frederick Taylor (above quote). The contemporary view proliferated in the literature views "human resources" as the organization's strategic asset, and a vital element of its arsenal, so to speak: It is through people that the organization accomplishes its mission and surpasses its competitors. In other words, if used effectively, human resources determine organizational effectiveness.[3] Therefore, *HRM effectively aligns and engages its people, or human resources to meet and exceed organizational goals. It is a logistics arm of the organization in the sense that it places the right people at the right place at the right time.*

Textbooks also describe functions or roles of human resource professionals, e.g., staffing, performance appraisal, job analysis and job design, compensation, motivation, safety and health, etc., and generally devote a chapter or two to global human resource challenges, e.g., culture shock and national culture's effect on organizational design, hiring, promotion, and occasionally unions. Diversity is generally a separate chapter and frequently Western-centric in describing the profile of diversity in the workplace.

International human resource management (IHRM)

IHRM is a relatively new domain that has developed over the last two decades, and one that continues to evolve due to the effects of globalization, workforce mobility, national culture, and more. As the acronym suggests, the management perspective prevails. Plus, there is a tendency to focus on the multinational enterprise and the challenges it faces during various stages of international development, cooperation, control and ownership, and design. While IHRM is generally viewed as an evolution of HRM in the Western world, in China (for example), HRM is considered a subset of IHRM.[4] The following quotations define the meaning and purpose of IHRM as is practiced today in all of its many functional variations internationally:

- IHRM "*is about understanding, researching, applying and revising all human resource activities in their internal and external contexts . . . to enhance the experience of multiple stakeholders, including investors, customers, employees, partners, suppliers, environment and society.*" The authors of this definition also emphasize the importance of ongoing attention to effective alignment of processes, capabilities, and competencies in accordance with the realities of workplace locales.[5]
- "The global HR challenge consists of how to effectively attract, engage, and retain the thousands of multinational enterprise (MNE) employees in many different countries to achieve strategic objectives. This includes engaging not only employees in different countries of the MNE but also the role and importance of globally mobile employees such as expatriates, inpatriates, and short-term international assignees."[6] This statement defines the IHRM function.

In 1995 Oded Shenkar writes, "An enhanced understanding of the organization-environment interface across sectors is . . . vital to the understanding of the dynamics of human resource management in a global era and must be gained if we are to reach beyond the confines of the domestic treatment of the field."[7] More than a decade later, the extent to which IHRM still remains a domestic treatment is uncertain, and certainly a topic deserving of further research.

Human resource development (HRD)

HRD as a recognized field of study is relatively "young academic discipline," although its definition(s) and interest in improving adult productivity in the context of the workplace are noticeable in the 1960s and beyond.[8] It is defined herein as, "any process or activity that, either initially or over the long term, has the potential to develop adults' work-based knowledge, expertise, productivity, and satisfaction, whether for personal or group/team gain, or for the benefit of an organization, community, nation, or, ultimately, the whole of humanity."[9] Obviously, there is some overlap with other fields addressing workforce performance.

While there are variations in the activities and roles that are included under the HRD umbrella, standard ones often include training and development, performance improvement, career development, coaching, change management, workforce planning, technology related to HR productivity, management and leadership development. Given an era of business to business (B–B) and business to consumer (B–C), not-for-profit, and government alliances throughout the world, many professionals and/or academicians alike view the future role of HRD as challenging: There is obviously the need to address leadership development, negotiation, "people systems"—rewards, recruiting, etc. for associates working outside of their home country.[10] Yet, as with HRM and IHRM, so has the discipline of IHRD evolved as a growing field of study, bringing us to the following section.

International human resource development (IHRD)

IHRD does not necessarily exclude any of the above considerations and functions that are ascribed to the practice of IHRM or HRM. The difference involves IHRD's focus on resources that will progress the competencies of individuals and groups who are "on the ground," so to speak—i.e., engaged to do work with others in physical and virtual spaces—and who wish to be effective and productive in diverse and sometimes unfamiliar settings. The extensive literature regarding expatriate failures overseas illustrates that employees cannot necessarily count upon the organization for attention to development of these competencies. Therefore, IHRD is defined as follows: *International Human Resource Development focuses on the commitment to progress the competencies and optimize the effectiveness and motivation of those engaged in work with individuals and groups in diverse multicultural internal and external settings.*

Arriving at a definition of IHRD is challenging for several reasons: In the HRM literature: (1) "Training" is often viewed as skill-based and focuses on correcting competency-based gaps that are required immediately (or soon) for the current job; while, (2) "development" generally involves competencies that are deemed useful to the organization over the long term or in the future. Yet, as we already know, time is very culturally constituted. Chapters 1–9 of this book point to a combination of KSAs—e.g., "breaking the code" involves research and analysis and transspection; other chapters point to the need for broadened communication skills; another points to the importance of technology choices and instructional design savvy. These are KSAs that do not fall compactly into the realm of training vs. development: And, who determines whether competencies are a current vs. a long-term requirement— the home or the host country?

It is argued that KSAs in diverse internal and external arenas are best viewed holistically, and personalized to address the IHRD needs of trainers, leaders, managers, executive education designers, and others. That "learning landscape" (Chapter 7), given the nature of globalization, is likely to be multidisciplinary in nature. In short, it appears the time has come to view IHR "development" as a continuum of personal growth that includes skill, knowledge-based, perspectives training and more, and is well aligned with the evolution of the organization–environment interface, as described by O. Shenker (above).

Figure 10.1 provides an illustration of a hypothetical developmental path, "wheel," or learning landscape for an individual who has been identified for an

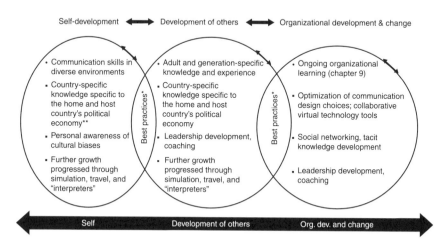

Figure 10.1 An International Human Resource continuum.

Notes: * "Best practices" refers to learning and use of effective methodologies in HR functions such as job analysis and design, as applicable.
** See Glossary.

international assignment. The circle to the left addresses formative KSA development in the area of communications, country- or countries-specific information and social development. Each KSA can be facilitated through simulations, role plays, and/or "interpreters"—cross-cultural informants and mentors who have extensive experience in international work, a host country or countries or regions, and/or are natives of those countries. Obviously, elements of this circle/wheel may be both generic, i.e., important to everyone regardless of location, and/or country- or region-specific. Language training, while not shown, may also be an important consideration on a KSA growth continuum.

As the wheel progresses, so does the level of advancement progress in accordance with the overseas political, economic, social and cultural realities involved. This individual may also be on a leadership growth track whereby he/she is mentoring others and developing internal and external tacit knowledge networks that will build future expertise and progress organizational learning. Other examples might include progression of negotiating skills. All these stages of growth are linked and monitored through application of "best practices": organizational audits, job analysis, workflow analysis, succession planning, mentoring, knowledge management systems, ethical policies, and more to assure the organization and its human resources are aligned and responsive to their environment and vice versa. This is the future of IHRD if the goal is to optimize the success of those engaged in working with others internationally or in domestically diverse environments. The following section addresses the intersection of organizational development with HR and implications to IHRD going forward.

The intersection of OD and HRM: implications for IHRD

Fieldwork by the author over the last few years shows that individuals who began their careers in HR frequently shift to other roles that fall within the realm of organizational development. While it is still too early to make sweeping generalizations across industries or organizations based on interviews to date, they do point to interesting trends that are worth exploring further to anticipate educational opportunities that may need to be addressed in the future. Several interview exchanges are provided herein and analyzed with this purpose in mind. First, however, we turn to a definition of organizational science and organizational development as a rubric for the following discussion.

Organizational science and organizational development (OD)

Organizational science (OS)

The field of Organizational Science, as a "science," attempts to observe, record, measure, and analyze data regarding organizations—defined in Chapter 9 and the Glossary. Organizational scientists construct explanations regarding the way organizations may work to enable those involved in the business of "work" (Chapter 1) to understand and predict future events involving effectiveness, health and well-being of their constituencies. A literature search points to numerous subtopic areas of study within the field, including but not limited to: communication effectiveness, change management, team performance and processes, workplace safety and health, job turnover, training and development, organizational culture, leadership, coaching, reward systems, and customer service. OS is generally recognized as an outgrowth of the collective influence of Behavioral Science, Industrial/ Organizational Psychology, Organizational Communication, Anthropology, and Organizational Behavior. The field, therefore, is multidisciplinary by nature, focusing on social behavior, alignment in an ecological sense with organizational surroundings, knowledge management (KM), and technology usage.

Organizational development (OD)

> Organizational development (OD) is a powerful set of concepts and techniques for improving organizational effectiveness and individual well being that had its genesis in the behavioral sciences and was tested in the laboratory of real-world organizations. It offers solutions that have been shown to work. Organizational development consists of intervention techniques, theories, principles, and values that show how to implement planned change efforts and achieve success.[11]

While there are numerous definitions of OD, the above quote effectively captures the definition and the importance of the field. OD is not to be construed as a haphazard approach aimed at general organizational improvement. Rather, it is planned, systematic, attention to the health and well-being of human and social systems—to include organizational culture, knowledge management and learning. OD nurtures and advances individual and organizational potential. Under the mantra of OD, organizational units work in tandem to anticipate and move effectively through change. Further, OD is supported and generally managed by senior line individuals in order for intervention, development and transformation efforts to be successful.

The intersection of OD and HR

Based on the above, it seems relatively easy to understand why there is an increasing tendency for OD and HR to intersect since the evolution of OD in the early 1970s. For several explanations of this phenomenon: OD effectiveness obviously requires robust and innovative reward systems that engage and grow individuals and groups; for another, if "form [ever] follows function"[12]—applied herein to mean that the purpose drives the organization and design of human activities—collaboration with HR appears vital and vice versa. Additionally, as goal setting becomes more collaborative and linked with external environments and factors of production throughout the world, feedback mechanisms to and from HR are vital. The following interview excerpts further support the above definitions and observations, and illustrate implications for formal and informal educational preparation for IHR development and developers.

Selected interviews[13]

Case 1: The following is an excerpt from an interview with the OD Manager for a multi-business company that predominantly services the heavy industrial and civil construction market and has clients throughout North America; company size is 2500 employees. Both the company and participant wish to remain anonymous. The interviewee, whom we'll call Joan, began her position as the Corporate Training and Development (T&D) Coordinator. She now is manager of OD. She describes her former role as T&D Coordinator:

> JOAN: That role really focused on supervisory and management training, working with regional operations and their training resources to ensure standard objectives and shared resources among the training that is available . . . and to look at competencies of the supervisors and management and look at the gaps that exist, and to help develop training to fill those gaps.

Joan describes her academic preparation for her roles as varied. She received an undergraduate degree in management information systems, and then went on for an MBA. She did not have a concentration in HR. Joan has "grown into" the positions she has held. Work as an intern in a not-for-profit economic development association placed her in a leadership development role, where several mentors guided her to manage their leadership development program. She later went back to school and obtained certifications in conflict resolution. Joan took a position in banking and was VP in charge of marketing and public relations. She acknowledged the value of marketing for doing focus groups and company image studies in markets where they were unknown and needing to attract new hires. Collectively, Joan feels that both her academic and personal experience prepared her for what she is doing now as Organizational Development Manager. I asked her to describe how that role is different from the T&D Coordinator.

> JOAN: Before I was doing one small aspect of what our organizational development offices is in charge of doing. When this department was formed, its first focus was putting together a stronger performance management program. *So organizational development oversees and provides the structure and process around performance management, compensation, the training and development area—all of those people systems that are inter-*

connected. Succession planning is tied to it as well, and we also try to look at diversity and other people issues in the organization, so there are other side projects that come from that.

Joan's discussion of OD parallels the above definition and its relationship to HRM. She also addresses succession planning through leadership facilitation. Joan's organization recognizes that they have an aging workforce; therefore, succession planning is vital to their future; she refers to future capabilities in terms of "bench strength":

JOAN: Well, if you focus on the competency areas asking, *What is it that we need to be good at in order to achieve success 5 years down the road? What are the strengths as a team that we need to have? What is the bench strength that we need to have developed by that point in time?*, considering the fact that we have an aging workforce and a huge amount of our superintendents and the people with the knowledge in their brains about how you build. They are all going to be retiring; and how do you make sure the next generation has the same capacity so that we can be self-performing our work 5–10 years from now? . . . When we talk about succession planning . . . we think about it from the organizational need, the individual capacity, and finding matches to how do we then develop and provide the right path for succession planning.

Joan's comments recall the core of the IHRD definition (above), providing instead an *HRD* perspective: She expresses "the commitment to progress the competencies, and optimize the effectiveness and motivation of those engaged in work with individuals and groups in diverse . . . settings."

Yet, she also provides the OD perspective to develop processes that nurture and advance individual and organizational potential:

JOAN: We tie everything to one process where a supervisor identifies and acknowledges the major contributions they have provided to us in the last year. They talk about strengths and areas for improvements, but they also talk about their career aspirations. They lay out their training and development plans. They talk about objectives for the next 12 months. They will update us on their skills and anything that they have acquired for knowledge; a certification, a license, or whatever.

. . . after that supervisor does that initial sit-down with the team member; then, the supervisor goes through a calibration review of their entire team among their peers and managers. So, it's that extra step where . . . what it does for us is a couple of things. Everybody gets to better know our team, and the quality of feedback to our team is higher, since other people who have worked with the individual gets a chance to chime in from their perspective as to their strengths and areas for improvement, and suggest how their developmental path can be strengthened. At the end of the calibration day, certain organizational development needs are always clarified and followed up upon.

The above illustrates that performance evaluation from an OD perspective is much more than an isolated department event; rather, it is part of a planned process. Joan also talks a great deal about connecting "people systems" to facilitate interconnections. It is here that she finds her IT background to be useful.

HR and OD at this organization are evolving structurally. Interestingly, OD is currently part of corporate HR where legal issues, policy-setting, and HR functions are addressed. Joan is very involved in both strategic and short-term planning. Staffing is done at the local HR level; but, according to Joan, they are trying to coordinate better at a corporate level. What KSAs does she view as vital to self-development going forward? Joan details those as follows:

- Self-Awareness and Organizational Awareness: (tied to listening skills and inquiry skills) which enables the individual to be strategically aware of underlying patterns of behavior and be able to better predict implications and consequences of things;
- Diagnostic capability: assessment skills, analytical skills; ability to identify root causes of issues and help translate those into practical solutions;
- Coaching and conflict management skills: to facilitate the wisdom of the conflict into productive outcomes;
- Facilitative leadership skills or the ability to influence change—i.e., generating a sense of purpose/shared vision, ability to engage others, gain commitment, and understand the dynamics of the change process.

In short, effective facilitative leadership skills, analytical/assessment skills, and conflict management skills are vital self-development areas going forward. Additionally, Joan points to the importance of developing a "ladder of inference," which she defines as a process that helps us understand human behavior—breaking down the thought processes that lead to actions. Understanding the ladder helps to avoid assumptions or jump to conclusions too quickly about a situation. Recognizing that "what we know" is likely only to be a small piece of what is fully happening. This approach, whereby we probe how and why we affix meanings to situations and obtain feedback that questions assumptions, is an application of Chris Agyris' ladder of inference model, later popularized by Peter Senge.[14] Further, it recalls the Chapter 2 discussion of "transspection" of the environment to learn what more there is to discover about the setting or the situation, and to see beyond symptoms and discover root causes of issues.

Case 2: The parent company of this retail grocery business is located in Europe and employed 26,000 at time of interview (2007). Their business environment is highly competitive, fast-paced, and getting faster. The company names, locations, and names of interviewees remain anonymous; each was interviewed individually. In this case example, the interviewees are referenced by the areas in which they work. Interviewees included: (1) a VP of "social relations" (SR)—an area that deals with policies and practices such as performance-based issues (e.g., absenteeism), American Disability Act (ADA) policies, and legal regulations. Their domestic operations are essentially non-union, except for one location where their labor relations group is occasionally involved. (2) VP of Strategic Staffing (SS)—an area that supports and develops processes for recruiting, internships, pharmacy, retail management. In aggregate, SS guesses that about 140 people work in the HR function, which *includes* social relations (SR), staffing (SS), learning and OD, loss prevention, food safety, risk management, benefit compensation, workers' compensation, workers' wellness, and retirement. SS and SR are one of four individuals who comprise the leadership team that heads these broad areas; *all* report to the VP of HR. Three out of four began in-house, in operations, all having done the jobs. Both SS and SR describe their relationships as "partnerships" and quite collaborative, indeed.

The third interview was (3) VP of Strategic Organizational Development and Learning (ODL) who primarily works with the 500 top echelons of the organization, and runs the "OD network," so that there is an OD person who reports to ODL for every one of their companies. Other responsibilities include succession/talent planning, executive coaching, and directing of their leadership college. Every year, ODL designs and executes a skill of the year that becomes integrated into a curriculum taught by "internal experts."

While the standardized interview questions did not address communications design choices (Chapter 9), it was clear that media choices are important considerations to these three individuals. In fact, ODL mentioned that the parent organization was planning a learning summit to address virtual blended and distance learning. ODL prefers, however, to do a lot of coaching by phone, and acknowledges the importance of video conferencing for executive meetings. ODL mentions this in the context of her role and responsibilities, which include travel to the parent company location and the US, and occasional travel to Indonesia, Romania, Athens, Luxembourg, and Germany.

The background of all three interviewees may be described as varied. SL has an undergraduate degree in economics and spent several years in marketing; SS has a BA in Business Administration and also worked in marketing for a short time. ODL has a BA with majors in psychology, literature and education, and a master's degree in OD, and credits Peace Core work in Latin America, in profit and not-for-profit training endeavors, and inner-city school teaching for important and useful learning experiences. All three interviews triangulate the value of multidisciplinary education and experiences in their careers. SR maintained that multifaceted teams will be very important to the business going forward.

How do they see the future of OD and HR? ODL believes the intersection of OD and HR should be viewed on a case-by-case basis, as it is dependent upon organizational maturity:

ODL: . . . it depends on which the company needs to be in the forefront, I think. If a company has matured and done a great HR foundation building, then I would put OD over that because OD can help design and create all of that architecture. But you first have to have that foundation built. And then I might put OD beneath organizational effectiveness and those processes that are needed to make our organization effective, and that could be OD, that could be HR, that could be project management, that could be change management. So I think it depends on where the organizational culture is and where their foundational skills are. [Our company], having [x number of companies], having a different approach going to market, OD has to be very prominent because you are really basing your strategies on differences.

ESP: Where would you see OD and HR overlapping?

ODL: They would overlap on the managerial and the executive development. So HR would have the traditional hiring and getting the talent and setting the policies to help keep people, and OD would be more to develop the talent, but not just the talent, the organization. What does this whole organization need to be healthy and fulfill its mission? Learning was one of my answers when I asked that question for [our company]. . . . So in our company, originally, when it was put together, HR was much more of the traditional compliance, policies, taking care of ex-pats, health and benefits, associate relations and the performance management system, and OD was more the training, talent development, team work, and organizational large system intervention. That is how we divided it up. It's going to shift to have pure HR to have everything but the executive development and management pulled out separately; and OD is going to be focused only on large group issues and the learning.

ODL maintains that OD can be as effective only as far the vision of the CEO can see, and is appreciative of the fact that she has had the good fortune to work with exceptional—enlightened—CEOs.

SS's comments parallel those of ODL, and SS adds,

SS: I think OD to me is looking at patterns throughout a system about maybe what is happening and why. I also think OD looks a lot more at learning and leadership and delivery systems and systemically what is either supporting or negating what you are trying to do . . . So here is OD and here are all the subsets that support it. . . . both done well create a healthy organization.

Similarly to SS, SR sees the intersection between OD and HR primarily with performance development of associates. SS's comments are also similar to Joan's comments in Case 1.

SR: The area where it [OD] really starts to intersect is when folks on my side, the associate relations side, start to get involved with that performance development piece. Because the development piece really starts to overlap with the OD piece as well. A lot of our work, whether it is with managers and how they are interacting with associates, or whether it is associates and how they are interacting with their managers or whatever issues they might have at that moment in time. It is a lot about helping folks to realize . . . more of their full potential, or change a style or adapt a style or work with someone who has some difference.

SR indicated that in five years it could be entirely possible that OD might evolve so that HR reports to OD, particularly because the organization is growing rapidly and because many "folks" are advancing internally. However, he acknowledges, as does ODL, that the future of their areas will depend on growth and business needs.

What KSAs do they feel are vital to self-development going forward?

SR: Communication, analytical, writing, and social networking skills, which includes the ability to provide feedback.
SS: Interpersonal communication, systems thinking, analytical skills—particularly, seeing patterns and relationships, facilitation and conflict resolution skills.
ODL: Understanding the dynamics of the business so that you can figure out the leverage points to intervene; cross-cultural ability; analytical ability—the ability to diagnose an organization as if [it] were a person and to design interventions that help it along; relational abilities. [ODL adds the importance of relating quickly and disconnecting to be able to go on to something else]; virtual skills—ability to utilize virtual collaborative tools; the ability to balance confidentiality or secrets, while still having your integrity.

All three interviewees mentioned HRM and OD challenges caused by generational differences between Baby Boomers, Generation Xers and the Generation Yers, who ODL described as "over-nurtured." They are studying these groups through qualitative methods such as focus groups.[15]

In short, both cases indicate that OD and HRM are interwoven, and are constructed in accordance with the emerging needs of the organization and of the individuals involved. However, while the above needs and interviewee perspectives are in no way generalizable to other organizations, they do support the literature review regarding trends in the fields addressed in this chapter.

The future of IHRD

In today's competitive global business environment, international human resource development (HRD) programmes are of significant importance for developing corporate managers. Although some companies have programmes to develop global executives, most of the programs are new, and many are in the planning stage suggesting that management and executive development with a global focus is still fairly uncommon.[16]

To address the future of IHRD without addressing developments in related fields (and the issues raised in previous chapters) would have been a very low-context, job task approach, indeed, by the author of this book. Alternatively stated, the future of IHRD is best understood in a larger context than that of an "enhancement" or extension of HRM or HRD. The high-context approach to IHRD is a holistic view of workforce development that integrates etic and emic perspectives regarding necessary competencies for self-development and development of others. It is true that country-specific knowledge and cross-cultural competencies will need to be progressed in individuals and groups due to an increasing number of strategic alliances throughout the world. At the same time, it will also be important to develop culture-free KSAs and best practices such as those partially illustrated in Figure 10.1—uncovered through interview, observation, or focus groups.

Effective practice of IHRD also requires multidisciplinary perspectives, as they are vital for transspection and development of collaborative forums. Looking forward, the field of IHRD should invite insight and research from the field of organizational science and organizational development and vice versa. Solving the "chicken or the egg"—the "which comes first" question—regarding OD and HRM does not appear to be of critical importance going forward. What does appear important is that the fields benefit from interdisciplinary collaboration, rather than co-exist in functional silo-ism; and that interdisciplinary perspectives be woven into collaborative higher-education OD and IHR curriculums where KSAs described herein and double-loop learning are nurtured in highly interactive feedback environments. This may require a rethinking of how HR and OD and other departments have been structured for decades in institutions of higher education.

Finally, the context in which workforce development is understood remains uncertain. Would the fields of IHRM and IHRD, today and in the future, be better served if HRM were viewed as a subset of both fields— as in China, rather than the other way around? And who will drive the future of these fields? Individuals? The enlightened private and public sector? Enlightened institutions of higher education? Or a combination of all three? Ideally, all three would take a leadership perspective in developing the learning landscapes of the future. Time will tell. This author encourages IHRD professionals and/or practitioners to take a leadership role in defining performance needs for the future, and sharing those through tacit and explicit knowledge systems in collaboration with institutions of higher learning in both virtual and physical spaces. True leadership creates followership, and so follows the final "Hallmarks of Leadership" for the book's second edition.

Hallmarks of leadership

You as Proteus

Proteus was the son of the Greek god, Poseidon, and god of the sea. Aside from the ability to see past, present and future, he had the amazing knack of changing his appearance to adapt to external threats. Leaders of the future might be inspired by the flexibility, adaptability, and individuality of Proteus, particularly as regards their own developmental path. In that regard, Douglas Hall noted the emergence of the "protean career" over three decades ago:

> The protean career is a process which the person, not the organization, is managing. It consists of all of the person's varied experiences in education, training, work in several organizations, changes in occupational field, etc. The protean person's own personal career choices and search for self-fulfillment are the unifying or integrative elements in his or her life. The criterion of success is internal (psychological success), not external.[17]

The leaders of the future will need to be adaptable, flexible, and prepared to reinvent themselves, with or without the help of the organization(s) for whom they work. As Hall further argues, "the traditional psychological contract in which an employee entered a firm, worked hard, performed well, was loyal and committed, and thus received ever-greater rewards and job security, has been replaced by a new contract based on continuous learning and identity change."[18] Pursuing a Protean path involves a high level of personal self-awareness and responsibility for development of those competencies that will be valuable to personal success. Douglas Hall's (1996) article, while not intended for an IHRD audience, provides a useful perspective that can be applied to future leadership in IHRD.

Leaders as "synthesizers"

It's been said and proven that leaders need to be particularly skilled at synthesizing information—"to perform the requisite sifting, weighting and stitching together" of information that may be biased or very narrowly focused.[19] This view of leadership seems particularly applicable to the future leaders in the field of IHRD, given developments in related fields as described in this chapter.

Leadership toolbox 10: The future of IHRD

1   *Assure that your IHRD function is more than an extension of your domestic operations. Build an organization that is responsive to external and internal environments and to ongoing research in the field of organizational science.*
2   *Much in the way that architect Louis Sullivan (1896) encouraged architects to develop "their own characteristic individuality," progress competencies that will optimize your effectiveness and engagement in work with individuals and groups in diverse multicultural internal and external settings. As an individual, recognize that this ongoing development may ultimately be your responsibility to advance through multidisciplinary education, job rotation, and mentoring.*

Key terms and concepts

HRM, OS, ladder of inference,
IHRM, OD, IHRD, HRD

Exercises

1   Search the Internet regarding Chris Argyris (1990) "ladder of inference," and/or review Peter Senge's discussion of discussion of it in *The Fifth Discipline Fieldbook* (1994). Additionally, review Chapter 2's discussion of "transspection" and this chapter's discussion of "cultural informants." How may these discussions be integrated and applied to develop future IHRD professionals?
2   Draw a visual diagram that represents what your IHRD developmental path is likely to be.
3   Research how globalization has influenced the curriculum in subjects such as organizational behavior (OB), HRM, and IHRM or IHRD in your college or university? Evaluate needs that may be required for the future.

Postscript

International Human Resource Development: A Leadership Perspective promised to navigate the reader—individuals entrusted with human resource development in varied organizational roles, and those IHRD professionals monitoring their own development—through a self-discovery process. The aim: to uncover self-assumptions and potential perceptual screens regarding work's meaning, preferred working and communication styles, learned communities of practice and more. It is argued that leading change begins with self-assessment—for one cannot know the road to travel or decide which portal to enter (and how) without knowing where one has been. To break that code, the new face of management, trainers, and others requires multiple disciplinary lenses to manage, develop, and integrate diverse working styles for leadership competitive advantage in an era where the only constant is change.

The use of the term "hallmarks," as in "Hallmarks of Leadership" described in previous chapters, is inspired from the English hallmark system that was introduced in the time of King Edward I in 1300. King Edward decreed that all gold or silver items be tested for "fineness," and stamped accordingly with a mark, prior to sale.

Developing the hallmarks of leadership, or the defining attributes of "fineness," involve an ongoing commitment to:

- Insight into the complexity of diversity in an age of globalization (i.e., granularity)
- Synthesizing skills
- Knowledge of media richness
- Protean flexibility
- Self-knowing
- Demographics savvy

As the globalized world of business and industry continues to be characterized by mobility, cultural and other diversities, and hypertext time, organizations of all kinds will continue to socially construct themselves on a daily basis. It is this world that is the real world of organizations. Organizations

Organizational learning	Continuous learning	Knowledge-seeking and self-discovery
Knowledge management	Broadened communication skills	Transspection
Followership development	Effective tools and communication design	Equifinality
Creativity and craftsmanship	Systems thinking	Storytelling
Cartography	Building learning landscapes	On-going organizational audits

are not—and never have been—static entities that can be deconstructed and constructed for all to see in perpetuity. Leaders are creatively challenged to influence people to action in all of the functions they are required to perform and oversee. Indeed, IHRM&D is an intensely creative activity.

Given it is generally agreed that people learn in gestalts, learning organizations will require deliberate attention to building of "learning landscapes" in order to develop shared meanings and organizational direction. Elements of a learning landscape include the types of communication assists discussed particularly in Chapters 6 and 7 and Appendices. However, a learning landscape may also be considered a developmental map that is constructed and systematically followed and updated in training and development. Examples of learning pieces can include, but are not limited to, elements of corporate philosophy, the architectural use of space to facilitate learning, the use of proxemics and creative activity of teamwork, and effective media choices. Diagramming of a corporate landscape should be a high-context training design piece that is utilized to balance and integrate differences in culturally constituted learning styles and orientations to work. Cross-disciplinary research on cross-cultural effects to the design of computer-based technologies will become increasingly important in transnational systems integration endeavors. Indeed, organizations live in a complex environment of relationships of loops and linkages—some readily seen, and others, unseen at the surface. The organizational audit will be key to planning. As such, it should be viewed as a process aimed to monitor the nature of work and advise planners accordingly as contexts change and evolve.

As firms face challenges of being quick to market without sacrificing quality, this fast pace impacts processes, structures and people. I would discourage a management-centric view to the application of the concepts, approaches, and understandings presented herein. Succession planning is an important consideration in all organizations. Therefore, the leadership should be developed at all levels through consideration of theory and practice discussed in this book. The future will belong to market-driven organizations that subscribe to *e pluribus unum*—where enriched communication strategies, knowledge management, and corporate culture nourish and integrate employee comparative advantage while instilling shared values. Indeed, navigating through change can be a noisy process.

As the writing of the first edition of this book draws to a close, I recall one of the many "Calls for Papers" from the Academy of Management that focused on "Special Research Forum on Change and Development Journeys into a Pluralistic World." Organizers encouraged "useful research data and models for understanding . . . change journeys in pluralistic settings" [that transcend] "the traditional linear and causal views of reality, [and] "include complex, nonlinear, and dynamic processes of change." In August of 2003, a conference that focused on "knowledge management" or "The Third International Conference on Knowledge, Culture and Change in Organisations" took place in Penang, Malaysia. Session participants were from many corners of the world, with Asia and the Mideast, the U.K., Canada, and the US apparently most heavily represented. Registrants had the option to participate virtually or on-site in Penang. Some chose not to participate on-site due to concerns with travel, terrorism, SARS and other contextual influences; or perhaps there are other combinations of explanations to include working and learning preference styles. It is ironic, in light of the themes that run through this book, how we can never forget that every organization works in an environment that is wider than its own.

A review of the KM conference program (above) shows that virtual and on-site presentations covered such topics as "e-commerce issues in Kuwait," "how cultures understand knowledge," "the relationship of knowledge to the management of change," "social talk and storytelling," "implications of knowledge management to human resource management," "the borderless world: globalisation, technology and human kind," "cross-cultural comparisons of ethnocentrism," and more.

Fast forwarding, a leadership "Best Practices" Conference met in Abu Dhabi in December, 2009 to address the importance of sharing best practices regarding leadership development. In 2010 the IES International HR Conference met in Mumbai, India to discuss "Dynamics of Change—Micro and Macro Perspective." Major tracks were syntheses of OD, Global HRM, Leadership, Marketing (e.g., "Building a Leadership Brand" and "E-Recruitment"), and Global HRM. As the reader can see, while there may be fields of study, apparently these fields need to be porous.

In a recent email exchange with Dr. Erika Bourguignon, noted psychological anthropologist, teacher, and often mentor to me, she reflects on the times in which we live,

> We have seen a dramatic worldwide economic downturn, an expansion of globalization, great economic development in India and China. "Outsourcing" has taken new forms. It is no longer limited to production, but includes such dramatic and often invisible developments as the growth of call centers abroad, particularly in India, with its educated population of speakers of English. There has been an ongoing dramatic series of

innovations in the area of electronic communication, including the rise of social media and electronic publishing, and more. The current year 2010 is both year of the Census in the United States and the International Year of Biodiversity. Previously unknown species are being discovered, many known species disappear daily. The US Census will point to the growth of the American population and its current distribution across the map. The Census forms now permit individuals to select more than one of the ethnic categories provided, so again a new snapshot of the population will become available, telling us what percentage of the population chooses to acknowledge more than one line of ancestry. However, since there are few and rather gross categories to choose from, this is at best a very rough measure of a complex situation. It does however have potential political and economic implications and consequences to the workforce.

The human resources manager of a company working in an international field will be aware of many of the issues raised in your timely and original book, but most likely not all of them. In fact, we may ask whether any company in the 21st century may be said to be unaffected by issues of international complexity and workplace diversity. Relevant materials from a broad range of disciplines, visual presentations, the charts and graphs, the interesting and diverse cases, the classroom-tested exercises, all will facilitate both learning and teaching.

(April 12, 2010, Columbus, Ohio)

I trust that this book has made a contribution of its own in furthering cross-disciplinary conversation about International Human Resource Development. Additionally, it is hoped that issues and arguments raised herein will be further informed and advanced in other nationally and culturally diverse forums to generate seeds for the next edition. For in these times, the circle of self-development can never be closed.

Elaine S. Potoker
September, 2010

Notes

Introduction

1 Culture herein refers to shared values, beliefs, and patterns of behavior that are learned from early childhood distinguishing one group of people and/or society from another. Culture's meaning is explored in depth in Chapter 2.
2 T. Bianco and S. Barkley (2001) offer a contemporary view of working styles in office work. The authors support the need to understand how individuals learn best, and to choose forms of communication accordingly to minimize the stress in working, optimize worker productivity, and to create more pleasant working relationships and environments.
3 "The emic approach generally yields a description of a cultural system from the inside, . . ." (Bourguignon, 1979, p. 216); it is a culturally laden view. The etic perspective is culture free, and considered to be a universalist view. Also refer to Glossary for term definitions.
4 R. Rosaldo (1989), *Culture and Truth*, p. 217. See also J. Van Maanen (1988), who comments in *Tales of the Field* that "Human culture is not something to be caged for display, put on a slide for inspection, read from an instrument, or hung on a wall for display," pp. 3–4.
5 J. Kotter (2001), p. 86.
6 The complete quote is: "My opponent won't rule out raising taxes, but I will. Congress will push me to raise taxes, and I'll say no, and they'll push, and I'll say no, and they'll push and I'll say, 'Read my lips: no new taxes.'" August 18, 1988.
7 R. Moss Kanter (1989), p. 89.
8 P. Senge (1990), p. 3.
9 Senge (1990), p. 10.
10 R. Hanvey (1975), p. 85.

1 Breaking the code

1 H. Applebaum (1996), pp. iii–iv.
2 C. deRoche (2001), p. 161. (Underlining is added in the quotation for emphasis.) Through a case study of women's work in Cape Breton, Nova Scotia, deRoche illustrates that in the industrialized world, work's perimeters generally include, *but are limited to* job-*paid* activities. This narrow view of work contrasts markedly from that of the Cape Breton community she describes. Her case study, therefore, calls into question how individuals perceive what constitutes work. These perceptions have implications for the way one views/reacts to, evaluates, and manages the work of others.

3 This definition is inspired by H. Applebaum (1984a), p. 2. His autobiographic note (1984b) is also insightful for understanding a broad definition of work: "My perspective on the study of work is humanistic and expressive, in the tradition of anthropology, which sees work as an intrinsic aspect of what it means to be human. Through work and language, humans became [and become] part of larger social groups, conscious of themselves as total beings, and a part of nature in a relationship of mutuality and reciprocity" (p. x).

4 See deRoche (2001) as an example.

5 F. Gamst (1995), p. 1.

6 Refer to F. Gamst (1995), and H. Applebaum (1984a; 1984b) for more information on these subjects.

7 H. Applebaum (1996), pp. 42–8.

8 There are those who argue that work without rewards (incentives, benefits, personal satisfaction) is mere drudgery or labor. The French term, *travail*, captures the latter meaning. Refer to H. Arendt (1958) for further discussion. Another extensive realm of research that informs this discussion is the field of semiotics, which focuses on the meaning of symbols. See C. Nippert-Eng (1995), who addresses the complexity of meanings related to work, home, leisure, privacy, and more.

9 G. Hofstede's work (see Hofstede (1980) as an example) is frequently referenced in discussions of risk (uncertainty) avoidance comparisons between cultures. Hofstede's work on national cultural tendencies and their implications for managerial practice is integrated throughout the book.

10 Refer to Charles Hill (2009), p. 185, for more explanation regarding "*advanced factors*" of production.

11 Refer to G. Morgan (2006), p. 153, for discussion of forms of political rule.

12 *The Universal Declaration of Human Rights* (1948) <http://www.un.org/Overview/rights.html>.

13 Refer to J. Rosenoer (2002) for further discussion on DRM.

14 As an example, "flex-time" in the US has been influenced considerably by the Family and Medical Leave Act of 1993 (FMLA) in businesses with 50 or more employees. Negotiating work, work at home, necessary tools such as modems, cell phones, and laptops, and flex-time around births, maternity, personal health issues, and care of aging parent(s) are workspace realities.

15 Consider the literature on national, regional and world organizational and other initiatives to reduce the number of working week hours. As an example, in 2000, the 35-hour working week was legislated in France for companies with more than 20 employees. Although research reflects attempts to compare statistics and initiatives across countries, it is questionable as to how "comparative" they really are. For example, some statistics incorporate sick leave and vacation times into the data, so it is difficult to determine if one is comparing apples to apples when statistics are not adjusted for comparability. Nor can one assume that motives for reducing work time involve a desire for more leisure. In France, Lionel Jospin initiated the reforms in 1997 to reduce unemployment. The social and economic impact of that legislation is still being debated; while reports in 2008 suggested that the government might reverse the legislation, that did not happen for continued want of more leisure time. President Sarkozy himself stated that the 35-hour limit is the base point for calculating overtime and therefore the reason why it would not be reversed (http://www.iht.com/articles/2008/01/10/europe/sarkozy.php). Refer to key indicators of labor markets: the International Labor Organization (www.ilo.gov); The Bureau of Labor Statistics (www.bls.gov); European Union related web-sites: e.g., <http://ue.eu.int/en/summ.htm; http://europa.eu.int/index_en.htm; http://www.eiro.eurofound.ie>; Organization for Economic Cooperation and Development (www.oecd.org); and Adam Sage (2001); "News and

Trends" (2001); Paul Johnson (2002) for statistics and debates, respectively. The information is useful as part of the "code of rules" (Figure 1.2) to be identified to inform managerial practice when traveling to other locations.

16 M. Baba, "Work and Technology in Modern Industry," in F. Gamst, (ed.) (1995), p. 121.

17 See Baba, in Gamst (1995) for more on this subject. Baba acknowledges that work and technology are not the same, the difference being what humans *do* vs. what humans *make*, respectively (p. 124). Organizational theorists and behaviorists might add that effective tools, i.e., *form*, follows *function*, i.e., intended goals.

18 Chapter 9, "Communications Design Issues of the Future," addresses how culture affects communication choices in the computer-based technology Information Age. Focus is on communication issues as they effect human computer interaction and working styles.

19 E. Hall (1976), p.154.

20 F. Gamst, "The Web of Rules in Comparative Work Relations Systems," in Gamst (ed.) (1995), p. 149. Gamst's discussion actually refers to the "web of rules" that drives each society's "gainful" work (p. 147). I've taken the liberty to delete the word "gainful" as it suggests a narrow view of work's meaning.

21 Technocentrism is ethnocentrism as it affects technology choices in the workplace. This subject is part of Chapter 9's discussion.

22 To do so would involve writing another book!

23 E. Hall (1976), p. 141.

24 Refer to G. Hofstede (1980).

25 Hofstede (1980).

26 Refer to W. Alan Randolph and M. Sashkin (2002) for further examples of how empowerment and development of self-managed teams were accomplished in relatively high power distance environments (Brazil and Argentina).

27 "Smart power" (2008), pp. 55–6, a *Harvard Business Review* interview with Joseph Nuy, Jr.

28 Refer to Harris Collingwood (ed.), *Harvard Business Review*. (2001), p. 8. This entire issue is devoted to the idea that leadership's commandments involve a voyage of self-discovery.

29 R. Hanvey (1975), p. 93. Italics are added for emphasis. Transspection is a term that was introduced by anthropologist and philosopher Magoroh Maruyama at an Anthropological Association Conference address in 1970. Hanvey viewed the transspection process as a developing psychic characteristic of postmodern peoples. This subject, along with culture's meaning, is discussed further in Chapter 2.

30 Refer to F. Elashmawi (1997) for knowledge-seeking as it relates to its importance in training for multinational assignments.

31 Harvard Business Review, roundtable discussion, All in a day's work (2001). *Harvard Business Review* 79(11, Dec.): 57, interview with respected leaders from the corporate, non-profit, and academic world.

32 S. Zaccaro and R. Klimoski (eds.) (2001), p. 8. Italics are added for emphasis. Boundary management involves the ability to balance and negotiate organizational goals with those of external and internal stakeholders.

33 As a knowledge-seeker, the reader is also encouraged to be a participant observer/fieldworker in the environment in which she/he works. C. Glesne and A. Peshkin's (1992) advice to researchers provides insight into what that entails: "Learning to be an effective participant observer takes some doing. We suggest by asking what there is about your identity or persona—such as gender, age, ethnicity, or country of origin—that might affect your access and data collection", p. 60.

Appendix 1.A

34 Refer to C. Hope (2008). http://www.telegraph.co.uk/news/uknews/1930010/
England-to-be-most-crowded-in-Europe.html;www.cia.gov; Religious Populations
(2001). http://www.statistics.gov.uk; Balanced migration. (2001–2008). http://
www.migrationwatchuk.com/balancedmigration.pdf; http://www.statistics.gov.
uk/cci/nugget.asp?ID=963&Pos=1&ColRank=2&Rank=320

35 The Human Development Index (HDI) is a very useful tool to those who wish to
anticipate human resource capabilities and training and development needs. It
rates countries based on literacy, educational attainment, GDP per capita, and
life expectancy.

36 *World Fact Book* (2009); *Human Development Reports* (2009).

37 *World Fact Book* (2009).

38 *International Populations* (2009).

39 *New Car Sales Industry Profile: India* (2008).

40 This is a fictitious place, but based on a real incident.

41 <http://www.igeme.gov.tr/english/turkey/pdfView.cfm?sec=tr&secID=2&subID=1>.

42 http://209.85.229.132/search?q=cache:WKrMIgr9-IoJ:cgft.sabanciuniv.edu/eng/
Haberler/documents/53.FamilyCompaniesinTurkey-B.Eczacibasi.doc+Bulent+
Eczacibasi,+at+International+Conference+on+Family+Firms+and+Corporate
+Governance&cd=1&hl=tr&ct=clnk&gl=tr&client=firefox-a>.

2 The limitations of language

1 See Glossary.
2 M. Matsumoto (1988), p. 14
3 See Glossary for a definition of NVC.
4 Erika Bourguignon (1979), p. 5.
5 Bourguignon (1979), p. 216.
6 Refer to earlier discussion; also see Edward Hall (1969).
7 A. Irving Hallowell (1955), p. 87.
8 Specific to the practices of the Quiché, refer to the writings of Nobel Peace
Prizewinner, Rogoberta Menchú.
9 J. Higgins (1991), p. viii.
10 E. Hall (1976), p. 6. Subsequent chapters explore how visual cues and diagramming may be used as heuristic tools of analysis to assist in viewing organizations
and culture from the "inside."
11 Another dimension of national culture discussed by G. Hofstede (1980) involves
national tendencies to stereotype specific gender roles for men, versus women.
This tendency is referred to as the masculinism/feminism dimension. My job
responsibilities and managerial level in this industrial sector would not be typical
for women in South America compared to the US, where equality in gender roles
is more common.
12 For an excellent overview of how conceptions of time ("time visions") vary across
cultures and influence behavior and attitudes of individuals and groups regarding
agenda-setting, deadlines and more, see C. Saunders, C. Van Slyke, and D. Vogel
(2007), pp. 297–316.
13 The idea of "discovering" culture recalls the work of E. Sapir. Sapir is remembered
as describing culture as something that is "gradually, gropingly discovered" (Spier
et al., 1941, p. 282).
14 E. Hall (1973), p. 30.
15 E. Sapir (1929), in D. Mandelbaum (1949).
16 M. Kunihiro (1976), p. 279.

17 Sapir (1929), pp. 90–1.
18 Sapir (1931), p. 578.
19 This is central to the idea of what became known as the "Sapir Whorf Hypothesis." Additionally, language defines habitual modes of experience into categories specific to gender, number, tense, and time. Also see H. Hoijer (1954). There is extensive literature which argues that habitual modes of behavior due to linguistic orientations can be modified; that, of course, is what this book (and previous chapter) advocates, i.e. broadening communication skills that may not be indigenous to the bearer.
20 E. Hall (1976); S. Philips (1972).
21 Kunihiro (1976). The author states, "I am especially interested in cognition, perception and logic, for I believe that difficulty in intercultural communication is closely related to those mental processes," p. 270.
22 Kunihiro (1976), p. 267.
23 These vignettes are based on the author's fieldnotes involving real-world experiences.
24 The individual from a country other than the US was actually from the Middle East. The letter's destination was in fact, N.Y. I deleted this information from the vignette after the World Trade tragedy of Sept. 11, 2001, as I was afraid that external events might cast unintended meanings on the exchange between the postal worker and the patron. Subsequently, however, I decided facts are facts, nothing more, and therefore hope the reader does not read any more into the exchange than what is intended. Recalling Chapter 1, one can appreciate the potential impact that external events can have on one's work.
25 In doing cross-cultural analysis, one often runs the risk of stereotyping. What is discussed in this section is a general *tendency* by the Japanese (as supported in the literature) of their orientation to language, high-context preferences, and the use of NVC. It does not imply the characteristics described are typical of *all* Japanese.
26 There are copious amounts of information regarding trade and labor force statistics regarding Japan. Refer to <http://www.state.gov/r/pa/ei/bgn/4142. htm>, <http://www.stat.go.jp/english/data/handbook/c02cont.htm#cha2_6>, and <https://www.cia.gov/library/publications/the-world-factbook/geos/ja.html> for more information.
27 Hall (1976), p. 49.
28 The pareto diagram is a specialized type of column graph used to prioritize the order in which problems are to be addressed.
29 M. Imai (1986), p. 62.
30 A. Yamamoto (1991), p. 3.
31 S. Ishinomori (1988).
32 C. Lewis (1988), p. 162.
33 S. Ramsey (1984), pp. 139–67.
34 Kunihiro (1976), p. 270.
35 Yamamoto (1991).
36 Hall (1976), pp. 75–6. There is support in the literature for the visual contextualizing that individuals perform; see P. Gouras and P. Bishop (1972) as an example. In training situations this has implications not only for the hierarchy of ordering stimuli (i.e., general to specific), but also for the utilization of visuals to optimize stimulation. The more neurons in the eye that can be stimulated, the greater the advantage for extracting more features from the external world.
37 Ishikawa (1985), p. 64.
38 See, for example, L. Crump (1989), pp. 48–55.
39 Hall (1976), p. 63.
40 D. Barnland (1989); M. Matsumoto (1988).

41 J. Morgan and J. Morgan (1991), p. 195.
42 D. Lu (1987), p. 19.
43 *Aizuchi* is generally acknowledged in linguistic literature as a word that was created by the Japanese to explain their nodding behavior to foreigners. Literally, it refers to "encouraging responses, including gestures." Foreigners should be careful not to assume that the Japanese individual is agreeing with what is being said, or even understands what is being said. Rather, he or she is likely to just be following along, acknowledging that something is being said.
44 J. Sherman (1989).
45 For comprehensive information regarding meanings of gestures across cultures, see N. Armstrong (2003).
46 L. Dalby (1985). S. Kakuchi (2001, p. 76) defines the 500 year-old Japanese geisha trade as follows: "Traditional geisha spent a lifetime learning the art of entertaining men by singing, dancing, making titillating conversation, pouring them drinks and sometimes sharing their beds. In return, they were paid handsomely by their wealthy clients. They held an exalted position in society and the most popular among them were showered with gifts like expensive kimonos by men who took on the role as patrons."
47 A. Yamamoto (1991), p. 3.
48 Hall (1976), p. 79.
49 Hall (1976), p. 80.
50 For further information regarding ways in which national culture and experiences may tend to influence world views, refer to Hofstede (1980).
51 Hall (1976), p. 77.
52 E. and M. Hall (1990).
53 Hall (1976), p. 94. Hall is apparently referring to *US* (American) courts, rather than *Latin* American ones when discussing characteristics of LC vs. HC cultures, respectively. In frequent use of the term "American" there is a tendency to equate American with US monochronic, LC tendencies, if "American" herein refers to "*the core culture of the United States [that] has its roots in northern European or Anglo-Saxon culture*" (Hall and Hall, 1990, p. 140).
54 See Hall (1976), p. 218. For information regarding the role and use of space in Japanese culture, see L. Di Mare (1990); E. Hall (1969, 1976); and Matsumoto (1988).
55 Frances Cairncross (2002).
56 Refer to W. Chan Kim and R. Mauborgne (1992), and their "Parables of Leadership."
57 The example aims only to illustrate the importance of tool choices. The analogy ends here!
58 W. Bennis and J. Goldsmith (1994), p. 104.

Appendix 2A

59 The following vignette is meant to be a brief introduction to potential applications of visuals—particularly of Figure 2.4 discussed in Chapter 2.
60 R. Shweder (1990), p. 18.
61 There is a tremendous need for gender study *across cultures* in transnational organizational settings. Gender considerations are added as the case unfolds, and withheld initially to illustrate that it is impossible to know intentional worlds of others through only one piece of the puzzle, or from a one-dimensional view of the web of rules that exist within and across cultures.
62 R. Carroll (1987 [trans. 1988]), pp. 6, 12.
63 Edward and Mildred Hall (1990), pp. xiii–ix.

64 Carroll (1987), p. 39.
65 Carroll (1987), pp. xi–xii.

3 Recognizing the "others" are us: demographic trends in countries around the world

1 S. Schieber (2000), p. 18.
2 "Home ageing society" (2002), p. 1; also see S. Schieber (2000).
3 "SELECTED" is emphasized as this is a huge topic. The author's intent is to briefly introduce the reader to factors influencing the changing and diverse nature of the international workforce of the future.
4 "International Migration Report 2006: A Global Assessment." See publication "Home Page" at <http://www.un.org/esa/population/publications/2006_MigrationRep/report.htm>.
5 R. Jackson and R. Strauss (2007).
6 N. Howe and R. Jackson (2006), p. 9.
7 The brain-gain or return migration issue is among the many issues that fall under the umbrella of international migration management. Yet, knowledge as to why individuals return to their home countries or take circulatory paths before returning is still an emerging area of research. This is a very important phenomenon to be understood by host and home countries alike since departures and arrivals have considerable impact on labor pools and training costs. For discussion of return migration in OECD countries, see *International Migration Outlook* (2008). Also see Ç. Özden and M. Schiff (eds.) (2007) for further discussion.
8 "International Migration Report 2006: A Global Assessment" (2009), p. xiii.
9 Refer to "Program Summary" (2009), IUSSP XXVI International Population Conference on <http://iussp2009.princeton.edu/ProgramSummary.aspx>.
10 For example, Pacific Rim population projections include countries from the Americas and Asia; many of these same countries are included in other regional projections—some time periods overlapping and others not at all—making comparisons challenging or impossible.
11 See N. Howe and R. Jackson (2006), and D. Kapur and J. McHale (2005), p. 11.
12 P. Peterson (1999), pp. 43–4, and 46.
13 Implications for learning, training and development are addressed in Chapter 4.
14 See the United Nations Human Development Reports (2008) at <http://hdr.undp.org/en/statistics/>.
15 Only significant and perhaps remarkable demographic trends are addressed in this section. Efforts to compile a comprehensive overview of migrant stocks for every region of the world are a daunting, but needed task. It is challenging, indeed, to corroborate information from the many agencies dedicated to demography studies. A highly respected researcher from the Center of Global Development shares, in an email exchange (2009), that the state of global migration statistics is quite poor; there is presently no standardized international database that captures international migrant flows.
16 Compiled from the *International Migration Report 2006: A Global Assessment* (2009), p. 2.
17 *Europe's Demographic Future: Facts and Figures* (2007), p. 9.
18 *Employment in Europe 2001: Recent Trends and Prospects* (2001), pp. 3–4. "To become the most dynamic knowledge-based economy in the world capable of sustainable economic growth with more and better jobs and greater social cohesion" is *the* strategic goal set for the Union by the Lisbon European Council; "labor markets will be open to all and accessible to all" (p. 7). Diverse demographics, social inclusion, and mobility were projected to characterize the EU workforce.

Immigration quotas are often influenced by a country's projected social priorities. In 2001 one might argue that there was a certain degree of tolerance toward immigration due to an inability to fill economic needs through native populations; quotas in some countries were less stringent or nonexistent as in the case of Germany. Immigration policy stands to be a subject of much debate in many countries in the years to come.

19 P. Ester and H. Krieger (2008), p. 2.
20 "Demography Report" (2008).
21 See F. Field and N. Soames (2008), "Balanced Migration: A New Approach to Controlling Migration," p. 10.
22 See F. Field and N. Soames (2008), p. 4.
23 "Migrant Stock Has Doubled . . ." (2009).
24 P. Peterson (1999), p. 46.
25 "World Migration 2008" (2008), p. 411.
26 See Jackson and Howe (2004), p. 2.
27 C. Haub and O.P. Sharma (2006).
28 J. Sudworth (2006).
29 "World Migration 2008" (2008), p. 444.
30 "World Migration 2008" (2008), pp. 443, 471. The Middle East is the most significant region as a destination for contractual workers, with most of them from Asia.
31 R. Jackson, R. Strauss, and N. Howe (2009), p. 1.
32 Jackson, Strauss, and Howe (2009), p. 1.
33 For discussion regarding the story of white-collar company men in the early twentieth century, with focus on California, refer to C. Davis (2000).
34 Source: M. Toossi (2006), p. 26.
35 See S. Sandall (1987).
36 Toossi (2006), p. 22.
37 Toossi (2006), p. 36.
38 Source: Toossi (2006), p. 20. "The long term labor force projections are done every couple of years. The basis for the labor force projections is the annual averages of the labor force participation rate. Those include: anyone working either full time, part time (self-employed are included) or anyone who has been actively looking for a job within the last 4 weeks prior to the data collection which happens at the 12th of each month. . . . The data collector asks the persons in the sample and if the responder says that they have been actively looking for a job even from their computers at home and have sent in resumes, then they are counted as part of the labor force. And of course you know that housewives' work is not counted in the gross domestic product!" (Toossi, email of May 19, 2009).
39 C. Bennett (2007), pp. 55–6.
40 Census categories, undoubtedly, can be confusing and misleading. However, the reader should bear in mind that data are based on what individuals choose to self-select to describe themselves when filling out the forms, and it is not uncommon for individuals to fill in more than one category.
41 The highlighted portion is editorial emphasis added by the author of this book. Tallies that show race categories for Hispanics and non-Hispanics separately are available through the Census. See <http://quickfacts.census.gov/qfd/meta/long_RHI725200.htm> for more information. Note that anthropologists often refer to "Hispanics" as those inhabitants from the Iberian Peninsula (Spain and Portugal). For a brief but excellent overview regarding implications of workforce diversity for management, refer to T. Bateman and S. Snell (1996), Chapter 13.
42 Toossi (2006), p. 36.
43 Toossi (2006), p. 36.
44 J. Allen and E. Turner (1988), p. 27. The authors' illustration was created based on information from the former US Immigration and Naturalization Service which is

now US Citizen and Immigration Services (USCIS) under the umbrella of the Department of Homeland Security.
45 R. Monger and N. Rytina (2009). LPR status as migrant stock is much more useful than data regarding ebbs and flows of immigration for obvious reasons.
46 Monger and Rytina (2009), p. 4. Refer to "Profiles on Permanent Legal Residents" from the Dept. of Homeland Security at <http://www.dhs.gov/ximgtn/statistics/data/DSLPR07s.shtm> for LPR population characteristics information. This site is also a good resource for population characteristics such as age and employment data. For example, 2007 employment data show that 10 percent of the LPRs in California were employed in management, professional and related occupations, 4 percent in the services, 4.5 percent in sales and office occupations, 5 per cent in production, transportation, and materials-moving occupations, and so on.
47 See endnote 43: "Profiles on Permanent Legal Residents" from the Dept. of Homeland Security at <fhttp://www.dhs.gov/ximgtn/statistics/data/DSLPR07s.shtm>. For example, in the case of California, males outnumbered females in management and professional-related, service, sales and office, and production, transportation and materials-moving occupations; yet, women occupied more sales and office positions than males.
48 Monger and Rytina (2009).
49 M. Baghai *et al.* (2009), pp. 88–9.

4 Learning: one size does not fit all

1 E. Hall (1976), p. 152.
2 P. Penland (1984), p. 47.
3 S. Merriam and R. Caffarella (1991).
4 Numerous topologies of learning styles can be found in the literature specific to adult learning. Style diagnosis in organizations often relies upon self-assessment inventories or observation (by the facilitator). For further information on Kolb's topology, see D. Kolb (1984) and Valerie Krahe (1993).
5 Some refer to the "processing" portion of this definition, i.e., how people receive, store, retrieve and transform information as "cognitive styles." Others view "learning styles" and "cognitive styles" as synonymous. For a review summary of both, see Merriam and Caffarella (1991) and B. Ash (1986); also refer to Kolb (1984).
6 Barriers to (adult) learning and change in organizations are frequently described in terms of corporate cultural differences, structure, cost, and conflicts between individual goals and corporate goals. Cognitive differences are often overlooked and are, therefore, addressed in this book along with other complexities (e.g., national cultural tendencies [G. Hofstede, 1980]).
7 B. Hoffman and H. Dukas (1972), p. 19.
8 Hoffman and Dukas (1972), p. 255.
9 M. Kunihiro (1976), p. 269.
10 For more on this subject, refer to E. Hall (1976) and E. Hall and M. Hall (1990).
11 See E. Nathan (2008), p. 19, for further discussion.
12 Refer to Figure 1.2 and discussion in Chapter 1.
13 Merriam and Caffarella (1991), pp.159 and 179, respectively.
14 H. Bee (1987), p. 125.
15 See Note 5 above.
16 J. Cannon-Bowers and S. Tannenbaum (1991), p. 287.
17 D. Lee (1950), p. 93.
18 The human factors literature solves man–machine design problems. Of primary concern is the mind, i.e., the "central processing unit" stripped of context;

engineering is *the* factor of concern. For a review of cognitive psychology and information processing models, see W. Howell and N. Cooke (1987). It is noted, however, that several disciplines, anthropology included, have long debated whether all individuals process information similarly. See R. Shweder (1990), and M. Cole and S. Scribner (1974) for further discussion of this issue.

19 S. Biesheuvel (1949), p. 65.
20 See early references to M. Kunihiro (1976) in Chapter 2; refer also to Cole and Scribner (1974).
21 D. Wagner (1982), p. 107.
22 Hall (1976), p. 9. He points out that biologically man's visual apparatus enables him [her] to see simultaneously in many different ways.
23 For three years I was assistant editor of a journal published by the Comparative and International Education Society. In a phone conversation with one of our authors, Dr. Elaine Gerbert (then) of the Department of East Asian Languages at the University of Kansas, I mentioned that penmanship was my worst subject in grammar school. I also recalled my comfort with polychronic behavior. Through questioning, we both constructed how differently a US child is oriented to space than a Japanese child. Dr. Gerbert supplied the grid shown in Figure 3.1. She also confirmed the use of charts and graphs to reinforce procedural skills during early childhood education in Japan.
24 B. Edwards (1989), p. xiv.
25 The chapters and subtitles in her book, e.g., "Getting to Know Both Sides of Your Brain," "Crossing Over: Experiencing the Shift from Left to Right," point to many avenues for communication training and self-analysis.
26 Subsequent chapters and Appendix 6A provide examples of use of drawing and metaphor in communicating concepts, strategic planning efforts, and other activities where border zones must become porous in order to integrate diverse communication styles and preferences.
27 For more information regarding generational characteristics, see D. and J. Oblinger (2005), *Educating the Net Generation*; J. Beck and M. Wade (2004), *Got Game: How the Gamer Generation Is Reshaping Business Forever.*
28 E. Nathan (2008).
29 N. Gordon, and M. Steele (2005), p. 26; J. Clarey (2009).
30 See M. Milliron *et al.* (2008).
31 Entertainment Software Association (2009) <http://www.theesa.com/facts/index.asp>.
32 A. Carstens and J. Beck (2005).
33 M. Conner (2005).
34 J Feiertag and Z. Berge (2008), p. 462.
35 Feiertag and Berge (2008), p. 458. The authors also add that Generation N tends to enjoy group activities and desires continuous feedback. From personal experience in both teaching and training in the US and others of the Americas, I can support that these characteristics are largely true.
36 Beck and Wade (2004), p. 4.
37 Entertainment Software Association (2009) <http://www.theesa.com/facts/index.asp>.
38 J. Ford (1992), p. 3; also see J. Ford and L. Ford (1995).
39 Also see D. Nadler, "Concepts for the Management of Organizational Change," in Tushman *et al.* (1989) for more on research on change. The authors argue that participation is important in change as it tends to "reduce resistance, build ownerships of the change, and thus motivate people to make the change work." Yet these and others, e.g., the work of P. Senge (1990) specific to "learning organizations" and Moss Kanter (1989), specific to "collaborative forums," do not address how access in the participation process is to be facilitated.

40 See R. Downs and D. Stea (1973) who state that "human spatial behavior is dependent on the individual's cognitive map of the spatial environment," p. 9.
41 Limitations of research relating to these issues involve the need to duplicate work-place realities. Focus is often too short-term and/or procedural task-oriented, too experimental in design and low in context, too language-laden, too single-cultural in orientation (e.g., U. S. or other), and too pedagogy-oriented (rather than andra-gogy, or adult learner-oriented). A further consideration is that "cognitive mapping" involves symbols and connections which may vary from group to group and individual to individual.
42 Hall (1976), p. 74. Hall further states, "the solution to the problem of coping with increased complexity and greater demands on the system seems to lie in the pre-programming of the individual or organization. This is done by means of the 'contexting' process," p. 75.
43 The section heading is inspired by the work of Robert Gagné (1962). According to Gagné, identification of "what is to be learned" is a key agenda item in training and development design, but is often overlooked by researchers and trainers. This advice seems right on target as much today as it was over half a century ago, since making design choices, regardless of the demographic landscape of the labor pool, is not advisable without first auditing learning needs.
44 F. Casmir (1991), p. 233.
45 This company is devoted to *kaizen*. Additionally, self-managed and cross-functional teams characterize work design.
46 P. Senge (1990), p. 340.
47 Senge (1990), p. 341.

5 Intermezzo: the changing face of management

1 An Internet search (May 2009) under "immigration of foreign born," or "debate in (country) regarding immigration of foreign born" yields thousands to millions of sites addressing the subject and its historical precedents. For selected examples, a search of "immigration from Nicaragua to Costa Rica" yields over 5 million sites; over 24 and 26 million appear for Australia and the U.K., respectively. Numerous countries have actually "earned" a place on Wikipedia for discussion of the topic, their histories, the debates on the issue, and the implications to policy. For select examples, see <http://en.wikipedia.org/wiki/Immigration_to_the_United_Kingdom_(1922-present_day)> for the U.K.; for Australia, <http://en.wikipedia.org/wiki/Migratory_history_of_Australia>.
2 See Glossary for a definition of "diversity."
3 M. Gordon (1964), p. 104.
4 J. Cuber (1955), pp. 557–8.
5 Quoted in Gordon (1964), p. 94.
6 Gordon (1964), p. 99.
7 See R. Bogdan and S. Biklan (1992) for an excellent overview of the rise of anthro-pology and schools of thought within the field of sociology during the nineteenth and twentieth centuries, pp. 1–57. See also F. Boas (1932), R. Benedict (1934), and M. Mead (1928); the work of E. Sapir (1929) and B. Whorf (1939) also bear on this issue.
8 Refer to A. Weiner (1992), who discusses the lessons anthropology can offer across disciplines concerning issues of cultural diversity.
9 J. Campbell (1971), p. 576.
10 Campbell (1971), p. 575.
11 N. Adler, R. Doktor, and S.G. Redding (1986), p. 295.
12 R. Noe and K. Ford (1992).

13 A common expatriation issue involves adjustment to the new environment for the international assignee, spouse, and family. See the *Society for Human Resource Management/Commerce Clearing House Survey (SHRM/CCH Survey)* (1992) for issues concerning repatriation and expatriation that were concerns for developmental agendas.

14 See G. Hofstede (1980); Y. Kim and W. Gudykunst (1988), and S. Ronen's taxonomy of skills and attitudes (1989), as examples. Y. Yun Kim (1986) addresses perceptions, attitudes and other communication-related concepts among ethnic groups. Also refer to S. Black and M. Mendenhall (1990).

15 For more information on this issue see J. Campbell and M. Dunnette (1968), and overview by E. Potoker (1994).

16 M. Timpane and L. Miller-McNeil (1991).

17 This subject is addressed further in Chapter 6.

18 According to Audrey Edwards (1991), "discomfort with difference within the US may well be grounded in the very principles upon which 'America' was founded—e.g., 'all men are created equal', 'one nation under God'," etc., p. 46.

19 Gordon (1964), p. 111.

20 Gordon refers to this phenomenon as "structural pluralism."

21 Gordon (1964), p. 130.

22 Refer to M. Imai (1986), K. Nishiyama (1981), and T. Peters (1988) for more on this issue.

23 For a discussion and overview of the decline of productivity in the US see T. Peters, "Facing up to the Need for a Management Revolution", in M. Tushman *et al.* (1989), pp. 7–32.

24 This was a case argued before the Supreme Court in 1970. Pursuant to Title VII of the 1965 Civil Rights Act which prohibits discrimination because of race, color, religion, sex, or national origin, Black employees at the Duke Power Co. Dan River plant in Charlotte, North Carolina challenged their employer's practice of requiring a high school diploma or the passing of an intelligence test as a condition of employment or transfer to other jobs at the plant, particularly when there was no proof that either standard would be predictive of successful performance. They argued that the practice showed disparate treatment of Negroes (compared to white employees) that inherently kept them from obtaining higher paid positions in other departments. Negroes were permitted to work in only the Labor Department, where the lowest wages were paid.

25 R. Noe and K. Ford (1992), p. 360. They also highlight the importance of mentoring and experience-centered learning. R. Hanvey's work and the field of applied anthropology are concerned with similar issues.

26 Gordon (1964), pp. 264–5. G. Hofstede (1980) stated this somewhat similarly: "The survival of mankind will depend to a large extent on the ability of people who think differently to act together," p. 9.

27 Indeed, this is by no means a new question. Anthropologists have been asking this critical and challenging question for over a century. Refer to Renato Rosaldo (1989) as one example.

6 Management's new face

1 I have attempted to research previous editions of management education textbooks to determine how perceptions of the functions of management had evolved since the time of H. Fayol ([1916] 1949). Unfortunately, as publishing companies have undergone many life cycle changes, to include maturity, mergers, and death, my wish became a mission formidable if not near-to-impossible. It would still be interesting to do. One outcome would be a chart that categorizes functions and

roles since 1916 to the present in order to see how much change is reflected in contemporary management education literature. Perhaps there is a reader out there (who kept those books) who might wish to undertake this collaborative with me.

2 Refer to E. Potoker (1994).

3 H. Mintzberg (1998), p. 142. This is an advanced view from Mintzberg's college thesis days, and the publication which grew out of that, *The Nature of Managerial Work* (1973). At that time, he identified ten functional roles and summaries of behaviors related to each, respectively.

4 Mintzberg (1998), p. 142.

5 C. Lehman and D. Dufrene (1999), p. 4. Italics are added for emphasis. Also refer to R. Vecchio (2003) for further complementary discussion of the communication process (p. 286).

6 Channels are the physical and/or virtual carriers of the messages: the individuals, and/or computer-based mediums such as email, texting, discussion and bulletin boards, etc. In the context of work, channel choices often are *very* culturally constituted. Recall the Chapter 2 discussion of the importance of "face" in Japanese culture, as only one example. This issue is explored further in Chapter 9, "Communications Design Issues of the Future."

7 In Spier, Hallowell, Irving and Newman, eds. (1941).

8 Interviews in 2009 with seasoned professionals from the maritime sector provide extensive testimony to the importance of cross-cultural competencies to optimize decision-making at sea. Graduate students in maritime management (US/Maine Maritime Academy) also echo this need, particularly as foreign flagged ships and diverse crews travel waterways here and abroad.

9 This quote is from a May 29, 2009 email. The company name, by request, is not divulged. The system name (LTV) is fictitious to assure that no association can be made with the company.

10 Chief Engineer, Wm. Donnini, January 24, 1999 email; 2009 email phone conversation May 29, 2009 in collaboration with Captain Wm. Gatchell.

11 May 29, 2009 email from Aaron Paulino, Master of Vessels of less than 500 tons; mate of ongoing tugs.

12 These graphic illustrations can be so useful in so many ways. As example, one of my clients owns a catering business, and depends on part-time employees. Charting the critical path helped her organize activities more efficiently; it also communicated to the employees at a glance what would have to be done and when. She claims that was particularly important, given the cultural diversity among her employees.

13 R. Chase, N. Aquilano, and R. Robert Jacobs (2009), p. 65.

14 The balanced scorecard was popularized by R. Kaplan and D. Norton of the Harvard Business School in their book of the same name in 1996. It refers to a strategic planning and management system aimed to align and monitor vision and strategy of the organization with business activities and expectations of stakeholders. Many books and journal articles have advanced the subject since their seminal work, applying the idea that organizations should be viewed from a number of perspectives in order to develop metrics, collect data, and analyze the relationships to one another.

15 A dashboard generally refers to the key performance indicators that drive a business. As example, for Starbucks, one key driver is customer waiting times. For discussion of the dashboard and how to design it, see McGovern (2004).

16 For a brief overview between the difference between TQM and Six Sigma, refer to T. Jacowski (2009) at <http://ezinearticles.com/?Six-Sigma-vs.-Total-Quality-Management&id=296184>.

17 E. Potoker (1994).

18 For further discussion of the use of these tools in marketing, refer to Appendix 6A.

19 B. Edwards (1989). See Chapter 4.
20 E. Tufte (1990), p. 9.
21 R. Daft (2001), p. 357.
22 Refer to C. Christensen (1997), p. 144. This view is also frequently expressed in marketing circles.
23 G. Shaw *et al.* (1998), p. 42.
24 P. Northouse (2001), p. 3.
25 E. Tufte (1990), p. 9.
26 Also refer to discussion of organizational creativity in Potoker (1994), p. 193.

Appendix 6A

27 Reprinted with permission from J. Henderson, formerly of the Boy Scouts of America, North Shore District.
28 Gareth Morgan (2006), pp. 263–69.
29 See M. Maruyama (1963), J. Forrester (1958), C. West Churchman (1968). Also refer to Potoker, *et al.* (2007), pp. 193–4.
30 Refer to <http://www.skymark.com/resources/tools/relations_diagram.asp> for a further elaboration of the process and examples. Or, a search of "Relations Diagram" under <www.google.com> turns up over 10 million!
31 For an illustration of marketing's evolution, see <http://www.scribd.com/doc/468522/Marketing-Definitions>.
32 "Definition of Marketing (2007)" (2009) <http://www.marketingpower.com/AboutAMA/Pages/DefinitionofMarketing.aspx?sq=definition+of arketing>.
33 Scott Adams, author of *The Dilbert Principle* (1996), in parodying the activities and lack of understanding of what *marketing* and *marketers* do, suggests that the entrée to marketing begins with a two-drink minimum (p. 131). My challenge was real!
34 This idea is not new. P. Drucker (1954) suggested that the purpose of a business lies outside of itself. "It is the customer who determines what a business is" (p. 37).
35 Theodore Levitt (1960).
36 Michael Porter (1996), p. 61.
37 Drucker (1954), p. 20.
38 Portions that are in [brackets] are editorial clarifications.
39 David Aaker (1996).

7 Building learning organizations through learning landscapes

1 J. Kotter (1995), pp. 60 and 67, respectively.
2 Polychronic environments and monochronic environments are discussed in Chapter 2. Refer to E. Hall (1976) and E. and M. Hall 1990) for further discussion.
3 R. Wax (1971), p. 13; see also Magoroh Maruyama and Arthur Harkins (eds) (1978) for further insight into this issue.
4 M. Herskovits (1948).
5 American is used interchangeably with US "American" is how the organization referred to its US location.
6 To protect firm identity, program names are referred to only as "[p]" Programs aim to train individuals at different levels of responsibility, e.g., first-line supervisor level, department manager level, etc. It is important to note AM's enthusiasm about her work and role; this too was a common denominator among respondents.

7 This conference was held in a room that seated about 75 people. About 50 people attended. The room had tier seating—similar to a theater. Each row had permanent swivel seats and a continuous desk ledge for papers and water. I sat in the back (highest tier), so it was easy to view the reaction of the audience to the speaker. DH's presentation was the first after lunch. In discussing the company corporate philosophy, I observed attendees shaking their head (as if to ask, "how do they make it work?"); of course, how they make it work involves the subject of this entire book.

8 The role of corporate culture was a "discovery" derived from data analysis, rather than a research objective formulated prior to doing fieldwork.

9 While I did not ask SL what she meant by this statement, I understood her to mean that visual aids offered another vehicle for communication to those who are more reserved or less inclined (for cultural reasons) to participate readily in verbal discourse.

10 I have included a large portion of this interview as it also illustrates how—through the interview—meaning was constructed by both the respondent and the researcher through varied communication modes that became shared. It illustrates the interactive nature of qualitative research, and also why the terms "constructivist" and "interpretist" are frequently used interchangeably to describe qualitative research endeavor.

11 AM states in her interview, "we believe that our associates are our most important asset." It is noted that not only is there triangulation of *perspectives* across managerial levels, but also verbatim use of words and expressions. Note, as an example, the reference to respect for associates as synonymous with the term "human being"—used by the lathe operator from the supplier firm and also by the SVP.

12 Reiterating, the program is a real situation; the name of this program cannot be revealed for reasons explained. The name, in itself, conveys an interesting visual image regarding group creativity.

13 A portion of that developmental map, as an example, could be Ronen's (1989) taxonomy for the international assignee.

14 Data show that the SVP played a key role in establishment of the site that I visited. According to C, the SVP had been to many "one horse" towns in the US, i.e., he traveled to see company customers and sites throughout the US This was among the many strategic stories that were shared by associates.

15 Refer to Appendices 2A and 6A for examples of how visuals may be used for numerous purposes addressed in this case.

16 Another group worked on "Why dogs may have fleas?"; another, "Why are children misbehaving?"

17 Refer to E. Tufte (1990), p. 9, and Chapter 6 discussion.

18 J. Kotter (1995), p. 61.

19 R. Kelley (1988), pp. 144–8.

20 G. [Morgan] (1994), p. B28.

8 Best practices in IHRD

1 G. Hofstede, 1984.

2 For further discussion, refer to W.R. Tracey (1992), *Designing Training and Development Systems*.

3 P. Drucker (1954), p. 37.

4 D. Aaker (1996), p. 95: Value proposition is a key element of brand and branding. "It is a statement of the functional, emotional, and self-expressive benefits

delivered by the brand that provide value to the customer. An effective value proposition should lead to a brand–customer relationship and drive purchase decisions."

5   J. Collins (2001), pp. 90–119.
6   I. Berlin (1953).
7   Refer to Collins (2001; 2005) for further insight into the Hedgehog Concept and organizational examples.
8   R. Keidel (1984), p. 10.
9   For examples, see R. Daft (2007), p. 269, and D. Ancona, *et al.* (2005), pp. 58–9.
10 J. Flanagan (1954), p. 327.
11 Flanagan (1954), p. 328. Subsequent studies identified essential requirements for officers; others focused on failures of bombing missions. All these efforts pointed to the need to establish best practices for recruiting the right people.
12 Refer to "Competency and Position Analysis Questionnaires" (1974–2009). <http://www.paq.com/index.cfm?FuseAction=bulletins.job-analysis-questionnaire>.
13 The Job and Worker Characteristic Matrix is referred to in Figure 8.3 as "The CIT Matrix." The specific quote from Flanagan (1954), p. 327, justifies why the terms are used interchangeably. Flanagan explains the meaning of the term "incident" in the context of discussion of critical incident technique as follows: "By an incident is meant any observable human activity that is sufficiently complete in itself *to permit inferences and predictions to be made about the person performing the act.*" [The italicized portion is added herein for emphasis.]
14 L. Carter and P. Carmichael (2009), p. 16.
15 Refer to K. Neupert, C. Baughn, and T. Lam Dao (2005), "International Management Skills for Success in Asia."
16 Collins (2005), p. 41.

9 Communication design issues of the future

1   R. Moss Kanter (1989), p. 90.
2   Moss Kanter (1989), p. 89.
3   Refer to R. Lengel and R. Daft (1988) who referred to executives as "media artists" and "critics," p. 230.
4   For an expanded definition to apply herein: "Knowledge is a fluid mix of framed experience, values, contextual information, and expert insight that provides a framework for evaluating and incorporating new experiences and information. It originates and is applied in the minds of knowers. In organizations, it often becomes embedded not only in documents or repositories, but also in organizational routines, processes, practices, and norms" (T. H. Davenport and L. Prusak, 1998, p. 5).
5   Kivrak, Serkan *et al.* (2008).
6   T. Kontzer (2002), p. 65.
7   J. Van Maanen (1988), p. ix.
8   R. Lengel and R. Daft (1988), p. 226.
9   A. Pentland (2009), p. 37.
10 Pentland (2009), p. 37.
11 "Once Dismissed . . ." (2009), p. 81.
12 H. Andres (2002).
13 N. Kock (2001).
14 Refer to J. Purdy, P. Nye, and P.V. (Sundar) Balakrishnan (2000) for more information on this subject.
15 G. DeSanctis, M. Wright, and Lu Jiang (2001).
16 E. Nathan (2008).
17 F. Gamst (ed.) (1995), p. 149.

18 O. Lee (2000), p. 198.
19 Refer to G. Hofstede (1980), and earlier chapters.
20 See E. Hall (1976) and earlier chapters.
21 A. Massey *et al.* (2001), p. 8.
22 Nathan (2008).
23 Nathan (2008), p. 19.
24 D. Foster (1992), p. 80.
25 J. Feiertag and Z. Berge (2008), p. 458.
26 Refer to Jen-Hung Huang (2001).
27 P. Han and A. MacLaurin (2002), p. 35.
28 Han and MacLaurin (2002), p. 38.
29 R. Guimerà *et al.* (2002). These researchers studied the 1700 users' email network of the University Rovira I Virgili (URV) in Tarragona, Spain, and their work is similar in objectives to the HP study discussed.
30 Refer to R. Daft (2007), p. 10. Daft defines organizations as "(1) social entities that (2) are goal directed, (3) are designed and deliberately structured and coordinated activity systems, and (4) are linked to their external environments." Italics are added for emphasis.
31 M. Baba (2003), p. 3.
32 Baba (2003), p. 2.
33 Baba (1999).
34 J. Tyler, *et al.* (2003).
35 M. Milliron *et al.* (2008), p. 7. The authors recall several lines from the movie, *Field of Dreams*. This article provides further insight to discussions heretofore, and into the blended technological and other strategies that deserve consideration to build a new generation for learning.
36 See P. Woolliams and D. Gee (1992).
37 P. Honold (2000), p. 328.
38 Refer to Chapter 2 discussion of back-channeling (*aizuchi*), and also to Hall and Hall (1990).
39 See J. Deregowski (1973), S. Biesheuvel (1949) and Chapter 2, and G. Jahoda and H. McGurk (1982), who explore how one acquires the ability to identify objects represented two-dimensionally in pictures (p. 78).
40 H. Ishii (1990), pp. 48, 50.
41 Ishii believes that the advance of technology is driving HCI focus to shift from human *interfaces* to "human-*interaction* [emphasis added] mediated by computer and communication," p. 49.
42 Woolliams and D. Gee (1992), p. 305.
43 J. Felici (2002), p. 11. For more on the subject of Unicode and its advantages, see Reuven Lerner (2003).
44 R. Chandrakar (2002).
45 Email exchange dated July 28, 2003.
46 A. Dix *et al.* (1998), p. 3. Also see A. Sears and J. Jacko (2009), p. xiii, who illustrate that while HCI began within the computing world, many other disciplines have since made contributions in designing solutions.
47 R. Spitz (1993), p. 57. At the Marketing Management Conference held March 17–19, 1999 in Chicago, Ill., Plenary Session speaker (March 18), Bill Wiggenhorn, Vice President of Training and Education, Motorola Inc., and President of Motorola University, mentioned that, in HR recruiting, they are turning more and more to graduates in the fine arts and music.
48 Spitz, p. 57.
49 R. Shweder (1990), p. 1.
50 Shweder (1990), p. 4.

51 Shweder (1990), p. 7.
52 Shweder (1990), p. 7.
53 Shweder (1990), p. 2.
54 C. Blakemore (1973), p. 9.
55 "Intentional worlds," according to Shweder, "are human artifactual worlds popu-
lated with products of our own design (p. 2)." The "intentional world" of Shweder
(1990) and the "culturally constituted behavioral environments" of Hallowell
(1955) are viewed to be synonymous. See Chapter 2 for discussion of culture and
Hallowell.
56 Sears and Jacko (2009), p. 64.
57 M. Marquardt and N. Berger (2000), p. 1.
58 D. Tapscott *et al.* (2000), p. ix.
59 W. Chan Kim, and Renée Mauborgne (1992), p. 128.

10 The future of IHRD

1 Note that there is no intention by the author to trace the evolution of IHRD from
HRM over the past century since a historical overview falls beyond the scope and
purpose of this book. Only those historical factors that are useful to formulate a
contemporary definition of IHRD are captured herein.
2 F. Taylor (1947), pp. 45–6.
3 Fieldwork by the author illustrates, however, that "human resources" *as a department* does not always garner a place alongside of strategic planners. This issue
remains a subject for another research endeavor.
4 C. Zheng and D. Lamond (2009).
5 D. Briscoe and R. Schuler (2004), p. 20.
6 D. Briscoe, R. Schuler, and L.Claus (2009), p. 20.
7 O. Shenkar (1995), p. 11.
8 R. Swanson, and E. Holton (2009), p. 4.
9 G. McLean, and L. McLean (2001), p. 322.
10 Swanson, and Holton (2009), p. 422.
11 W. French, C. Bell, and R. Zawacki (2005), p. viii.
12 L. Sullivan (1896). See <http://academics.triton.edu/faculty/fheitzman/
tallofficebuilding.html> for the origin of this famous, and often misquoted
statement by the famous US architect.
13 All interviews followed a structured, open-ended format; the standardized questions were sent in advance of the personal interview. This is a work in progress;
while the qualitative research goes forward, it is not just in time (JIT) enough to
meet publication deadlines for the second edition of this book.
14 For further information regarding the "ladder of inference," see C. Argyris (1990)
and P. Senge (1994, pp. 242–61). Also refer to G. Morgan (2006) and his discussion of "double-loop" learning, pp. 84–91.
15 See Chapter 4 for discussion of generational differences and implications for
organizational challenges.
16 A.M. Osman-Gani and W. Tan (2005), p. 42.
17 D. Hall (1976), p. 201.
18 D. Hall (1996), p. 8.
19 H. Gardner (2006), p. 37.

Glossary

1 Erika Bourguignon (1979), p. 216.
2 L. Gómez-Mejía, D. Balkin, and R. Cardy (2010), p. 156.

3 D. Brisco and R. Schuler (2004), p. 20.
4 R. Monger and N. Rytina (2009). LPR status as migrant stock is much more useful than data regarding ebbs and flows of immigration, for obvious reasons.
5 Robert Lengel and Richard Daft (1988), p. 225.
6 C.W. Hill (2009), p. 43.

Glossary

action chains: refer to the sequencing of events, the protocols, that characterize and guide social activities (E. Hall, 1976).

assimilation (and "acculturation"): these are used interchangeably in this discussion, and generally refer to the meeting of individuals and/or groups of different cultures that result in changes in the original cultural patterns of either or both.

asynchronous courses (and delivery modes): are courses that allow students to attend class on their own schedule. The student logs in to lectures for a certain amount of time per week to view text, presentations, exercises, audio/video clips, and/or leave messages on discussion boards.

best practice: refers to identifying and consistently executing the optimum way of doing a particular activity or process(es).

brain gain: herein this is conceptually synonymous with *returning migration*, referring to those people who return to their country of origin for at least a year having been hosted by another country previously for short- or long-term stay. See the "International Migration Outlook: SOPEMI—2008," pp. 164. <http://www.oecd.org/datapecd/30/13/41275373.pdf>

business: activities involving the production and/or exchange of goods, and/or the rendering of services to the public (Houston, 1990, ERIC Thesaurus). "Business" and "industry" are used interchangeably in this discussion.

code of law: the legal system that influences work practices.

cognition: refers to how individuals perceive, process and organize information from their environments.

command economy (or a planned economy): an economy that relies on a centralized government to control all or most factors of production. Government makes allocation and production decisions, or what to produce, how much to produce, and for whom to produce.

communication: the interchange of thoughts or opinions through shared symbols.

computer-based technologies: refer to those of computer-mediated communication, business-to-business and consumer transactions via electronic commerce, and management information systems within and between individuals, groups, and within and across organizations. A **computer**

may include any technology ranging from a desktop computer to a large-scale computer system, a process control system or an embedded system. The system may include non-computerized parts, including other people.

computer-mediated communication systems (CMCS):   refer to technology networks associated with electronic mail and other computerized conferencing and "social space" type of software. This is not an all-encompassing definition, but one that serves the scope and focus of this book.

critical incident technique (CIT):   refers to a particular methodology of collecting significant information about the job itself, and the worker behaviors that are associated with incidents themselves.

critical path: refers to "the longest sequence of [consecutive] connected activities to be completed [for a project] with zero slack time." (Richard Chase, Nicholas Aquilano, and F. Robert Jacobs (1998), p. 57.

culture: no one definition adequately defines culture. Please see Chapter 1.

data mining: refers to retrieval of information from electronic databases.

data warehousing: refers to storage of information on electronic databases.

demographic profile: refers to workforce characteristics such as age, ethnicity, income, gender.

demographics: the gender, income, racial, age, ethnic, educational attainment, and nationality profile of a population.

digital capital: refers to the ability to store information such as sound, graphics, text, and video by computer. It is considered a critical component among other elements of capital required for effective knowledge management in contemporary times. See Chapter 7 for further information.

dimensions: categories of job performance.

diversity: refers to variance in educational levels, age, gender, race, ethnicity, sexual orientation, disability, world views, patterns of cognition among individuals. Diversity training focuses on *both* similarities and differences among peoples.

effective: achieving goals.

efficient: achieving goals with the least (optimum) amount of resources.

emic perspective: "the emic approach generally yields a description of a cultural system from the inside," or a culturally laden view. Also refer to **etic perspective** below.[1]

enculturation: refers to the socialization process that societies pursue to integrate new members into their ranks.

ethnic group: refers to a social group that distinguishes themselves from others by race, religion and/or national origin.

ethnocentrism: refers to the expectations that one acquires over time as a member of a particular cultural or subcultural group. Alternatively stated, it is the expectation that work "happens"—meaning it is organized, has similar meanings, and is driven by the same web of rules as in one's own culture.

etic perspective: the etic perspective is culture-free, and considered to be a universalist view.

explicit knowledge: knowledge that can be codified rather easily.

extranets: refer to computer networks that allow the flow of information via the Internet between the organization and elements of its external environment.

globalization: is defined herein from an economic perspective. It refers to the integration of national economies through technology, migration, capital flows, and trade.

HCI: the field of human–computer interaction (HCI) addresses the relationship between people and computers, by asking how one should design computer systems to meet the needs of the people who use them.

Hispanics: are generally defined as Spanish-speaking of *any* race. See Chapter 3 for more detailed discussion.

human–computer interaction (HCI):   refers to the relationship between people and computers. HCI is a field of study concerned with the design of computer systems to meet the needs of users, i.e., the people who use them. Also refer to **computer-based technologies** (above).

human resource management: is a field devoted to effective alignment and engagement of its resources to meet and exceed its strategic objectives.

human resource planning: refers to "the process an organization uses to ensure that it has the right amount of people to deliver a particular level of output or services in the future."[2]

hypertext and hypertext systems: these are generally those communication choices that contain a combination of text—a broad term for written words, graphics, and other kinds of media such as audio, video, and animation. They are non-linear in nature.

industry: enterprises of production or manufacturing that utilize relatively large amounts of labor and capital (Houston, 1990). Also see "business" (above).

information: is derived from raw data—facts and figures—that have been organized to explain some phenomenon.

interaction: means "any communication between a user and computer, be it direct or indirect (Dix et al., 1998, p. 3)."

international human resource development (IHRD):   focuses on the commitment to progress the competencies, and optimize the effectiveness and motivation of those engaged in work with individuals and groups in diverse multicultural internal and external settings.

international human resource management (IHRM):   "is about understanding, researching, applying and revising all human resource activities in their internal and external contexts . . . to enhance the experience of multiple stakeholders, including investors, customers, employees, partners, suppliers, environment and society"[3] (emphasis in original removed).

intranets: refer to computer networks that enable data sharing and communication within an organization and its various workstations.

job analysis: refers to the process of capturing work-related information important to job decision-making and job design. This is often done through observation, interviews, and/or through diaries kept by the employee/employees.

job design: a process where work is organized around job tasks, responsibilities and duties of a particular job position or job positions.

kaizen: generally associated with the quality control movement, and is Japanese for "continuous improvement."

knowledge: refers to information that is learned and applied to use.

knowledge management: how an organization develops its capacity to warehouse, mine, share and utilize information with its stakeholders.

language: the expression of thoughts and feelings through verbal or written communication. The term "discourse" is also used to refer to communication, whether oral or written. Verbal language or discourse refers to communication via the use of words and articulate speech. "Language" generally refers to a system of voice sounds, gestures, written symbols and rules to communicate thoughts and feelings.

learning: changes in individual, group and/or organizational knowledge and/or behavior due to formal and informal training and/or experience.

learning landscapes: a holistic visual representation of planning, processes, developmental agendas and other organizational activities that contemporary and future managers are challenged to create in order to maximize organizational and intercultural communication (Potoker, 1994).

legal permanent resident: a legal permanent resident (LPR), or "green card" recipient is defined by immigration law as a person who has been granted lawful permanent residence in the United States. Permanent resident status confers certain rights and responsibilities. For example, LPRs may live and work permanently anywhere in the United States, own property, and attend public schools, colleges, and universities. They may also join certain branches of the Armed Forces, and apply to become US citizens if they meet certain eligibility requirements.[4]

management: a creative process involving the integration of planning, communicating, organizing, directing (leading) and controlling of human and material resources to accomplish goals and objectives.

media richness: refers to "the information-carrying capacity of media."[5]

migrant stock: generally this refers to the numbers of non-nationals residing in a specific location at a particular point in time.

nationality: refers to one's country of origin.

network planning and control methods: refer to graphic representations of project steps and the timing and linkages between the steps (Dessler and Phillips, 2008, p. 240.)

nonverbal communication (NVC): communication other than oral and written discourse, e.g., visual cues and spatial relationships. Chapter 1 discusses the scope of this term in more detail (see also "**communication**" above).

"NVC strategies": are nonverbal communication skills utilized in managing and planning. See also, **"strategy."**

OECD: the Organization for Economic Cooperation and Development. See <http://www.oecd.org>.

operations control methods: these aim to reach medium-term goals (**tactical goals**), which also move the organization to satisfying its long-term objectives (**strategic goals**).

operations management: the everyday work that converts factors of production into goods and services.

organization: a structured social system consisting of groups and individuals working together to attain a common goal (Greenberg and Baron, 1993, p. 8). Another definition—a favorite one used by the author of this book in teaching organizational behavior, theory and design—is by R. Daft (2007), who describes organizations as, "(1)social entities that (2) are goal-directed, (3) are designed as deliberately structured and coordinated activity systems, and (4) are linked to the external environment. My favorite part of Daft's perspective is the following: "Organizations are hard to see. We see outcroppings, such as a tall building or a computer workstation or a friendly employee; but the whole organization is vague and abstract and may be scattered among several locations" (p. 10). To help managers transspect (Hanvey, 1975), decode, and communicate the "unseen" and the unheard is a primary intention of this book.

organizational audit: refers to a periodic review of alignment/fit between the organization's strategic direction—or its mission and vision, with its environment, human resources, mid- and short-term activities, and its organizational architecture or design.

organizational culture: those shared values and norms that differentiate one organization from another. Shared values and norms define "what is important around here. They provide direction, meaning, and energy for organizational members as they pursue organizational success" (Higgins, 1991, p. 387). "Organizational culture" is used interchangeably with "organizational philosophy" and "corporate culture." Alternatively stated, "corporate culture" refers to the pattern of assumptions and the organizational philosophy that drives a business when dealing with its internal and external environments.

perspectives consciousness: "the recognition or awareness on the part of the individual that he or she has a view of the world that is not universally shared, that this view of the world has been and continues to be shaped by influences that often escape conscious detection, and that others have views of the world that are profoundly different from one's own" (R. Hanvey, 1975, p. 85).

PERT: a program evaluation review technique that shows each event in relationship to another.

political economy: refers to "the interdependent combination of a country's political, economic and legal systems."[6]

project: "a series of interrelated activities aimed at producing a major, coordinated product or service" (Dessler and Phillips, 2008, p. 240).

qualitative research: research that focuses upon context,—i.e., where data tend to be collected in the field as opposed to laboratories or other researcher-controlled sites; the researcher generally frequents places in which events naturally occur (Bogdan and Biklen, 1992, p. 3). The term "case study" refers to an examination of one (organizational) setting.

quality: a standard that meets (and exceeds) the expectations of an organization's internal and external customers.

quality improvement tools (of *communication*): the visual representation of processes and interrelated activities for control of **quality** (above).

race: refers to genetically transmitted and inherited traits of physical appearance, e.g., Negroid, Caucasian, Malayan, Native American, Mongoloid.

relationship marketing: generally refers to the development of long-term relationships with internal customers and stakeholders,—e.g., "associates," and external customers and stakeholders along the physical supply chain.

strategic planning: this level of planning aims at the long-term reason for the business to exist and to continue to satisfy customer needs. **Strategic planners** are informed by research of the external and internal and external business environments. The organization's *raison d'être* is embodied in its vision and mission statements.

strategy|strategies: "skill[s] in managing or planning . . ." (1983, Webster's New Twentieth Dictionary, p. 1799).

supply chain management: cooperatively integrating the functions of management with suppliers, customers—with all who provide inputs contributing to the organization's outputs. The supply chain may also be considered the **value chain**.

synchronous courses (and delivery modes): courses that take place in real time with live instructor–student and/or student–student participation and interaction. As an example, it might be a course that is offered three times per week, with attendance required. Live chat rooms, audio/video conferencing, and/or real-time presence of teachers and students are examples of synchronous deliveries.

system: a group of related entities that receives inputs, adds value to them, and produces outputs to achieve goals at a strategic, tactical and/or operational level. (Inspired by Nadler and Hibino, 1990.)

training (also **training methods and training design**): planned learning experiences, approaches, and/or procedures designed to help groups or individuals improve, acquire (and/or recognize the need for) skills, attitudes and knowledge required for specific activities or functions in an organizational setting or settings.

training rigor: generally refers to the degree of cognitive involvement of the trainee and the duration and intensity of the program.

training system variables: are "interacting and integrated subsystems" of the workplace (see Tracey, 1992, pp. 196–7 for further discussion). They include, but are not limited to, contextual characteristics—e.g., the instructors, the trainees, the nature of the organization and its goals, and the organization's external environments.

transspection: a process of placing oneself in the mind of another and endeavoring to learn their beliefs and assumptions.

visual cues: refer to actions or symbols that are representative of a concept and/or something to be said or done.

wikis: refer to sites that allow simultaneous content development by multiple authors.

work: refers to all those purposeful activities that contribute to achieving human (to include organizational, community, and societal) needs, and aimed to affect in whole or in part physical and/or virtual environments.

workflow analysis: a review of how work moves from the customer through the organization.

working styles: refers to preferred ways of accomplishing work, learning, and communicating.

Bibliography

Aaker, David. (1996). *Building strong brands*. New York: The Free Press.

Adams, Scott. (1996). *The Dilbert principle*. New York: HarperBusiness.

Adler, Nancy, Doktor, Robert, and Redding, S. Gordon. (1986). From the Atlantic to the Pacific century: Cross-cultural management reviewed. *Journal of Management*, 12: 295–318.

'All in a day's work.' (2001). *Harvard Business Review*, 79(11): 54–66.

All-Academy-Journals call for papers: Special research forum on change and development in a pluralistic world. *Academy of Management Executive*, 12(4): 7–9.

Allen, James, and Eugene Turner. (1988). Where to find the new immigrants. *American Demographics*, 10(9), 22–7.

Ancona, Deborah, Kochan, Thomas, Scully, Maureen, Van Maanen, John, and Westney and D. Eleanor (2005). *Managing for the future*, 3rd edn. Cincinnati: Thomson-South-Western College Publishing (Cengage).

Andres, Hayward. (2002). A comparison of face-to-face and virtual software development teams. *Team Performance Management*, 8(1/2): 39–48.

Applebaum, Herbert. (1981). *Royal blue: The culture of construction workers*. New York: Holt, Rinehart and Winston.

—— (1984a). *Work in market and industrial societies*. Albany: State University of New York Press.

—— (ed.). (1984b). *Work in non-market and transitional societies*. Albany: State University of New York Press.

—— (1996). *Colonial Americans at work*. Lanham, MD: University Press of America, Inc.

Arendt, Hannah. (1958). *The human condition*. Chicago: The University of Chicago Press.

Argyris, Chris. (1990). *Overcoming organizational defenses: facilitating organizational learning*. Wellesley, MA: Allyn and Bacon.

Armstrong, Nancy. (2003). *Field guide to gestures: How to identify and interpret virtually every gesture known to man*. Philadelphia: Quirk Books.

Ash, Barbara. (1986). Identifying learning styles and matching strategies for teaching and learning. (ERIC Document Reproduction Service No. ED270142). *ASTD Communicator*. (1993, April). Central Ohio Chapter, pp. 1–2.

Ausubel, David. (1960). The use of advance organizers in learning and retention of meaningful material. *Journal of Educational Psychology*, 51: 267–72.

Awanchara, Susumu. (1990). Latin America's *nikkei* flock "home" to the Land of the Rising Yen. *Far Eastern Economic Review*, 149: 34–6.

Baba, Marietta. (2003). *Applications: Anthropological practice*. Retrieved, April 10, 2003 from <http://www.msu.edu/~mbaba/anthro_practice.html>.

—— (1999). Dangerous liaisons: Trust, distrust, and information technology in American work organizations. *Human Organization*, 58(3): 331–46.

—— (1995). Work and technology in modern industry. In Frederick Gamst (ed.), *The Meaning of Work: Considerations for the Twenty-First Century* (pp. 120–46). Albany: State University of New York Press.

Baghai, Mehrdad, Smit, Sven, and Viguerie, Patrick. (2009). Is your growth strategy flying blind? *Harvard Business Review*, 87(5): 86–96.

Ball, Stephen. (1990). Self-doubt and soft data: Social and technical trajectories in ethnographic fieldwork. *Qualitative Studies in Education*, 3: 157–71.

Barker, Roger G. (1968). *Ecological psychology*. Stanford, CA.: Stanford University Press.

Barnes, Sue, and Greller, Leonore. (1994). Computer-mediated communication in the organization. *Communication Education*, 43(2): 128–42.

Barnland, Dean (1989). *Communicative styles of Japanese and Americans: Images and realities*. Belmont, CA: Wadsworth Publishing Co.

Bartlett, Christopher, and Ghoshal, Sumantra. (1991). *Managing across borders: The transnational solution*. Boston, MA: Harvard Business Press.

Bateman, Thomas, and Snell, Scott. (1996). *Management: Building competitive advantage* (3rd edn). Chicago: Irwin.

Beck, John, and Wade, Mitchell. (2004). *Got game: How the gamer generation is reshaping business forever*. Boston, MA: Harvard Business School Press.

Bee, Helen. (1987). *The journey of adulthood*. N.Y.: Macmillan Publishing Co.

Benedict, Ruth. (1934). *Patterns of culture*: Cambridge, MA: The Riverside Press.

Bennett, Christine. (2007). *Comprehensive multicultural education*. 6th edn. Boston, MA: Pearson.

Bennhold, Katrin. (2008). Sarkozy reverses himself on 35-hr. week. *International Herald Tribune*. <http://www.iht.com/articles/2008/01/10/europe/sarkozy.php>.

Bennis, W. and Joan Goldsmith. (1994). *Learning to lead: A workbook on becoming a leader*. Reading: Addison-Wesley Publishing Company, Inc.

Berlin, Isaiah (1953). *The Hedgehog and the Fox: An Essay on Tolstoy's View of History*. New York: Simon and Schuster.

Bianco, T., and Barkley, S. (2001). Working style or annoying habit? *Office Pro*, 61(6): 19–21.

Biesheuvel, S. (1949). Psychological tests and their application to non-European peoples. In Douglas Price-Williams (ed.) (1970). *Cross-Cultural Studies: Selected Readings* (pp. 57–75). Baltimore, MD: Penguin Books.

Black, J. Stewart, and Mendenhall, Mark. (1990). Cross-cultural training effectiveness: A review and a theoretical framework for future research. *Academy of Management Review*, 15(1): 113–36.

Blakemore, Colin. (1973). The baffled brain. In R. L. Gregory, and E. H. Gombrich (eds.), *Illusion in Nature and Art* (pp. 9–48). New York: Charles Scribner's Sons.

Boas, Franz (1932). *Anthropology and modern life*. N.Y.: W. W. Norton & Co., Inc.

Bogdan, Robert, and Biklen, Sari. (1992). *Qualitative research in education: An introduction to theory and methods*. Boston, MA: Allyn and Bacon.

Bourguignon, Erika. (1979). *Psychological anthropology: An introduction to human nature and cultural differences*. New York: Holt, Rinehart and Winston.

Briscoe, Dennis, and Schuler, Randall. (2004). *International human resource management*. Abingdon: Routledge UK.

Briscoe, Dennis, Schuler, Randall, and Claus, Lisbeth. (2009). *International human resource management: Policies and practices for multinational enterprises*. Abingdon: Routledge UK.

Cairncross, Frances. (2002). *The company of the future*. Boston, MA: Harvard Business School Press.

Campbell, John. (1971). Personnel training and development. *Annual Review of Psychology*, 22: 565–602.

Campbell, John, and Dunnette, Marvin. (1968). Effectiveness of T-Group experiences in managerial development. *Psychological Bulletin*, 70: 73–104.

Cannon-Bowers, Janis, and Tannenbaum, Scott. (1991). Toward an integration of training theory and technique. *Human Factors*, 33: 281–92.

Carroll, Raymonde. (1988). *Cultural misunderstandings: The French-American experience* (trans. Carol Volk; French edn. 1987). Chicago: University of Chicago Press.

Carstens, Adam, and Beck, John. (2005). Get ready for the gamer generation. *TechTrends*, 49(3): 22–5.

Carter, Louis, and Carmichael, Patrick. (2009). Best practices go beyond benchmarking. *Leadership Excellence*, 26(11): 16–17.

Casmir, Fred. (1991). Introduction: Culture, communication and education. *Communication Education*, 40(3): 229–34.

Chandrakar, Rajesh. (2002). Multi-script bibliographic database: An Indian perspective. *Online Information Review*, 27(4): 246.

Chase, Richard, Nicholas Aquilano, and F. Robert Jacobs. (2009). *Production and operations management: Manufacturing and services*. 8th edn. Burr Ridge: Irwin McGraw-Hill.

Christensen, Clayton. (1997). Making strategy: Learning by doing. *Harvard Business Review*, 75(6): 141–56.

Churchman, C. West (1968). *The Systems Approach*. New York: Dell Publishing Company.

Civilian labor force and participation rates with projections: 1970 to 2005. Table No. 627. (1995). *Statistical Abstracts of the United States*: Washington, D.C.: U. S. Bureau of the Census.

Clarey, Janet. (2009). Multi-generational learning in the workplace. Retrieved February 28, 2009 from <http://www.brandon- hall.com/publications/generationallearning/generationallearning.shtml>.

Cole, Michael, and Scribner, Sylvia. (1974). *Culture and thought: A psychological introduction*. N.Y.: John Wiley & Sons.

Collingwood, Harris. (ed.). (2001). Leadership's first commandment: Know thyself. *Harvard Business Review*, 79(11): 8.

Collins, James. (2001). *Good to great: Why some companies make the leap—and others don't*. N.Y.: Harper Business.

—— (2005). *Good to great and the social sectors: Why business thinking is not the answer: A monograph to accompany Good to great*. Boulder, CO: Jim Collins.

Competency and position analysis questionnaires. (1974–2009). Paq Services, Inc. online at <http://www.paq.com/index.cfm?FuseAction=bulletins.job-analysis-questionnaire>.

Conner, Marcia. (2005). Andragogy + pedagogy. *The Ageless Learner*. Retrieved January 5, 2005 from <http://agelesslearner.com/intros/andragogy.html>.

Crump, Larry. (1989). Japanese managers—Western workers: Cross-cultural training and development issues. *The Journal of Management Development*, 8: 48–55.

Cuber, John. (1955). *Sociology: A synopsis of principles*. N.Y.: Appleton-Century-Crofts.

Daft, Richard. (2007). *Organizational theory and design* 9th edn. Cincinnati: South-Western College Publishing.

Dalby, Liza (1985). *Geisha*. N.Y.: Vintage Books.

Davenport, Tom, and Prusak, Laurence (1998). *What do we talk about when we talk about knowledge?* Boston, MA: Harvard Business School Press.

Davis, Clark. (2000). *Company Men: White-collar life & corporate cultures in Los Angeles, 1892–1941*. Baltimore, MD: Johns Hopkins University Press.

Decker, Phillip, and Nathan, Barry. (1985). *Behavior modeling training*. New York: Praeger.

"Definition of Marketing (2007)," (2009). Retrieved May 27, 2009 from <http://www.marketingpower.com/AboutAMA/Pages/DefinitionofMarketing.aspx?sq=definition+of+marketing>.

Demography report: Meeting social needs in an ageing society. Executive Summary. Brussels: Commission of the European Communities. Retrieved May 3, 2009 from <http://ec.europa.eu/social/main.jsp?langId=en&catId=89&newsId=419>.

Deregowski, Jan. (1973). Illusion and culture. In R. L. Gregory, and E. H. Gombrich (eds.), *Illusion in nature and art* (pp. 161–92). New York: Charles Scribner's Sons.

deRoche, C. (2001). Women's work in an Acadian Village. In Eileen Smith-Piovesan and Carol Corbin (eds.), *Women shaping Cape Breton cultural communities* (pp. 161–79). Sydney, Nova Scotia: University College of Cape Breton Press.

DeSanctis, Gerardine, Matthew Wright, and Lu Jiang. (2001). Building a global learning community. *Communications of the Association of Computing Machinery (ACM)*, 44(12): 80–2.

Dessler, Gary, and Phillips, Jean. (2008). *Managing NOW!*: Boston, MA: Houghton Mifflin.

Dicle, Ulku, et al. (1988). Human resources management practices in Japanese organizations in the United States. *Public Personnel Management*, 17: 331–9.

Dictionary of Occupational Titles (DOT). (1991). US Dept. of Labor, Office of Administrative Law Judges.

Di Mare, Lesley. (1990). *Ma* and Japan. *The Southern Communication Journal*, 55: 319–28.

Dix, Alan, Finlay, Janet, Abowd, Gregory, and Beale, Russell. (1998). *Human-computer interaction*. Hertfordshire (UK): Prentice Hall Europe.

Downs, Roger, and Stea, David. (1973). Cognitive maps and spatial behavior: Process and products. In Roger Downs and David Stea (eds.), *Image and Environment* (pp. 8–26). Chicago: Aldine Publishing Co.

Drucker, Peter. (1954). *The practice of management*. New York: Harper & Row.

Dunnigan, James, and Daniel Masterson. (1997). *The way of the warrior: Business tactics and techniques from history's twelve greatest generals*. New York: St. Martin's Press.

Earley, P. Christopher. (1987). Intercultural training for managers: A comparison of documentary and interpersonal methods. *Academy of Management Journal*, 30: 685–98.

Edwards, Audrey. (1991). The enlightened manager: How to treat all your employees fairly. *Woman's World*, 16: 45–51.

Edwards, Betty. (1989). *Drawing on the right side of the brain*. N.Y.: Penguin Putnam, Inc.

Elashmawi, Farid. (1997). Problems and possibilities in the global marketplace. *Trade & Culture*, 5(2): 15–16.

Employment in Europe 2001: Recent trends and prospects. (2001). Luxembourg: European Communities. Retrieved May 4, 2008 from <http://www.eurofound. europa.eu/eiro/2001/07/feature/eu0107230f.htm>.

English silver hallmarks 1736–1975. (2003). Retrieved November 22, 2002 from <http://www.horologia.co.uk/hallmarks1.html>.

Entertainment Software Association (2009). *Industry facts*. Retrieved May 15, 2009 from <http://www.theesa.com/facts/index.asp>.

Ester, Peter, and Krieger, Hubert (2008). *Labour mobility in a transatlantic perspective—Conference Report*. European Foundation for the Improvement of Living and Working Conditions. Retrieved May 3, 2009 from <http://www. eurofound.europa.eu/publications/htmlfiles/ef0826.htm>.

Europe's demographic future: Facts and figures. (2007). Brussels: Commission of the European Communities. Retrieved May 3, 2009 from <http://ec.europa.eu/social/ main.jsp?langId=en&catId=89&newsId=419>.

Eurostat Yearbook (2002), 1–26. Retrieved June 28, 2002 from <http://europa.eu.int/ comm/eurostat/>.

Fayol, Henri. ([1916]1949). *General and industrial management* (C. Storrs, Trans.). London: Pitman.

Feiertag, Jeff, and Berge, Zane. (2008). Training Generation N: How educators should approach the Net Generation. *Education + Training*, 50(6): 457–64.

Felici, Jim. (2002). Unicode: The quiet revolution. *The Seybold Report Analyzing Publishing Technologies*, 2(10): 11–15.

Field, Frank, and Soames, Nicolas. (2008). Balanced migration: A new approach to controlling migration. *Migrationwatch UK*. Retrieved Feb. 2, 2009 from <http:// www.migrationwatchuk.com/balancedmigration.pdf>.

Flanagan, John. (1954). The critical incident technique. *Psychological Bulletin*, 51(4): 327–58.

Ford, Jeffrey. (1992). *Producing change in organizations: Getting into communication*. Working Paper. The Ohio State University.

Ford, Jeffrey, and Laurie Ford. (1995). The role of conversations in producing intentional change in organizations. *The Academy of Management Review*, 20: 541–70.

Forrester, Jay. (1958). Industrial dynamics: A major breakthrough for decision makers. *The Harvard Business Review*, 38: 37–66.

Foster, Dean. (1992). *Bargaining across borders: How to negotiate business successfully anywhere in the world*. New York: McGraw-Hill.

Freedman, Audrey. (1982). Japanese management of US work forces. *Research bulletin*, 119, N.Y.: The Conference Board, Inc.

French, Wendell, Bell, Cecil, and Zawacki, Roberta. (2005). *Organizational development and transformation*. New York: McGraw-Hill/Irwin.

Gagné, Robert. (1962). Military training and learning. *American Psychologist*, 17: 83–91.

—— (1984). Learning outcomes and their effects. *American Psychologist*, 39: 377–85.

Gamst, Frederick. (ed.). (1995). *The meaning of work: Considerations for the twenty-first century.* Albany: State University of New York Press.

Gardner, Howard. (2006). The synthesizing leader. *Harvard Business Review,* 84(2): 36–7.

Garfinkel, Harold, and Sacks, Harvey. (1970). On formal structures of practical actions. In John McKinney and Edward Tiryakian (eds.), *Theoretical sociology* (pp. 337–66). New York: Meredith Corporation.

Glaser, Barney, and Strauss, Anselm. (1967). *The discovery of grounded theory: Strategies for qualitative research.* Chicago: Aldine.

Glaser, Robert. (1990). The reemergence of learning theory within instructional research. *American Psychologist,* 45: 29–39.

Glesne, Corrine, and Peshkin, Alan. (1992). *Becoming qualitative researchers: An introduction.* White Plains, NY: Longman Publishing Co.

Goffman, Erving. (1971). *Relations in public.* N.Y.: Basic Books, Inc.

Goldstein, Irwin. (1986). *Training in organizations: Needs assessment, development, and evaluation.* (2nd edn). Pacific Grove, CA.: Cole Publishing Co.

Goldstein, Irwin, and Gilliam, Patrice. (1990). Training system issues in the year 2000. *American Psychologist,* 45: 134–43.

Gómez-Mejía, Louis, Balkin, David, and Cardy, Robert. (2010). *Managing human resources.* 6th edn. Upper Saddle River, NJ: Prentice Hall.

Gordon, Milton. (1964). *Assimilation in American life: The role of race, religion, and national origins.* New York: Oxford University Press.

Gordon, Virginia, and Steele, Margaret. (2005) The advising workplace: Generational differences and challenges. *National Academic Advising Association Journal (NACADA),* 25(1): pp. 26–30.

Gouras, Peter, and Bishop, Peter. (1972). Neural basis of vision. *Science,* 177: 188–89.

Greenberg, Jerald, and Baron, Robert. (1993). *Behavior in organizations: Understanding and managing the human side of work.* Needham Heights, MA: Allyn and Bacon.

Guba, Egon, and Lincoln, Yvonna. (1989). *Fourth generation evaluation.* Newbury Park, CA: Sage Publications.

Guimerà, R., L. Danon, A. Díaz-Guilera, F. Giralt, and A. Arenas. (22 Nov. 2002). *Self-similar community structure in organisations.* Retrieved April 11, 2003 from <http: xxx. arxiv.org/abs/cond-mater/0211498>.

Hadamitzky, Wolfgang, and Spahn, Mark. (1991). *A guide to writing Kanji and Kana, Book I.* Rutland, VT.: Tuttle Co.

Hall, Douglas. (1976). *Careers in organizations.* Glenview, IL: Scott Foresman.

—— Protean careers of the 21st century. *Academy of Management Executive,* 10(4): 8–16.

Hall, Edward. (1969). *The hidden dimension.* N.Y.: Anchor Press/Doubleday.

—— (1973). *Silent language.* N.Y. Anchor Press/Doubleday.

—— (1976). *Beyond culture.* N.Y.: Doubleday.

Hall, Edward, and Mildred Hall. (1990). *Understanding cultural differences.* Yarmouth, ME: Intercultural Press.

Hallowell, A. Irving. (1955). *Culture and experience.* Prospect Heights, Ill.: Waveland Press, Inc.

Han, Peter, and Angus MacLaurin. (2002). Do consumers really care about online privacy? *Marketing Management,* 11(1): 35–9.

Handwriting: A way to self-expression. (1993). Columbus: OH: Zaner-Bloser, Inc.

Hanvey, R. (1975). An attainable global perspective. In W. Kniep (ed.). (1978). *Next steps in global education: A handbook for curriculum development* (pp. 83–114). N.Y.: American Forum.

Harvard Business Review (2001). All in a day's work (roundtable discussion), *Harvard Business Review*, 79(11, Dec.): 57.

Hatakeyama, Yoshio. (1992). What makes an organization appealing? *JMA*, 2(2): 2–3.

Haub, Carl, and Sharma, O.P. (2006). India's population reality: Reconciling change and tradition. *Population Bulletin*, 61(3): 1–20. Washington: Population Reference Bureau. Retrieved on May 9, 2009 from <http://www.prb.org/pdf06/61. 3IndiasPopulationReality_Eng.pdf>.

Herskovits, Melville J. (1948). *Man and his works: (The science of cultural anthropology)*. N.Y.: Alfred A. Knopf.

Higgins, James (1991). *The management challenge: An introduction to management*. N.Y.: Macmillan Publishing Co.

Hill, Charles. (2009). *Global business today*. 6th edn. N.Y.: McGraw-Hill/Irwin.

Hoffmann, Banesh, and Dukas, Helen. (1972). *Albert Einstein creator and rebel*. N.Y.: Viking Press.

Hofstede, Geert. (1984). *Culture's consequences: International differences in work-related values*. Newbury Park, CA: Sage Publications.

—— (1980). *Culture's consequences: International differences in work-related values*. Beverly Hills, CA: Sage Publications.

Hoijer, Harry. (1954). The Sapir-Whorf hypothesis. In H. Hoijer (ed.), *Language and Culture*. Chicago, IL.: The University of Chicago Press.

Home ageing society. Retrieved June 27, 2002 from <http://oecd.org/EN/home>.

Honold, Pia. (2000). Culture and context: An empirical study for the development of a framework for the elicitation of cultural influence in product usage. *International Journal of Human-Computer Interaction*, 12(3&4): 327–45.

Hope, Christopher. (2008). England to be the most crowded in Europe. *Telegraph. co.uk*. <http://encarta.msn.com/encyclopedia_761572205/England.html>.

Houston, James. (1990). *Thesaurus of ERIC descriptors*. Phoenix, AZ: Oryx Press.

Howe, Neil, and Jackson, Richard. (2006). *Long-term immigration projection methods: Current practice and how to improve it*. Washington, DC: CSIS Global Aging Initiative.

Howell, William, and Cooke, Nancy. (1989). Training the human information processor. In Irwin Goldstein (ed.), *Training and development in organizations*. San Francisco: Jossey-Bass, Inc.

Huang, Jen-Hung. (2001). Consumer evaluations of unethical behaviors of Web sites: A cross-cultural comparison. *Journal of International Consumer Marketing*, 13(4): 51 pp.

Human Development Reports. (2009). United Nations Development Program. Retrieved December 17, 2009. <http://hdr.undp.org/en/statistics/>.

Imai, Masaaki. (1986). *Kaizen*. N.Y.: Random House.

International migration outlook: SOPEMI—2008. (2008). *Transition economies*, 2008(10): 1–398.

International Migration Report 2006: A Global Assessment. (2009). N.Y.: Department of Economic and Social Affairs—Population Division, United Nations. Retrieved May 8, 2009 from <http://www.un.org/esa/population/publications/2006_ MigrationRep/report.htm>.

International Populations. (2009, December 15). US Census Bureau. Retrieved December 26, 2009. From <http://www.census.gov/Press-Release/www/releases/archives/international_population/014499.html>.

Ishii, Hiroshi. (1990). Cross-cultural communication & computer-supported cooperative work. *Whole Earth Review*, 69(winter): 48–53.

Ishikawa, Akiharo. (1982). A survey of studies in the Japanese style of management. *Economic and Industrial Democracy*, 3: 1–15.

Ishikawa, Kaoru. (1985). *What is total quality control? The Japanese way* (D. Lu, Trans.). Englewood Cliffs, N.J.: Prentice-Hall, Inc.

Ishimori, Nobuo et al. (1992). *Shogaku kakikata sannen.* Tokyo: Mitsumura Tosho.

Ishinomori, Shotaro. (1988). *Japan Inc.: An introduction to Japanese economics.* Los Angeles: University of California Press.

Ito, Kinko. (1987). *Organizational adaptation of Japanese companies in the United States.* Columbus, OH.: The Ohio State University Press.

Jackson, Richard, and Howe, Neil. (2004). *The graying of the middle kingdom.* Washington, DC: CSIS Global Aging Initiative. Retrieved May 2, 2009 from <http://www.csis.org/media/csis/pubs/grayingkingdom.pdf>.

Jackson, Richard, and Howe, Neil. (2008). *The graying of the great powers.* Washington: CSIS Global Aging Initiative. Retrieved May 9, 2009 from <http://www.csis.org/media/csis/pubs/080630_gai_majorfindings.pdf>.

Jackson, R., Nakashima, K., and Howe, N. (2009b). *China's long march to retirement reform: The graying of the middle kingdom revisited.* Washington, DC: Center for Strategic and International Studies.

Jackson, Richard, and Strauss, Rebecca. (2007). *The geopolitics of world population change.* Washington, DC: CSIS Global Aging Initiative. Retrieved Feb. 9, 2009 from <http://www.csis.org/component/option,com_csis_pubs/task,view/id,5357/>.

Jackson, Richard, Strauss, Rebecca, and Howe, Neil. (2009a). *Latin America's aging challenge: Demographics and retirement policy in Brazil, Chile, and Mexico.* Washington, DC: Center for Strategic and International Studies. Retrieved April 30, 2009 from <http://www.csis.org/media/csis/pubs/090324_gai_english.pdf>.

Jacobs, Robert, Chase, Richard, and Aquilano, Nicholas. (2009). *Operations and supply management.* 12th edn. New York: McGraw-Hill Irwin.

Jacowski, Tony. (2009). Six Sigma Vs. Total Quality Management. *Ezine Articles.* retrieved May 22, 2009 from <http://ezinearticles.com/?Six-Sigma-vs.-Total-Quality-Management&id=296184>.

Jahoda, Gustav, and McGurk, Harry. (1982). The development of picture perception in children from different cultures. In David Wagner, and Harold Stevenson (eds.), *Cultural Perspectives on Child Development* (pp. 77–104). San Francisco: W. H. Freeman and Company.

JMA Management News (1991, Autumn), 2(1).

Johnson, Paul. (2002). The two sick men of Europe. *Forbes*, 169(13): 41.

Kakuchi, Suvendrini. (2001). Geisha do, Geisha don't. *Asian Business (Hong Kong)*, 37 (5): 78.

Kapur, Devesh, and McHale, John. (2005). *Give us your best and brightest: The global Hunt for talent and its impact on the developing world.* Washington, DC: Center for Global Development.

Keidel, Robert (1984). Baseball, football, and basketball: Models for business. *Organizational Dynamics.* New York: American Management Association.

Kelley, Lane, Whatley, Arthur, and Worthley, Reginald (1987). Assessing the effects of culture on managerial attitudes: A three-culture test. *Journal of International Business Studies*, 18: 17–31.

Kelley, Robert. (1988). In praise of followers. *The Harvard Business Review*, 66(6): 142–8.

Kim, W. Chan, and Renée Mauborgne. (1992). Parables of leadership. *Harvard Business Review*, 70(4): 123–8.

Kim, Young Yun. (ed.). (1986). *Interethnic communication: Current research.* Newbury Park, CA: Sage Publications.

Kim, Young Yun, and Gudykunst, William. (eds.). (1988). *Cross-cultural adaptation: Current approaches.* Newbury Park, CA: Sage Publications.

Kivrak, Serkan, Arslan, Gokhan, Dikmen, Irem, Birgonul, and M. Talat. (2008). Capturing knowledge in construction projects: Knowledge platform for contractors. *Journal of Management in Engineering*, 24(2): 87–95.

Knowles, Malcolm. (1980). *The modern practice of adult education: From pedagogy to andragogy.* N.Y.: Cambridge Books.

Kock, Ned. (2001). Compensatory adaptation to a lean medium: An action research investigation of electronic communication in process improvement groups. *IEEE Transactions on Professional Communication*, 44(4): 267–85.

Kolb, David A. (1984). *Experiential learning: Experience as the source of learning and development.* Englewood Cliffs, NJ: Prentice-Hall.

Kontzer, Tony. (2002). Share the knowledge. *Information Week*, 915 (Nov. 18): 65.

Kotter, J. (1995). Leading change: Why transformation efforts fail. *Harvard Business Review*, 73(2): 61–7.

—— (2001). What leaders really do. *Harvard Business Review*, 79(11): 85–96.

Krahe, Valerie Ann. (1993). The shape of the container. *Adult Learning*, 4: 17–18.

Kunihiro, Masao. (1976). The Japanese language and intercultural communication. *The Japan Interpreter*, 10: 267–83.

Kvale, Steinar. (1989). To validate is to question. In Steinar Kvale (ed.). *Issues of Validity in Qualitative Research* (pp. 73–92). Sweden: Studentlitterature; Chartwell-Bratt.

Lave, Jean. (1990). The culture of acquisition and the practice of understanding. In James Stigler, Richard Shweder and Gilbert Herdt (eds), *Cultural Psychology: Essays on Comparative Human Development* (pp. 309–27). Cambridge, UK: Cambridge University Press.

Lee, Dorothy (1950). Linear and non-linear codification of reality. *Psychosomatic Medicine*, 12: 89–97.

Lee, Ook. (2000). The role of protocol in media choice in a Confucian virtual workplace. *IEEE Transactions on Professional Communication*, 43(2): 196–200.

Lehman, Carol, and Debbie Dufrene. (1999). *Business communication.* Cincinnati: South-Western College Publishing.

Lengel, Robert, and Richard Daft. (1988). The selection of communication media as an executive skill. *Academy of Management Executive*, 11(3): 225–32.

Lerner, Reuven. (2003). Unicode. *Linux Journal* (107): 18–20.

Levitt, Theodore. (1960). Marketing myopia. *Harvard Business Review*, 38(4): 45–56.

—— (1983). The globalization of markets. *Harvard Business Review*, 61: 92–102.

Lewis, Catherine C. (1988). Japanese first-grade classrooms: Implications for US theory and research. *Comparative Education Review*, 32: 162.

Lincoln, Yvonna, and Guba, Egon. (1985). *Naturalistic inquiry.* Newbury Park, CA: Sage Publications.

Lu, David. (1987). *Inside corporate Japan: The art of fumble-free management*, Stanford, CT: Productivity Press.

Mandelbaum, David (ed.). (1949). *Selected writings of Edward Sapir in language, culture and personality*. Los Angeles: University of California Press.

Marquardt, Michael, and Berger, Nancy. (2000). *Global leaders for the twenty-first century*. Albany: State University of New York Press.

Martinsons, Maris, and Westwood, Robert. (1997). Management Information systems in the Chinese business culture: An explanatory theory. *Information and Management*, 32(5): 215–28.

Maruyama, Magoroh. (1963). The Second Cybernetics. *American Scientist*, 51: 164–79.

—— Epistemology of social science research. *Dialectica*, 23: 229–80.

—— (1970). Toward a Cultural Futurology, Cultural Futurology Symposium, American Anthropological Association national meeting, published by Training Center for Community Programs, University of Minnesota.

Maruyama, Magoroh, and Harkins, Arthur. (eds.). (1978). *Cultures of the future*. Paris: Mouton Publishers.

Massey, Anne, Yu-Ting Caisy Hung, Mitzi Montoya-Weiss, V. Ramesh, (2001). *When culture and style aren't about clothes: Perceptions of task-technology "fit" in global virtual teams*. Proceedings of the ACM 2001 Group Conference, Boulder, CO, September, 2001.

Matsumoto, Minchihiro. (1988). *The unspoken way*. Tokyo: Kodansha International.

May, Linda. (1991). Sociolinguistic research on human–computer interation—A perspective from anthropology. *Social Science Computer Review*, 9(4): 529–41.

McGovern, Gail. (2004). Bringing customers into the boardroom. *Harvard Business Review*, 82(11): 70–88.

McLean, Gary N., and McLean, L.D. (2001). If we can't define HRD in one country, how can we define it in an international context? *Human Resource Development International*, 4(3): 313–26.

Mead, Margaret. (1928). *Coming of age in Samoa*. New York: Morrow.

Merriam, Sharam, and Caffarella, Rosemary. (1991). *Learning in adulthood: A comprehensive guide*. Jossey-Bass Publishers: San Francisco.

Migrant stock has doubled since 1991 immigration problem "Home Grown"—not a Result of globalization. (2009). Retrieved May 11, 2009 from <http://www.migrationwatchuk.com/pressreleases/pressreleases.asp?dt=09-March-2009>.

Milliron, Mark, Plinske, K., and Noonan-Terry, C. (2008). Building a new *generation* of learning: Conversations to catalyze our construction. *Planning for Higher Education*, 37(1): pp. 7–14.

Mintzberg, Henry. (1998). Covert leadership: Notes on managing professionals. *Harvard Business Review*, 76(6): 140–7.

—— (1973). *The nature of managerial work*. N.Y.: HarperCollins.

Mishler, Elliot. (1979). Meaning in context: Is there any other kind? *Harvard Educational Review*, 49(1): 1–19.

—— (1986). The joint construction of meaning. In *Research interviewing: Contexts and narratives*. Cambridge, MA.: Harvard University Press.

Monger, Randall, and Rytina, Nancy. (2009). US legal permanent residents: 2008. *Annual Flow Report*. Washington, DC: Office of Immigration Statistics, Department of Homeland Security. Retrieved May 15, 2009 from <http://www.dhs.gov/xlibrary/assets/statistics/publications/lpr_fr_2008.pdf>.

Moore, Jana, and Gordon, Sallie. (1988). Conceptual graphs as instructional tools. *Proceedings from the Human Factors Society—32nd Annual Meeting*, Anaheim, CA: Human Factors Society.

Morgan, Gareth. (1994). It's all in the water. *Globe and Mail*, B28 (November 29).

—— (2006). *Images of organization*. Updated from 1997. Thousand Oaks, CA: Sage Publications.

Morgan, James, and Morgan, Jeffrey. (1991). *Cracking the Japanese market: Strategies for success in the new global economy*. New York: The Free Press.

Moss Kanter, R. (1989). The new managerial work. *Harvard Business Review*, 67(6): 85–92.

Nadler, David. (1989). Concepts for the management of organization change. In Tushman, Michael, O'Reilly, Charles, and Nadler, David. (eds.), *The management of organizations: Strategies, tactics, Analyses*. (pp. 490–504). N.Y.: Harper & Row.

Nadler, Gerald, and Shozo Hibino. (1990). *Breakthrough thinking: Why we must change the way we solve problems, and the seven principles to achieve this*. Rocklin: Prima Publishing.

Nathan, Edward. (2008). Global organizations and e-learning. Leveraging adult learning in different cultures. *Performance Improvement*, 47(6): 18–24.

Neupert, Kent, Baughn, Christopher, and Lam Dao, Thi Thanh (2005). International management skills for success in Asia. *Journal of European Industrial Training*, 29(2): 165–80.

New Car Sales Industry Profile: India. (2009). *Datamonitor*. New York, NY.

News and trends: Study reveals global work week averages. (2001). *Occupational Health & Safety*, 70(8): 12.

Nippert-Eng, Christina. (1995). *Home and work: Negotiating boundaries through everyday life*. Chicago: The University of Chicago Press.

Nishiyama, Kazuo. (1981). *Japanese quality control circles*. Paper presented at the Annual Meeting of the International Communication Association, Minneapolis, MN. (ERIC Document Reproduction Service No. ED206031), May.

Noe, Raymond, and Ford, Kevin. (1992). Emerging issues and new directions for training research. *Research in Personnel and Human Resources Management*, 10: 345–84.

Noffke, Susan. (1990). Researching together: Curriculum Inquiry with, not on teachers. Paper presented at the Twelfth Conference on Curriculum Theory and Classroom Practice, Dayton, Ohio.

Northouse, Peter. (2001). *Leadership theory and Practice*. (2nd edn.). Thousand Oaks, CA: Sage Publications, Inc.

Oblinger, Diana, and James. (2005). *Educating the Net generation*. Boulder, CO.: Educause. Retrieved February 2, 2009 from <www.educause.edu/ir/li8brary/pdf/pub7101.pdf>.

Once dismissed, social media is fast becoming a priority. (2009). *Internet Retailer*, 11(7): 81.

Osman-Gani, AAhad M., and Tan, Wee-Liang. (2005). Expatriate development for Asia-Pacific: A study of training contents and methods. *International Journal Human Resources Development and Management*, 5(1): 41–56.

Ouchi, William. (1981). *Theory Z: How American business can meet the Japanese* challenge. Reading, MA.: Addison-Wesley Publishing Co.

Özden, Çağlar, and Schiff, Maurice. (eds.) (2007). *International migration, economic development, and policy*. Washington, DC: World Bank/Palgrave Macmillan.

Pagonis, Gen. William, with Jeffrey Cruikshank. (1992). *Moving Mountains: Lessons in Leadership and Logistics from the Gulf War*. Boston, MA: The Harvard Business School Press.

Pascale, Richard, and Maguire, Mary Anne. (1980). Comparison of selected work factors in Japan and the United States. *Human Relations*, 33: 433–55.

Pascarella, Perry. (1987). Create breakthroughs in performance by changing the conversation. *Industry Week*, 233: 50–7.

Patton, Michael. (1990). *Qualitative evaluation and research methods*. Newbury Park: CA.: Sage Publications.

Penland, Patrick. (1984). What we know about adult learning. In Carol Shulman (ed.), *Adults and the Changing Workplace: 1985 Yearbook of the American Vocational Association* (pp. 67–87). Arlington, VA.: American Vocational Association. (ERIC Document Reproduction Service No. ED252663).

Pentland, Alex (2009). How social networks network best. *Harvard Business Review*, 87(2): 37.

Peters, Tom. (1988). *Thriving on chaos: Handbook for a management revolution*. New York: Alfred A. Knopf.

Peterson, Peter. (1999). Gray Dawn: The global aging crisis. *Foreign Affairs*, 78(1): 42–55.

Philips, Susan. (1972). Participant structures and communicative competence: Warm Springs children in community and classroom. In Courtney Cazden, Vera John and Dell Hymes (eds.), *Functions of Language in the Classroom* (pp. 371–94). New York: Teachers College Press.

Population pyramid summaries. (2009) *US Census Bureau International Data Base (IDB)*. Retrieved May 3, 2009 from <http://www.census.gov/ipc/www/idb/pyramids.html>.

Porter, Michael. (1996). What is strategy? *Harvard Business Review*, 74(6): 61–78.

Potoker, Elaine. (1994). Management and training across cultures: The importance of non-verbal communication strategies—A case study. Unpublished dissertation.

Potoker, Elaine, Soucie, Rachael, and Jain, Navneet (2007). The supply chain and its management: Should we be thinking loops, not lines? *Marketing Management Journal*, 17(2): 190–201.

Profiles on permanent legal residents. (2007). Washington, DC: Dept. of Homeland Security at <fhttp://www.dhs.gov/ximgtn/statistics/data/DSLPR07s.shtm>.

Program summary. (2009), *IUSSP XXVI International Population Conference*. Retrieved May 8, 2009 from <http://iussp2009.princeton.edu/ProgramSummary.aspx>.

Purdy, Jill, Nye, Pete, and P.V. (Sundar) Balakrishnan. (2000). The impact of communication media on negotiation outcomes. *The International Journal of Conflict Management*, 11(2): 162–87.

Qureshi, Sajda. (1995). Meeting and working on an electronic social space: Behavioral considerations and implications for cross-cultural end user computing. *Journal of End User Computing*, 7(4): 12–21.

Ramsey, Shiela (1984). Nonverbal behavior East and West. In Aaron Wolfgang (ed.), *Nonverbal behavior* (pp. 139–67). N.Y.: C. J. Hogrefe, Inc.

Randolph, W. Alan, and Marshall Sashkin. (2002). Can organizational empowerment work in multinational settings? *The Academy of Management Executive*, 16(1): 102–15.

Ronen, Simcha. (1989). Training the international assignee. In I. Goldstein (ed.), *Training and Development in Organizations* (pp. 417–54). San Francisco, CA: Jossey Bass.

Rosaldo, R. (1989). *Culture and truth*. Boston, MA: Beacon Press.

Rosenoer, Jonathan. (2002). Safeguarding your critical business information. *Harvard Business Review*, 80(2): 20–2.

Sage, Adam. (2001). Le weekend gets longer and longer. *New Statesmen*, 130(4531): 35.

Sandall, Steven. (ed.). (1987). *The problem isn't age: Work and older Americans*. N.Y.: Praeger.

Sapir, Edward. (1927). The unconscious patterning of behavior in society. In E. Dummer (ed.), *The unconscious: A symposium* (pp. 114–42). New York: Knopf.

—— (1929). The status of linguistics as a science. In David Mandelbaum (ed.), (1949). *Selected writings of Edward Sapir in language, culture and personality*. Los Angeles: University of California Press.

—— (1931). Conceptual categories in primitive languages. *Science*, 74: 578.

Saunders, Carol, C. Van Slyke, and Vogel, Douglas. (2007). My time or yours? Managing time visions in global virtual teams. In Mark Mendenhall, Gary Oddou, and Günter Stahl (eds.), *Reading and Cases in International Human Resource Management*, 4th edn. (pp. 297–316), Milton Park: Routledge UK.

Schieber, Sylvester. (2000). The global aging crisis. *Electric Perspectives*, 25(5): 18–28.

Schuler, Randall, and Jackson, Susan. (1987). Organizational strategy and organizational level as determinants of human resource management practices. *Human Resource Planning*, 10: 125–40.

Scott, William. (1965). Field methods in the study of organizations. In James March (ed.), *Handbook of organizations* (pp. 261–305). Chicago: Rand McNally & Company.

Sears, Andrew, and Jacko, Julie. (2009). *Human-computer interaction: Fundamentals*. Boca Raton, FL: CRC Press/Taylor and Francis Group.

Senge, Peter. (1990). *The fifth discipline: The art and practice of the learning organization*. N.Y.: Doubleday.

—— (1992). Mental models. *Planning Review*, 20: 4–10, 44.

—— (1994). *The fifth discipline fieldbook: Strategies and tools for building a learning organization*. N.Y.: Currency, Doubleday.

Shaw, Gordon, Robert Brown, and Philip Bromily. (1998). Strategic stories. *Harvard Business Review*, 76(3): 41–50.

Shenkar, Oded. (1995). *Global perspectives of human resource management*. Upper Saddle River: Prentice-Hall, Inc.

Sherman, James (1989). Japan: Body language and etiquette as a means of intercultural communication. *Proceedings of the Annual Eastern Michigan Conference on Languages and Communication for World Business and the Professions*. Ann Arbor, MI. (ERIC Document Reproduction Service No. ED 324937).

Shweder, Richard. (1990). Cultural psychology: What is it? In James Stigler, Richard Shweder, and Gilbert Herdt (eds.), *Cultural psychology: Essays on comparative human development* (pp. 1–43). Cambridge, UK: Cambridge University Press.

Smart power. (2008). *Harvard Business Review*, 86(11): 55–9.

Society for Human Resource Management/Commerce Clearing House Survey (SHRM/CCH). (1992). Chicago: Commerce Clearing House, Inc.

Spier, Leslie, Hallowell, A. Irving, and Newman, Stanley (eds.), (1941). *Essays in memory of Edward Sapir*. Menasha, WI: Sapir Memorial Publication Fund.

Spitz, Rejane. (1993). Computer graphics as a cross-cultural experience. *Media information Australia*, 69(August): 55–7.

Steiner, Dirk, Dobbins, Gregory, and Trahan, Wanda. (1991). The trainer-trainee interaction: An attributional model of training. *Journal of Organizational Behavior*, 12: 271–86.

Stewart, Lea. (1982). *Comparison of Japanese management and participative decision making: Implications for organizational communication research.* Paper presented at the Annual Meeting of the Eastern Communication Association, Hartford, CT.

Sudworth, John (2006). Indians head home in "brain gain." *BBC News.* Retrieved May 9, 2009 from <http://news.bbc.co.uk/2/hi/south_asia/5290494.stm>.

Sullivan, Louis H. (1896). *The tall office building artistically considered.* Online at <http://academics.triton.edu/faculty/fheitzman/tallofficebuilding.html>.

Swanson, Richard, and Holton III, Elwood (2009). *Foundations of human resource development.* San Francisco: Berrett-Koehler Publishers, Inc.

Tannenbaum, Scott, and Yukl, Gary. (1992). Training and development in work organizations. *Annual Review of Psychology*, 43: 399–441.

Tapscott, Don, Ticoll, David, and Lowy, Alex. (2000) *Digital capital: Harnessing the power of business webs.* Boston, MA: Harvard Business School Press.

Tatsuno, Sheridan. (1990). *Created in Japan: From imitators to world-class innovators.* Grand Rapids: Ballinger.

Taylor, Frederick. (1947). *Scientific management.* New York: Harper & Brothers.

The new demographics: How to live with an ageing population. (2001). *Economist*, 361(8246): 5–8.

Timpane, Michael, and Miller-McNeil, Laurie. (1991). *Business impact on education and child development reform.* N.Y.: Committee for Economic Development.

Toossi, Mitra. (2002). A century of change: The US labor force, 1950–2050. *Monthly Labor Review.* Retrieved April 24, 2009 from <http://www.bls.gov/opub/mlr/2002/05/art2full.pdf>.

—— (2006) A new look at long-term labor force projections to 2050. *Monthly Labor Review.* Retrieved April 24, 2009 from <http://www.bls.gov/opub/mlr/2006/11/art-3full.pdf>.

Tracey, William. (1992). *Designing training and development systems.* 3rd edn. New York: AMACOM, American Management Association.

Tufte, Edward. (1990). *Envisioning information.* Cheshire, CT: Graphics Press.

Tushman, Michael, O'Reilly, Charles, and Nadler, David. (eds.) (1989). *The management of organizations: Strategies, tactics, analyses.* N.Y.: Harper & Row.

Tye, Kenneth (ed.). (1991). *Global education: From thought to action.* Washington, DC: Association for Supervision and Curriculum Development (ASCD) 1991 Yearbook.

Tyler, Joshua, Dennis Wilkinson, and Bernardo Huberman. (2003). *Email as spectroscopy: Automated discovery of community structure within organizations.* Retrieved April 17, 2003 from <http://lanl.arXiv.org/abs/cond-mat/0303264>.

United Nations (2009). *International Migration Report 2006: A Global Assessment.* N.Y.: Department of Economic and Social Affairs—Population Division, United Nations. Retrieved May 8, 2009 from <http://www.un.org/esa/population/publications/2006_MigrationRep/report.htm>.

Universal Declaration of Human Rights (1948). Online at <http://www.un.org/Overview/rights.html>.

Van Maanen, John. (1988). *Tales of the field: On writing ethnography*. Chicago: University of Chicago Press.

Vecchio, Robert. (2003) *Organizational behavior: Core concepts*. 5th edn. Cincinnati: South-Western/Thomson Learning.

Wagner, David. (1982). Ontogeny in the study of culture and cognition. In David Wagner, and Harold Stevenson (eds.), *Cultural Perspectives on Child Development* (pp. 105–21). San Francisco: W. H. Freeman and Company.

Wax, Rosalie. (1971). *Doing fieldwork: Warnings and advice*. Chicago: The University of Chicago Press.

Webster's New Twentieth Century Dictionary (1989). New York: Simon and Schuster.

Weiner, Annette. (1992) Anthropology's lessons for cultural diversity. *Chronicle of Higher Education*, B1–2 (July 22).

Wexley, Kenneth, and Latham, Gary (1981). *Developing and training human resources in organizations*. Glenview, IL.: Scott Foresman.

Whorf, Benjamin. (1939). The relation of habitual thought and behavior to language. In Leslie Spier, A. Irving Hallowell and Stanley Newman (eds.) (1941), *Essays in Memory of Edward Sapir* (pp. 75–93). Menasha, WI: Sapir Memorial Publication Fund.

Woolliams, Peter, and Gee, David. (1992). Accounting for user diversity in configuring online systems. *Online Review*, 15(1): 303–11.

World Fact Book. (2009). CIA. Retrieved December 17, 2009. <https://www.cia.gov/library/publications/the-world-factbook/>.

World migration 2008: Managing labour mobility in the evolving global economy. (2008), 4, pp. 1–562. Geneva: International Organization for Migration (IOM). Retrieved May 1, 2009 from <http://www.iom.int/jahia/Jahia/cache/offonce/pid/1674?entryId=20275>.

Yamamoto, A. (1991, Autumn). Keys to cross-cultural technical education. *JMA*, 2(1): 2–3, 8.

Zaccaro, Stephen, and Richard Klimoski. (2001). *The nature of organizational leadership: Understanding the performance imperatives confronting today's leaders*. San Francisco: Jossey-Bass.

Zheng, Connie, and Lamond, David. (2009). A critical review of human resource management studies (1978–2007) in the People's Republic of China. *The International Journal of Human Resource Management*, 20(11): 2194–227.

Index

In this index figures and tables are indicated in **bold** type; notes are indicated by n.